# A HISTORY OF BLACKBURN

*To my family. Judith my wife, Emma, Cordelia and Naomi my daughters, James and Nicholas my sons in law and William, George, Isobel, Matilda and Caspar my grandchildren. Life would be empty without them.*

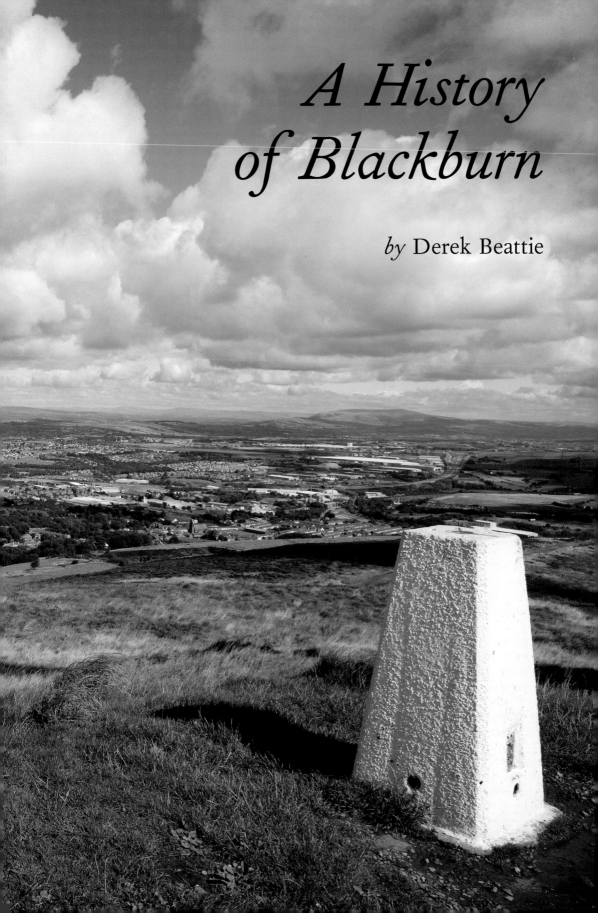

# A History of Blackburn

*by* Derek Beattie

Also published by Carnegie:
Prof. David Hey, *A History of Yorkshire: 'County of the Broad Acres'* (2005)

Town and city histories available from Carnegie:
Prof. David Hey, *A History of Sheffield* (2005)
Prof. John K. Walton, *Blackpool*
Prof. Graham Davis and Dr Penny Bonsall, *A History of Bath: Image and Reality* (2006)
Peter Aughton, *Bristol: A People's History*
Dr John A. Hargreaves, *Halifax*
Dr Andrew White (ed.), *A History of Lancaster*
Peter Aughton, *Liverpool: A People's History* (3rd edn, 2007)
Prof. Alan Kidd, *Manchester* (2006)
Dr Jeffrey Hill, *Nelson*
Malcolm Neesam, *Harrogate Great Chronicle, 1332–1841* (2005)

Forthcoming town and city histories:
Prof. Carl Chinn, *Birmingham*
W. A. Maguire, *Belfast*
Dr John Doran, *Chester*
Michael Baumber, *A History of Haworth*
Dr John A. Hargreaves, *Huddersfield*
Dr Andrew White, *Kendal*
Dr Trevor Rowley, *A History of Oxford*
Dr Mark Freeman, *A History of St Albans*
Prof. Bill Sheils, *A History of York*
Peter Shakeshaft, *St Anne's*
Dr Evelyn Lord, *Cambridge*
Anthea Jones, *Cheltenham*

Full details on www.carnegiepublishing.com

Copyright © Derek Beattie, 2007

Published by Carnegie Publishing Ltd
by Carnegie Publishing Ltd
Carnegie House
Chatsworth Road, Lancaster LA1 4SL
www.carnegiepublishing.com

ISBN: 978-1-85936-113-9 *hardback*

*British Library Cataloguing-in-Publication data*
A catalogue record for this book is available from the British Library

Published with the support of Blackburn with Darwen Council

Designed and typeset by Carnegie Book Production, Lancaster
Printed and bound in China by 1010 Printing International Ltd

*frontispiece*
Blackburn, nestling in its valley setting, seen from the trig point at Darwen Tower in summer, 2006.
PHOTOGRAPH: CARNEGIE

# Contents

In 1759 R. Lang drew 'A Map of the Glebe of the Rectory of Blackburn belonging to the Most Revd the Archbishop of Canterbury'. This is the south-west quarter of the map, showing lands held by the Church in and around the town of Blackburn. Within the north-east quarter of the map there is a more detailed plan of the town centre, which is reproduced in full on page 96. In this view are shown the main roads to Darwen (Roman Road, as Bolton Road was then a country lane) and to Tockholes and Bolton (Hey Lane), meeting on Blackburn Moor. The main road north from the little town is Shear Brow, as Preston New Road and Whalley New Road did not then exist.

BY COURTESY OF LAMBETH PALACE LIBRARY, TD 20

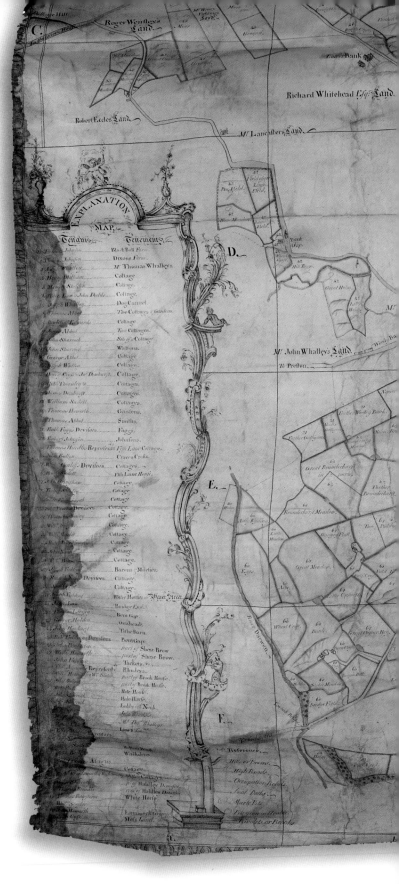

vi

# List of tables

# *Acknowledgements*

My thanks to the staff of Blackburn Museum, Blackburn Library, Blackburn College Library and Lancaster University Library. One person who stands out from all others deserves special thanks and that is Diana Rushton. Diana is one of the very knowledgeable guardians of Blackburn Library's local history collection and virtually the sole guardian of the superb Cottontown Project which allows people all over the world to access much of the collection. Whatever she earns, it should be doubled. My thanks also to Jim Halsall, a volunteer on the Project, for advice and help in tracing some of the illustrations. His extensive local knowledge also helped clear up a number of points for me. Thank you, too, to the helpful staff of Lambeth Palace Library who managed to track down and photograph so professionally Lang's superb town plan of 1759.

Thanks also must be given to Dr Stephen Constantine of Lancaster University for encouraging me to embark on the original work and for overseeing the first edition, and to Dr Alan Crosby for reading the revised manuscript and for making numerous helpful suggestions; he also drew many of the informative and useful maps which appear in this book.

This updated and expanded edition by Carnegie Publishing owes much to the staff there. Advisors seem to have come and gone as events such as motherhood intervened, but one thing they all had in common was the quiet certainty that no problem was insurmountable. Thank you, Claire, George and Anna, and not forgetting, of course, Alistair Hodge, who was the driving force behind it all.

The publishers would like to acknowledge the help and support of Blackburn and Darwen Borough Council. It has been a pleasure working with the various council departments, including Communications, the Museum and the Library. The Council also generously contributed towards the cost of reproducing so many superb illustrations held in their collections and elsewhere, as well as helping to advertise the book to local residents. Thank you to all those involved.

Now part of a
conservation area
the Georgian
pavilions at the top
of Church Street
have been rescued
from decline and
the entire area
pedestrianised
and filled with
seating and street
sculptures.

# Introduction

I N   M A N Y   N O R T H E R N   T O W N S such as Blackburn the industrial revolution changed everything. It is impossible to trace with certainty the precise date when the changes really began, but contemporaries started to take serious note of what was going on during the third quarter of the eighteenth century. Canals, cotton mills, foundries, engineering works and mines all excited great interest, while the novel, cramped and inadequate living conditions during this early 'heroic age' of urban development provoked an equal measure of social and political concern.

Places such as Blackburn, which had slumbered through the centuries, or at most been just local markets towns or centres of local government or religion, suddenly and dramatically grew and changed during this industrial and urban revolution. The results were unplanned expansion of the built environment, and mass migration from country to town, rural to urban, agricultural to industrial. Just six or seven generations separates the town shown in a map of 1759 (page 96) with that depicted by the Ordnance Survey in 1893 (for example, page 109), but they are, quite literally, a world apart. Superficially Blackburn's experience was similar to that of many other places, yet many of the characteristics which came to be identified with the town were quite distinctive and different to those of towns not far away. An understanding of what really happened lies with the small ruling elite thrown up by the industrial revolution, an elite which shaped virtually every aspect of Blackburn – economic, political, social, cultural and religious. And the key to appreciating exactly why Blackburn has evolved into the town we know today lies in that crucial period of urbanisation between around 1750 and, say, 1914. During this period Blackburn became a cotton town, and was confident of its purpose in the world.

When decline set in – absolute in the case of cotton, relative in the case of the town itself – it became harder to identify what Blackburn's post-industrial role might be: as late as 1992 I wrote, 'Blackburn is finding it difficult to find a new *raison d'être*. It is still looking.' Much has happened even since then, and regeneration has begun to transform, once more, the physical appearance and the economic and social nature of Blackburn. Now is a highly appropriate time to assess the true nature of Blackburn's historical legacy.

The map which was used by Edward Baines in his *History of Lancashire* was surveyed by James Gillies and published in 1824. This detail shows the town centre, with the recently rebuilt parish church just south-east of the site of the old church; by this date St Peter's (left) and St John's (right) had also been built. The building marked by the letter K on Clayton Street is the town's Methodist church, while 'B' on Thunder Alley is the National School. The river from which Blackburn derives its name has not yet been culverted, and is still a fairly prominent feature in the early townscape.

BY COURTESY OF DAVID BRAZENDALE

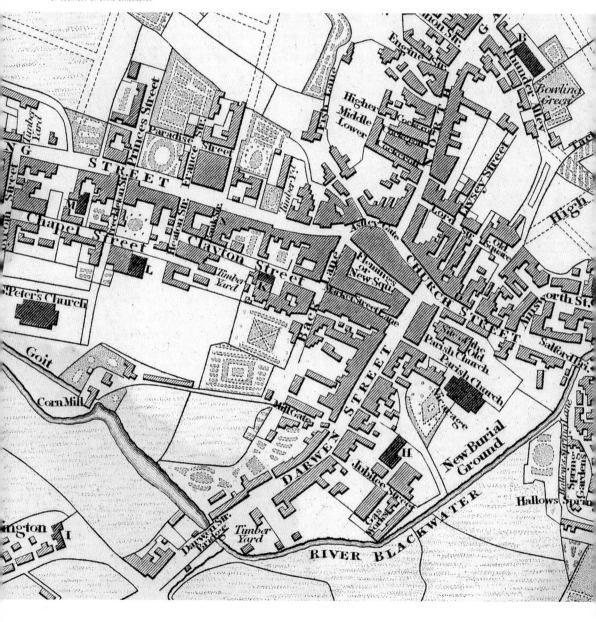

# CHAPTER ONE

# Blackburn before 1750

B Y 1880, WHEN IT WAS NEARING ITS HEYDAY as one of the world's greatest textile manufacturing centres, Blackburn had over 100,000 people. Only a century before that time, though, it had an estimated population of just 5,000, so its growth as a major urban centre was relatively recent. That change was largely due to the rise of cotton, which brought about Blackburn's prominence and ended its comparative obscurity. Without cotton the town's growth would not have been so rapid or so great. However, this dependence on one key industry was not only the reason for growth but also the main cause of decline, for if a town's economy is based on one industry, the contraction of that industry will inevitably harm the town itself. But of course, there is, and always has been, a lot more to Blackburn than cotton. The town has had many industries, it has a long history, and its present state of change and renewal is another chapter in a lengthy and complex story. Blackburn has a strong and distinctive personality, which is in considerable measure the consequence of its particular historical development. It is not like Burnley and it is not like Preston, even though those two rival towns are only ten miles distant. Its accents are different, its character is different, and its economic and social structure are different.

Blackburn sits in the valley of the little river Blakewater, which flows westwards from the low watershed just above Rishton and Oswaldtwistle, and is fed by streams flowing north from the northern fringe of the Rossendale uplands, a western spur of the Pennines. A mile below the modern town centre the Blakewater joins the Darwen, a larger river flowing north from the high moors above Darwen town and Turton, and thence its waters eventually reach the lower Ribble. The site of Blackburn is very varied and distinctive topographically, something which not only gives the town its shape but also gives it views out to the hills – and allows views in, for from vantage points such as Darwen Tower the town can be seen nestling in its valley and spreading up the adjacent slopes. On both sides of the centre the land rises sharply, reaching 229 metres above sea level at Revidge and almost the same height at Guide on the south side of the town. On the north-west, in particular, this combination of elevation above the congested and, in the past, smoky industrial and poorer housing areas, and fine views across the adjacent country-side, has long provided attractive sites for the development of higher-class housing. This is important in Blackburn's history because, as in many other larger industrial centres, during the nineteenth century its increasingly complex social structure was reflected in the town's developing geography. In appear-ance, layout and subtle variations of society and landscape it was anything but uniform, monotonous and dull. The town's physical setting also played an important part in its industrial development: with an average annual rainfall of 45 inches there were ample supplies of excellent soft water draining from the local gritstone, and in the early phases of industrialisation this meant not only a source of power but also permitted many water-based industrial processes. In the surrounding area, too, there were plentiful supplies of coal, so that in the later phases of industrial growth fuel for steam engines was also obtainable locally.[1] But this, inevitably, is not the beginning of the story, and Blackburn's history can be traced back many centuries before the dramatic changes which took place from the mid-eighteenth century onwards.

The Revidge urn.
BLACKBURN MUSEUM

Blackburn's earliest beginnings are obscure and undocumented, and there is almost no archaeological evidence to provide even fragments of the story. That should occasion no surprise, for the same limitation holds true for many places in Lancashire and even in the better known places such as Manchester a great deal remains unclear and conjectural. Blackburn lies directly on a Roman road but that, despite its historical promise, does not appear to have influenced the location or development of the later town. During the pre-Roman period the area around Blackburn, like the rest of the lands west of the Pennines, was loosely under the authority of Brigantia, a British kingdom which was a confederation of many smaller tribes living in the area of modern Lancashire and Yorkshire. After AD 69 the Roman military presence in this troublesome kingdom was rapidly strengthened, and by AD 80 the region was under tight Roman control. The military presence required, as it did everywhere in the empire, a network of roads and the construction of forts. In this area there was, at least in the first and second centuries, a potential threat to security from possibly discontented people living in the Pennines, and firm control was required. A high-level road, essentially a military highway, was therefore constructed along the axis of the hills from Manchester to Carlisle. Its route runs through Radcliffe and Affetside, and then to the east of Darwen, before crossing the Blakewater in the centre of the modern town of Blackburn and heading northwards over Ramsgreave to Ribchester. Whether there was any native or British settlement in the vicinity of the river crossing is unknown, though it remains a possibility, but there is nothing to suggest any Roman military presence in the town itself. The nearest Roman fort was at Ribchester,

*The huts of the inhabi-tants erected of crooks pegged together; clay, plaster, and straw, or such thatched roofs; windows latticed, necks and semi-doors . . .'*

PAVEMENT OF THE ROMAN ROAD AT BLACKAMOOR.

Protographed by R. P. Gregson in 1890

a more strategically significant location where the main north–south route crossed an important east–west road from Kirkham along the Ribble valley to Ilkley and York. There was, however, a Roman site, which was probably a signal station, on the hilltop at Mellor. Nevertheless, it is apparent that as was also the case with many other Lancashire towns (but unlike Manchester, Lancaster and Wigan) Blackburn was not a significant Roman site.

The name Blackburn is derived from the stream which later was called the Blakewater. The place-name element 'burn', from the Old English *burna*, a stream, is typically found in north-east England, and this is a relatively rare instance of its occurrence so far south. It is generally regarded as a Northumbrian form, and it has apparently survived here despite the prevalence of the Scandinavian equivalent 'beck' and the alternative Midland English 'brook' or 'stream'. The 'black' element is probably derived from the very dark peaty waters of the stream, flowing from the Rossendale moors. The name of the village, and later town, evidently followed from the name of the watercourse, and 'Blakewater' therefore means exactly the same as 'Blackburn'.

The first evidence, albeit very circumstantial, of a significant settlement on the site of the later town does not appear until the Anglo-Saxon period. The absence of archaeological evidence means that dating its origins is as yet impossible, and because of the repeated redevelopment and intensity of urbanisation in the vicinity of the first village, around the parish church, now the cathedral, it is possible that all trace has in any case been destroyed. However,

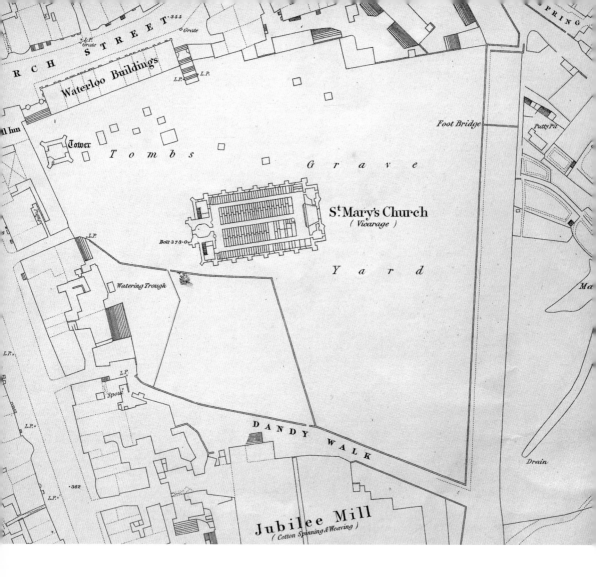

it is clear that the church of St Mary was an important Saxon foundation, of the type which is often known as a 'minster' – a church which is the focus of an extensive parish, the 'mother church' of a substantial district embracing many separate communities. The most revealing evidence for the early origins and importance of the church is not the building itself, but its evident high status in the medieval period. Blackburn parish was, like those of Whalley, Preston and Lancaster, extremely large. It included numerous townships and extended from the Ribble southwards to the moors above Darwen, and from Great Harwood in the east to Walton-le-Dale in the west. Most historians consider that such churches were the building blocks of the structure of the faith in the pre-Conquest period and here, as elsewhere in the county, the great ancient parishes retained their importance until the late eighteenth and early nineteenth centuries. Only then, as a result of population growth and urbanisation, were they gradually broken up into smaller units. The church stood on the bank of the Blakewater at a central point where several hill and valley routes converged. Although nothing is known of the origins of the church, there is no doubt that it predated the Norman Conquest, for it is mentioned in the very brief entry for Blackburn which is given in the Domesday Book of 1086. A nineteenth-century historian, using his imagination, described the infant community: 'The Parish Church of St Marie, the inn of the Lord, and the abode of the Parson, are the only buildings of any note. The huts of the inhabitants erected of crooks pegged together; clay, plaster, and straw, or such thatched roofs; windows latticed, necks and semi-doors.'[2]

But the site of St Mary's, ancient though it certainly is, may have come into use rather later than an even older religious site nearby. A tantalising hint of a very early Christian site is the place-name Eccleshill, for the word *eccles-* is derived from the British (or Celtic) term for 'church', which is itself a direct borrowing from the Latin word *ecclesia*. Place-names with this element (of which there are six in pre-1974 Lancashire) are now usually considered to have been the locations of Christian worship before the Anglo-Saxon settlement of the seventh century, since after about AD 600 the British language was no longer used for the creation of place-names. Whether that was the case at Eccleshill and, if so, precisely where the site was and in what form, are questions which cannot yet be answered and may never be clarified, but the possibility is clearly of major historical interest. The implication is that the earliest Christians in the area had a place of worship on the hill above the town, and that subsequently, after the arrival of the Anglo-Saxon people in

| DI | DINCKLEY |
| EC | ECCLESHILL |
| LH | LITTLE HARWOOD |
| OS | OSBALDESTON |
| PB | PICKUP BANK |
| PL | PLEASINGTON |
| RA | RAMSGREAVE |
| WI | WITTON |
| YA | YATE |

Names in capitals are townships

Names in lower case are other parishes

⊕ parish church

⊕ chapels recorded before 1650

The medieval parish of Blackburn, showing constituent townships and pre-1650 chapels.

MAP BY DR ALAN CROSBY

the years after AD 620, the focus shifted down to the valley bottom and a new church was built at the meeting of the routeways. This, and the adjacent Church Street, formed the heart of the later town, even though in the eighteenth and nineteenth centuries the commercial centre gradually moved a short distance northwards to its present location.

After the Norman Conquest William I allotted extensive areas of land to leading supporters, those knights who had helped him in the successful campaign which centred on the Battle of Hastings. The aim was twofold. First, these men were rewarded for their support, and by giving them large estates the king could hope to command their gratitude and loyalty; and second, the creation of powerful baronies, held by supporters, in the more distant and less manageable parts of the country was a way of trying to ensure that royal control was maintained. Most of what subsequently became the county of Lancashire was given to one Roger de Poitou, who established his power base at Lancaster, where he built the castle; this choice of location was sensible, for he also held the lands of Furness and Cartmel over the sands. As often happened, Roger in his turn granted lands to his own supporters and retainers, and two of these, Roger de Busli and Albert Grelley, obtained lands in and around Blackburn. The pattern of land-holdings was, however, partly that which had been inherited from the past.

One of several fragments of early glass, apparently early modern in date, now incorporated into a later window in the cathedral.

PHOTOGRAPH: CARNEGIE

Throughout the medieval period and beyond, Blackburn was the administrative centre of the huge 'hundred' of Blackburn, which extended across east Lancashire from the edge of Preston to the Yorkshire border, and from the high moors of Bowland beyond Chipping to the watershed above Rossendale. The hundreds were the sub-county divisions of medieval England, but in Lancashire, as in other northern counties, there is clear evidence that they had originated very much earlier. Several of the Lancashire hundreds, like those in for example County Durham and Northumberland, were known as 'shires', and so we often find reference to Leylandshire, Salfordshire and Blackburnshire. The current view is that these were certainly units of administration in the Scandinavian period, and they may well already have been ancient when the Norse settlers appeared in the north of England from the late ninth century onwards. Some authorities suggest that these are in fact based on pre-Roman tribal territories. If this is so, it means that Blackburn,

though it was still small by later standards, was recognised as a 'central place' from a very early date, a view reinforced by the clear importance of its parish and parish church, and by its geographical position at a major meeting of routeways. The conclusion might well be that the Roman choice of Ribchester, rather than Blackburn, as the site of a major fort was actually something of an aberration in historical terms.

It is not easy to reconstruct the appearance of the landscape at the time of the Norman Conquest, although local place-names do give some indications. Thus, some names relate to wetter and marshy tracts, such as Feniscowles (*Feinyscholes*, 1276) which is derived from Old Norse words that mean 'muddy or dirty huts', or Livesey, which means 'Leof's island' and implies drier ground within a marshy or wetland area close to the river. There are many woodland names in the area, such as Harwood ('the old or grey wood'), Ramsgreave ('the grove of the ram'), Ewood ('wood by the river') and the river name – and hence place-name – Darwen, which is the same as the more common river-name 'Derwent' and is derived from a Celtic word meaning 'oak river'. Other names refer to cultivation and settlement, such as Eanam ('land taken in from the waste') and Beardwood which, despite appearances, does not come from 'wood' but from 'worth', and means 'the enclosed place belonging to Bearda'. There is nothing particularly distinctive about any of these names, for they are characteristic of those found very widely along the Pennine edges of Lancashire. They imply a landscape which, in the years around 800–1000, comprised valleys with substantial areas of wetland and carr (overgrown swampy ground) along the riversides and streams; wooded hills; substantial areas of open moorland on the upper slopes and summits; and extensive cleared and cultivated areas. Places such as Audley, Mellor, Ramsgreave, Eccleshill, Livesey and Pleasington had already emerged as distinct townships and identifiable communities by the end of the eleventh century but, as noted above, there was always a greater importance attached to Blackburn. The nearby communities did not acquire their own churches or chapels for many centuries and, in terms of religion and civil administration, were always to some extent subordinate to Blackburn itself.

*Blackburn: 'black stream'*

*Feniscowles: 'muddy or dirty huts'*

*Livesey: 'Leof's island'*

*Harwood: 'the old or grey wood'*

*Ewood: 'wood by the river'*

*Darwen: 'oak river'*

*Eanam: 'land taken in from the waste'*

*Beardwood: 'the enclosed place belonging to Bearda'*

By the twelfth century the manor of Blackburn had passed into the hands of the de Blackburn family, who, as with many other locally important families across Lancashire, derived their name from that of the place in which they lived. In 1180 Henry of Blackburn divided the manor between his two sons, Richard and Adam, and it remained separated into different portions until the end of the eighteenth century. The half that belonged to Adam of Blackburn was sold by his son Roger to John de Lacy, earl of Lincoln. The de Lacy family were the lords of the honour of Clitheroe, the baronial holding that included much of east Lancashire and the Ribble valley, and they were also patrons of Stanlaw Abbey in Cheshire. They granted their Blackburn estate to Stanlaw and when in 1296 the monks moved from there to Whalley the property passed to Whalley Abbey. When Henry VIII dissolved the monasteries in the sixteenth century the estates passed to the Crown, which in turn regranted the land to the archbishop of Canterbury. Half of the manor was now in the hands of the Church of England, which leased it out to the Talbot family. In the thirteenth and fourteenth centuries the other half of the manor passed from Richard of Blackburn by marriage to the Hultons, then the Radcliffes and the Bartons, until in the sixteenth century it came, again by marriage, into the hands of the 1st Viscount Fauconberg. His family remained in possession through to the time of the 4th Viscount, who sold the Blackburn estates to several different landowners in 1721.[3]

Blackburn's emergence as a market town is no less obscure than other aspects of its early history, but in this case we have a particular problem. Whereas for many market centres in Lancashire, as in other counties, there is at least the record of a formal grant of market rights, by means of a charter, in the medieval period, Blackburn apparently did not have such charter. Its market, through to the nineteenth century, was 'customary', that is, it had arisen by a casual process, rather than being formally created, and it was governed by 'custom', not by regulations and byelaws. The earliest reliable written record of a market being held in the town comes as late as 1526, in the court rolls of the honour

Wulf Cragg

Scotford row

Cloughho Hill

Conder R

Coker R

Wirr

Wiersdale Forest

Wiersdale

Scurton

Waddiker

Greenhaugh Cast.

Claughto Broke

NESS HUN

the Lodge

Barton

S. Laurence

Catford Hall

Broughton

Plumpton

Sowick

Cotham

Clifton

Lea

Preston

Penwortham

Walton Hall

Langton Chap.

The Moss

Howte

Bretherton

Bankhall

Croston

Rufford Chap.

LAYLAND HUN.

Biʃpham

Hartock Hall

Parbad

Dowe

newbrugh

Lathom

Croʃhall

Aʃhurst

Shelmarsdale

Holland Chap.

Bickerſta

YE HUNDRED

Raynford Chap.

Billing

Simons Wood Forest

the Brigantes

Moʃbarrow

ork by

Eggleſton

Knowesley

St. Helens Chap.

Prescot

Hyton

Roby

Ranhill

Childwall

Farnworth

Bold

Sankey

The Pele

Waarring

Edmarsh Chap.

The Laund

Chipping

Longridg Hill

Bowland Forest

Radholm Park

Baʃhall

Mitton

Stony hurſt

Longridg Chap.

Ribodunum or Ribcheſter

Salesbury

Osbaldeston

Samʃbury

Samʃbury Hall

Keuerdale

Law

Darwen R

Houghton Tower

Brindall

Clayton Hall

Laland

Werden

Exton burgh

Charno

Chorley

Aʃley

Hill

The Pele

Raventon

Smethels

Yarrow R.

Longworth

Walmeʃley Chap.

Egberden Hall

Hall of the Wood

LUND HUN.

Adlington

Standiʃh

Blak Rode

thington

Hay

Houghton Chap.

Wigan

Ince

Leigh

Abram

Aʃhton Chap.

Kilcheth

Newchurch

Newton Chap.

Rixley

Winwick

Southworth Hall

Bewsey

Brich

Wolston

Lym

Slatborn

Newton

Bardford

Waddington

Baterby

Eʃington

Grinleton

YORK

Giʃborn

Braʃewell

Sawley

Gilkirk

Chatburn

Rimington

Fawbridg

Barnside

Downham

Worston

Colne

Wicol

Clethero

Pendleton

Pendle Hill

Gawthrop

Newe church

Marſhden

Wiswall

Whaley

Read

Paddingham

Simonſton

Habergham

Burnley

Townley

Holm

Ribble R.

Langho

Great Harwood

Altham

Shutleworth

Dunkinhill

Hapton tower

Catder R.

Martholm

Rishton

Church

Little Harwood

BLACK BURN HUN.

Haudley

Accrington

Rossendale

Todmer

Blackburn

Haʃlingden

Bacup

Irwel R.

Darwen R

Darwen

Whitworth

Spodden R.

Tockholes

Hawcolm Chap.

The K. Mannor of

Ivtenfeld Chap.

Newhall

Wolsten holme

Entwiſel

Turton

Tottington

Brandleʃham

Ashworth Chap.

Roched Chap. Mar

Bradshaw

Coccium

Cockley Chap.

Griʃhurst

Bury

Heywood Chap.

Hop wood

SALFORD HUNDR

Little Bolton

Amʃworth hall

Little Lever

Y Stand

Roche R

Middle

Dean

Haſtok

Bolton

Great Lever

Farnworth

Rathf

Pilkington Park

Heaton

Preʃtoke

Preswi

Foxi

Brinsap

Highfield

Hulton Park

Shakerley

Ringley Chap.

Wordley

Ellynbrugh

Cliften

Rhodes

Edgecroft

Stangwes

Newto

Black

Lowcon

Tilsey

Atherton

Booths Hall

Aſtley

Morelees

Byram

Worsley

Barton

Eckles

Sakford

wordsall

Manche

Garret

Whickleſwith

the Colledg

Gort

Chatmoʃs

Denholm

Flixton

Urmſton

Holme

Traford

Hugh hall

Chawerton Ch

Barlow

Holcroft

Holly Grene

Ashton

Carrinton

Sale

Diddeʃbury

Northen

Rixton

Partinton

Chedle

Warberton

Altrincham

Irwel R.

Thelwall

of Clitheroe when it is described as being 'the King's Market at Blackburne', but there is no doubt at all that the market was very much older than this. Many early markets were closely associated with a parish church and were held on Sundays. While we cannot be absolutely categorical that this happened at Blackburn, there is very good reason to suppose that, given the importance of the church, a market was held in the vicinity of St Mary's from the early medieval period onwards. Why no market charter was ever granted, in contrast to the experience of almost all other Lancashire towns, is unclear. However, it is possibly because the control of the township of Blackburn was shared between the two manorial lords (in the Middle Ages, one half by Whalley Abbey and the other, in turn, by the Blackburn, Hulton and Radcliffe families). Since market charters were usually granted to manorial lords, it may be that this division of power militated against such a grant.

There was no formal market place, but old maps show a widening of the street at the junction of Church Street, Darwen Street, Northgate and Astley Gate, with the church gate at its south-east corner. This situation, with a broad street beside a church, is very typical of many medieval market sites (other local examples are at Preston, Burnley and Bolton) and so we can be sure that this is where the medieval market was held. It was also here that the market cross, which had three steps up to it and a carved niche in which was the figure of Mary,[4] and town stocks were situated, and a well which was one of the main sources of water for the little town. The well was surrounded by a circular stone wall and water was drawn up using a windlass. The remains of this well were discovered in 1860 during excavations for the installation of a sewerage system.[5] By the end of the medieval period the use of Sundays for market trading had fallen into disfavour, and Blackburn market was held on a Monday, though in 1774 the market day switched to Wednesday. Blackburn is also noted as having at least three fairs a year by the middle of the sixteenth century, the most important being that held on 1 May, which was especially noted for cattle and other livestock. As a market centre Blackburn was inferior to Preston, the county's main market apart from Manchester, but by the sixteenth century it was clearly at least as successful as, for example, those at Burnley and Bury.

Table 1 *Blackburn St Mary the Virgin, annual totals of burials, 1600–41*

| Year | No. of burials | Year | No. of burials |
|------|------|------|------|
| 1600 | 70 | 1621 | 111 |
| 1601 | 102 | 1622 | 131 |
| 1602 | no data | 1623 | 402 |
| 1603 | 114 | 1624 | 203 |
| 1604 | 74 | 1625 | 122 |
| 1605 | 70 | 1626 | 105 |
| 1606 | 86 | 1627 | 93 |
| 1607 | (27) | 1628 | 119 |
| 1608 | 88 | 1629 | (64) |
| 1609 | 72 | 1630 | 103 |
| 1610 | (53) | 1631 | 111 |
| 1611 | (51) | 1632 | 84 |
| 1612 | (26) | 1633 | 174 |
| 1613 | no data | 1634 | 120 |
| 1614 | 76 | 1635 | 142 |
| 1615 | 81 | 1636 | 139 |
| 1616 | 79 | 1637 | 133 |
| 1617 | 139 | 1638 | (96) |
| 1618 | 131 | 1639 | (41) |
| 1619 | 100 | 1640 | (96) |
| 1620 | 71 | 1641 | 145 |

*Note*: Figures in brackets are years with defective data.

These statistics not only indicate the slow yet steady growth of Blackburn's population but also highlight the fact that the townspeople suffered from intermittent outbreaks of disease or plague. For example in the year 1623 the death rate quadrupled and only partly fell back the following year. Ten years later, in 1633, mortality doubled yet again.

Conventionally, the 'interest' of history used to be measured by how many great events and colourful happenings took place in a locality. If that criterion is adopted, Blackburn's history in the medieval period and into the eighteenth century was very unremarkable. It played no part in stirring events such as the Wars of the Roses, and it was neither the resort of kings nor the scene of important occasions. Blackburn's state of military preparedness can be seen in the militia returns compiled in 1595, almost at the end of the long reign of Elizabeth I. Blackburn parish as a whole could muster 532 men, of whom 210 could supply some form of weapon. The township of Blackburn itself could only raise 63 men in total, of whom just eight were armed: two with bills, one with a bow and five with shot.[6] Blackburn failed to sleep through the English Civil War, though not for the want of trying. There were six hundreds in

This is Bank House on Adelaide Terrace, probably one of the oldest properties in Blackburn, dating back to the early seventeenth century. It was from here that during the Civil War the royalist Sir Gilbert Hoghton ineffectually bombarded the town using a small cannon around Christmas 1642. Later occupants of the house included William Eccles MP.

COTTON TOWN PROJECT

Lancashire, and in four of these the great majority of the local gentry supported the cause of King Charles, while in only one (Salford Hundred) was there as clear majority for parliament. Blackburn hundred was the exception. Here the gentry had mixed opinions and there was no definite allegiance to either side. The district was unsure and uncommitted. Outsiders, however, ensured that Blackburn did become involved. The first action occurred in October 1642 when the Royalist commander Sir Gilbert Hoghton of Hoghton Tower, west of the town, successfully seized a weapon store held at Whalley Abbey and then prepared to settle down for the night in Blackburn on his way home. His forces were surprised by 200 parliamentarian soldiers led by Colonel Shuttleworth of Gawthorpe Hall near Burnley, and the evening of 27 October saw fighting along Darwen Street and Church Street. Houghton's forces had to flee, so this counted as a minor victory for Parliament. The second action occurred on Christmas Eve of the same year. Hoghton returned, set up a small cannon near Bank House at the top of Dukes Brow and opened fire. The only casualty was a frying pan. Not wishing to miss their Christmas festivities the besiegers then left to return to Hoghton Tower. The remainder of the civil war passed Blackburn by, although Prince Rupert rode through on his way to the battle of Marston Moor. He lost. The only lasting result of these years was the destruction of the market cross by rowdy parliamentarian soldiers. Presumably they vented their wrath on it because it had a statue of Mary, which was anathema to the puritan soldiery. It was never repaired and for years to come the 'Blackburn Stump' sat forlornly in the very centre of the town.

Blackburn was comparatively isolated, and unimportant, in strategic terms, and this was seen again during the Jacobite Rebellions of 1715 and 1745. Though Preston was occupied for the Stuarts in 1715 no march on Blackburn was made. The town was too insignificant, and the main aim of the rebels was to head south towards Manchester or Chester. The nearest anyone came was when a forage party penetrated as far as Darwen via Tockholes. Captain Aynesworth of Pleasington had organised barricades across Blackburn's streets but they were not needed. In 1745 Preston was again occupied for the Stuart cause as Bonnie Prince Charlie marched his Highlanders south. Sir Henry Hoghton now left his tower and visited Blackburn to organise the local levies in defence of the Hanoverian succession. On hearing that the rebels might be advancing on Blackburn he sensibly decided to march in the opposite direction. He need not have bothered. The Jacobites carried on southwards. They even failed to visit Blackburn on their eventual retreat.[7] But do these things really matter? The absence of great events, in the dramatic and colourful sense, is nothing to do with steady commercial progress. Indeed, it could well be argued that

Blackburn was very fortunate not to have been the location of major fighting and military action: Bolton was largely destroyed, and many of its inhabitants killed, during sieges in 1643 and 1644, Preston was partly burned and experienced savage street-fighting in 1715. Blackburn escaped such traumas. Since it was not on any major north–south route, nor on a main east–west route Blackburn was never of strategic importance to anyone, and few could argue that it was the worse for that.

It was, however, growing in local influence. There are no reliable population figures until the beginning of the nineteenth century, but the limited evidence that is available suggests that in the late sixteenth century the population was probably only about 1,500. This can be compared with perhaps 2,500 in Preston and Wigan, and 5,000 for Manchester, the largest town in Elizabethan Lancashire, and is broadly comparable in size with places such as Bolton, Liverpool and Lancaster. The layout of the town was based on the crossroads where Church Street, Darwen Street, King Street and Northgate join. Here,

Top-o'-th'-Coal Pit (1893): Roughley Lane, at the bottom of the map, follows the alignment of what is now Manxman Road, while the existence of the former Mowbray Lodge is recalled by the name Mowbray Avenue. There were numerous small coal pits in the area, working shallow and poor-quality seams during the first half of the nineteenth century. Almost all had been abandoned by 1880.

DETAIL OF THE 1893 ORDNANCE SURVEY MAP, REPRODUCED BY KIND PERMISSION OF THE COUNTY ARCHIVIST, LANCASHIRE RECORD OFFICE

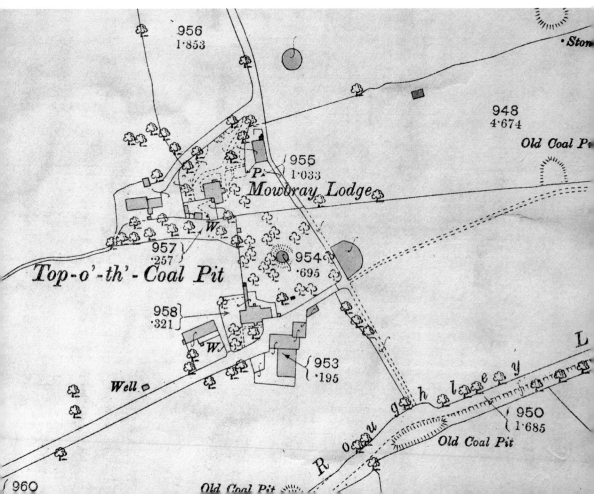

In the late nineteenth century Charles Haworth drew a number of sketches for the *Blackburn Times*, this one was titled Top o'th'Coal Pits. This old coal mine was at Grimshaw Park though other examples could be found dotted all around the town. Coal mining as a local industry was never on a large scale with pits often employing just a handful of men and with the coming of the canal and the arrival of cheaper coal by barge, most had ceased working by the middle of the nineteenth century.

as already noted, was the market place and parish church. Nothing survives of the medieval and Tudor town, since all trace of the buildings was swept away during the wholesale changes of the industrial period. However, engravings show that the parish church, which was rebuilt in the middle years of the fourteenth century and again in the 1540s, was a long and somewhat irregular stone building, with a chancel that was longer than the nave, and a squat battlemented tower. The buildings around were irregular and haphazard. Some may have been of stone but most were undoubtedly timber-framed, and many, even in the centre of the small town, were probably no more than single storey dwellings. Blackburn appears to have had no examples of the spectacular multi-storeyed black and white inns which were found in, for example, Preston, Wigan and Warrington. These were all thriving and commercially buoyant towns on a main routeway, whereas Blackburn, like Burnley and Bury, was more local in its catchment and less ambitious in its architecture. It was, however, a commercial centre of growing significance, and its existing role as a market centre was supplemented, from the end of the fifteenth century onwards, with industrial development. This was during the period which historians now term 'proto-industrialisation', the long run-up to the major expansion of industry in the mid-eighteenth century. By the 1590s there is some documentary evidence for industrial development in the Blackburn area. Many trades and crafts were conducted which were of the sort found anywhere – for example, blacksmithing and small-scale metal-working, milling and brewing. In turbaries nearby, turf (peat) was cut for burning as a domestic fuel and also for minor industrial use, a pattern which was found very widely across Lancashire. Thus, an indenture of 1618 gave a local man the right to 'dig and carry two hundred loads of turves out of the moss and Turbary at Livesaye to be spent and burned at the

King Street (1848): Until the commercial centre of the town shifted some distance to the north, with the laying out of the new market place in the mid-1840s, King Street was one of the main thoroughfares and was an address with some social cachet – indeed, well into the mid-nineteenth century it still had a sprinkling of well-to-do residents, as well as banks, the Royal Hotel, and one of the main post offices. The 'Infantry Barracks (Temporary)' is a reminder that Blackburn, like many of the cotton towns, was regarded with apprehension by those in authority at this time of political unrest, although, in reality, Blackburn was politically the very opposite of a radical town. Note, also, the poor rate office near the Wesleyan Methodist chapel on Clayton Street.

DETAIL OF THE 1848 ORDNANCE SURVEY MAP, REPRODUCED BY KIND PERMISSION OF THE COUNTY ARCHIVIST, LANCASHIRE RECORD OFFICE

This print shows the old windmill at Eanam, which produced flour for many of the local bakers, set against the steam-powered mills with their tall smoking chimneys. It highlights the changing face of energy that the industrial revolution brought with it.

kiln appertaining to the mill for the drying of corn to be ground at the same mill'.[8]

By that time, though, coal was also being mined from local seams on the northern rim of the great Lancashire coalfield. The parish registers for the seventeenth century state the occupations of a number of those who were married or buried, and some are referred to as 'coliers' or 'colegitters'. The mines in which they worked were scattered around the edges of the town but the focus of activity appears to have been Coal Pit Moor to the east of Ewood between Blackburn and Darwen. The 1844 Ordnance Survey map shows six old pits in this area, and around 1720 when John Bailey built a farm there he called it Coal Pit Farm. Further evidence of the mining past of this area was found in 1935. Two quarrymen descended a number of 50-foot shafts near the farm, which were clearly the ancient workings of one of the sixteenth- or seventeenth-century pits. At the bottom of one they found they could crawl along old coal seams that varied from 2 feet 3 inches to 4 feet. The tunnels ran for a distance of about 50 feet towards and under the grounds of Park Lee Hospital. Other pits were near Bank Hey. The type of workings in and

*'Coliers' and 'colegitters' are mentioned in the registers in the seventeenth century.*

College Ward Hall Clough Bank Hacking Hall Bank End Wha
Spout Lower Buckley Dewhurst Potter Ford
House College Francis Hall Houses Hough Dinkley Lango Gr 26
Green Butcher Dewhurst Dinkley Billington 15
Fold Ribchester New Hall Salisbury Moor Whalley Milton 6
Carwood House Parsonage York Whilpshire Fold A
Hothersall Madge Westwood Jack White
Fell Bank House New Hall Whinney Green Carr M
Bristroughs Hall Shirley Long Capster Lane Carr 13 Breadley Hall Cowa
Boot Hall Hall Lane Green Lovely Hall Hall Clayton le Dale Carr Green Cliff Low
Sun Ashland Pepperhouse Osbaldeston Clayton Hay Fold Pyethorn 12 Cow Cowa
Hawkers Main Lane End Green Thistle Nest New Ann Hey
Balderston Pilsley Smalleys Ramsgreave Hole 11 Dove 3 Hen Dewhurst
Pickerings Darwens Hall Steady Cots Close Nook
6 7 8 Call 9 10 Holes 2 Cunliffe Lee Oake
House Barker Sidebeet Rushton
Mascow Warble Hay Lane Little Eichill 81
Smithy Mellor Whinny Lane Harwood 9 New
New Inn Bolton Kings Town Lane Harwood Barn
Sowerbutts Fold Stanley Bank Rough Hey End Hall 10 Cow Hill
Gr Nab House Cuckow 1 Eichill New
Spring Head Ravens Beardwood Hall Barn
River Wings Green Hurst Scar Sheer Hole Ho. White Church
Wood Billing Yat End Brow Bottom Birk Stand
Bottom Fold Wood Witton Gate Knuzden Hill
Hall Hall Witton 25 BLACKBURN
Pleasington Stocks Stakes 24 Grimshaw Oswaldtwistle
Houghton Livesey Hall Abbots Park Shadsworth Jack
Tower Hall Rolling Bank 21 24 House
Printing 2 Moor Yate Langshaw 23 Holker
Hullart Works Fold 23 Lower Barn
Hall 5 Moulding Livesey Fernhurst Darwen 20 Pickering Stoney Kn
Dicksons Water Bogg Fold Height Lower Belthorn 22
Hill Marsh Stanworth Darwen Wood
Head Tockhole Edcraft Cotton Head 19 Bank Fold
Marsh Briner Fold Hare Groft Hall 22 Windy Bank 21
Lythe Withnell Height Eccleshill Crane
New Ho. Hay Head
Breworth 5 School Lower New Fold Water Haslingden
Fold 6 Wood Fold Hill House Livesey Darwen Side 18 Booth
Wheelton Fine Fold Chapel Moss
Peters Over Darwen Over Side
Wheelton Dale Fold Gantan Darwen 20 Longshaw
Stocks Winty Arbor Ryds Darwen White Hall 17 Head Stoops Hillock
Hall Lower House Moors Hollingshead Moor 19 Combs Grime
Fold Hall Fold Hills
Eagle Tower Low Fold Pins Overt 16
Nook
Warth Pasture Bull Hill Coal Pit Edgew
Barn Pike House
High Bullow Bromeleys Moors Hulton Pasture 18 Entwistle 15
Moors Pasture The Edge Hob
Whitaker Top Whitacre Lan
Entwistle Hall
Barnb
17

around Blackburn varied. Some were bell pits, where a vertical shaft was dug down to the coal and then the seam was dug out in all directions, producing a cross-section that resembled a bell-shape. Other workings involved digging outwards along the coal seams for some distance, with the roof shored up with pit props or sometimes with pillars of coal being left unworked to support the roof. Some had shafts of 200 feet, but most were much shallower. Yet others were adit mines, where a tunnel was driven horizontally into the hillside. The mining operations were almost always very small, the majority employing only three to five miners. Most of the coal was sold locally but some was carried by packhorse to neighbouring areas.[9]

The growth of the textile industry was, however, of the greatest importance to the future development of Blackburn. Although there is no specific evidence, we can be sure that for many generations past, local families had spun thread and woven cloth for domestic use, using the wool from sheep which grazed on the moorland slopes. In the late medieval period, though, it is likely that some farming families began to produce cloth not just for their own use but also for sale, to provide a second income which would supplement that earned from farming or other trades. The cloth they produced was sold to clothiers or chapmen who, after bleaching and then perhaps dyeing it, took it to surrounding markets. Contemporary evidence from Rossendale indicates that in the later sixteenth century there was a major increase in the numbers of sheep grazed on the moors between Haslingden, Oswaldtwistle and Darwen, and economic historians correlate this evidence with other indications of growing commercial activity to suggest that in the years between about 1560 and 1590 the Lancashire textile industry underwent a major expansion, one which set in train the pattern of development that led towards the Industrial Revolution itself. Gradually, during the sixteenth and seventeenth centuries, south-east Lancashire, from the Ribble valley to the Mersey, began to specialise in woollen cloths, and towns such as Blackburn, Burnley and Colne began to function as the commercial centres for the expanding trade. Under an Act of Parliament of 1566 Blackburn, together with Bolton, Bury, Rochdale and Manchester, was designated as one of the towns where inspectors of cloth were to be located, suggesting that it was by then recognised as having a special significance in the textile trade and was considered to be one of the main centres in Lancashire. The town was noted for its woollen cloth, though by the middle of the seventeenth century

A section of Aikin's map, published in 1795 as part of his *Description of the Country From Thirty to Forty Miles Around Manchester*. Note that although Bolton Road, through Ewood to Darwen, had been turnpiked, the old route, Roman Road, is still shown very prominently. However, there was still no good way out of the town north-westwards: Preston New Road was not constructed for almost another thirty years. As river navigations and canals were all the rage in the 1790s, Aikin tried wherever possible to show these on his map, but the construction of the Leeds and Liverpool canal through Blackburn lay well in the future, too.
CARNEGIE COLLECTION

its output was increasingly concerned with mixed-fibre cloths and those which included cotton. Among these was Blackburn Checks, which had a linen warp and a cotton weft, one or both of which were dyed to give it its distinctive check appearance. Blue and white became the pattern most associated with Blackburn. Alongside the Checks, the town also produced Blackburn Greys, a plain unfinished cloth. Blackburn's growing involvement with, and reliance upon, the textile industry can be seen by a study of the parish register of 1723. Of the 149 baptism entries, 68 were for the children of weavers, and of the 60 burial entries for heads of families, 34 were weavers.[10] Textiles were already the major industry. The scene was set for Blackburn to arise from relative national obscurity as the industrial revolution, led by cotton, got under way. How Blackburn and its people adapted to rapid urbanisation is the subject of the following chapters.

*'Of the 149 baptisms, 68 were for the children of weavers, and of the 60 burial entries for heads of families, 34 were weavers.'*

PARISH REGISTER, 1723

# The economy, 1750–1914

B LACKBURN WAS ALREADY NOTED for textiles by 1750. Thereafter, the manufacturing of cotton cloth expanded rapidly and the town expanded with it. Here, as elsewhere in the county, the cotton industry was at first dominated by the domestic system of production. Merchants purchased the raw cotton and took it to cottagers, who spun it first into thread and then wove it into cloth. They were paid by the piece. The merchants then had the cloth bleached and dyed – in the Blackburn area sites for bleaching and dyeing extended along the banks of the Blakewater. By 1750 this system, known as putting-out, was in its heyday, but it depended entirely on the domestic spinning and weaving processes, which were physically constrained by space, the human power for machinery, and the need for one man or woman to operate one loom. From the early eighteenth century onwards inventors and innovators sought to free production from these constraints, by introducing new forms of spinning and weaving machinery and by harnessing new sources of power – first water, then steam. The spinning process was the first to be mechanised, and by the late 1780s the application of steam power to more efficient and effective spinning equipment was transforming the industry. Steam-powered spinning mills became a new element in the industrial landscape, and the factory replaced the domestic system of manufacture, with the result that Blackburn itself was transformed: 'For years cotton merchants flourished so exceedingly in Blackburn, and such fabulous fortunes were amassed in a short time, there was a general rush to get into it ... The trade in a very short time not only absorbed the whole town but spread out into the country districts around, and the banks of the Blakewater are covered with great mills right up the valley to Accrington.'[1]

Thus, the first mills in Blackburn were for spinning and most of those in the earliest days of mechanisation were in were converted warehouses or corn mills. Not until 1797 was the first purpose-built spinning mill was constructed, at Wensley Fold. Even thereafter, the adoption of steam power for spinning was relatively slow, but after 1816 the mechanisation of the industry acceler-ated rapidly and in 1824 there were 24 mills, employing 10,460 hands; by 1831 the 15,000 spinners looked after 170,000 spindles, and in 1849 the town had

1.1 million spindles.[2] The zenith of spinning in Blackburn was reached in 1870, following two decades in which over 20 new spinning mills had been built. However, from this point onwards, long before the collapse of the Lancashire cotton industry, the fortunes of the town's spinning trade went into reverse. From 2.5 million spindles in the early 1870s the industry shrank to 1.1 million by 1900, and during that thirty-year period sixteen spinning mills either closed down or converted to weaving. Only four new ones replaced them, and the number of joint spinning and weaving mills also fell, from 45 to 29 over the same period.[3] The focus of the spinning industry moved to South Lancashire, and especially Bolton and Oldham. In its place came the rise to dominance of the power loom and the weaving mill. It is clear from this that the story of cotton is far from straightforward, and even in the nineteenth century there were long-term fundamental changes in the structure of the industry, as well as the shorter term ups and downs of trade depressions and booms.

The advent of steam-powered spinning had a dramatic impact upon weaving, for the application of steam to the weaving process was long delayed. As a result, although steam-spinning produced enormous quantities of yarn, all of this still had to be spun at home on domestic looms, a process managed by the putting-out system. This in turn meant that, because the industry depended on them, the handloom weavers could command exceptionally high rates of pay. Between the 1780s and the 1830s handloom weaving enjoyed a golden age, becoming one of the dominant elements in urban and rural economies in mid-Lancashire. Handloom weavers in and around Blackburn in the eighteenth century worked under what was known locally as the 'fested' system. They lived in small communities up to six miles from the town, in areas such as Little Harwood, Whitebirk, Stanhill and Knuzden, and each weaver signed up with a local cotton merchant, such as Robert Hopwood or George Briggs. The latter had up to 800 weavers on his books at any one time. It was estimated that in 1800 there were more than 20,000 such handloom weavers within a three-mile radius of Blackburn. At this time they mainly produced heavy jaconets, checks and shirting.[4]

Bank Top and Wensley Fold (1893): this was where Blackburn's history as cotton town started, for the first mill was opened at Wensley Fold in 1778, powered by the waters of the Blakewater. Along this stretch of the river a series of sizeable mills was developed in the next fifty years, together with ancillary industries including one of the town's five gasworks. Their noxious effluent was partly responsible for the gross pollution of the watercourse by the end of the century. As this area industrialised early, its housing was particularly poor and cramped – for example, the tiny homes around a communal yard with a central privy block on Chicken Street (*centre right*), and the densely packed hovels on the south side of Whalley Banks (*bottom right*).

DETAIL OF THE 1893 ORDNANCE SURVEY MAP, REPRODUCED BY KIND PERMISSION OF THE COUNTY ARCHIVIST, LANCASHIRE RECORD OFFICE

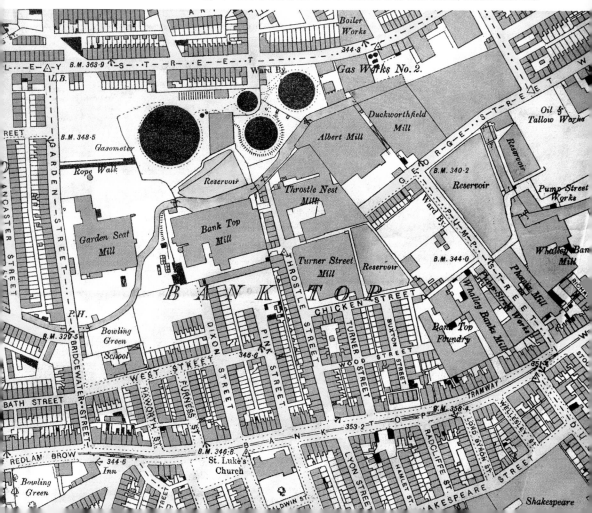

Nevertheless, even before the advent of the power loom in Blackburn (from the 1820s) there were indications that the golden age had departed, and significant indicators of difficulties, stress and tension were becoming evident. Handloom weavers began to experience a reduction in their standards of living, partly because its very success had encouraged too many people to enter the weaving trade. The consequent overmanning, especially after 1815 when men returned from the Napoleonic wars, resulted in a decline in piece rates, which had reached a peak as early as 1797. There were 170,000 handloom weavers in Lancashire in the 1820s, and in Blackburn alone there were, it has been calculated, some 14,750 in 1821. As wages began to decline slowly, the numbers employed in the domestic side of the industry also started to fall, not just in the Blackburn area but also throughout the county's cotton districts. In theory this should have led to the redressing of the balance, and the restoration of higher wage levels, but the gradual introduction of steam-powered technology in the weaving industry, which gathered pace in the mid- to late 1820s, accelerated an existing trend and further undermined the position of the handloom weavers. This pincer movement, whereby the handloom weavers were trapped between an overcrowded industry and the advent of new technology, reduced their

*'For years cotton merchants flourished so exceedingly in Blackburn, and such fabulous fortunes were amassed in a short time, there was a general rush to get into it ...'*

THE TIMES, 1862

standard of living and also changed the nature of their work. They had always been involved in the quality end of the market, producing 'fancy' goods and cambrics, but this now became the mainstay. They retained only that part of the market in which power looms could not yet compete. By 1838 the number of handloom weavers living in and around Blackburn was estimated at 7,000 and still declining, and one source in 1841 claimed that the number had diminished to just over 1,000.[5]

Though open to some dispute, these figures may well tell roughly the correct tale. A recent study of the 1851 census returns has shown that in the hamlets surrounding Blackburn handloom weaving still survived as a significant element of the employment structure.[6] Accurate figures for all townships are difficult to determine, since some census enumerators failed to differentiate between handloom and power loom weavers, but the figures for Blackburn town suggest a minimum of 986 and a maximum of 4,257 handloom weavers, representing anything between 2 per cent and 9 per cent of the working population. The lower of the two figures is probably nearer the true figure since it matches previous estimates. Moving away from the centre of Blackburn, however, the proportion of handloom weavers in the workforce gradually increased. In Livesey there were between 180 and 267, representing 7–10 per cent of the working community, while at Little Harwood there were 51 representing 16 per cent. A little further out, in Ramsgreave, the figure was 155, or 35 per cent of the workers, while in Wilpshire the figures were 76 and 32 per cent respectively; in Mellor between 371 and 706, representing 22–44 per cent; and in Tockholes 219–223 or 24–25 per cent. It appears that even in 1851, in the nearby outlying rural areas around Blackburn handloom weavers not only survived but also made up a sizeable proportion of the local workforce. Within Blackburn the handloom weavers tended to congregate in small communities, possibly signed up to the same 'putter out'. In the Mile End area in 1851, out of a total population of 279, 130 of the 162 employed people were handloom weavers.[7] One reason for the survival of such communities is that despite all the improvements of the power loom it was still more economical for handloom weavers to produce the fine, fancy and mixed cloths. The existence of a cheap and flexible supply of such weavers also gave entrepreneurs the choice of labour intensive or capital-intensive production. For men with a modicum of capital, 'putting out' was still a viable alternative to the expense of opening a mill.

By the end of the 1830s the living standards of handloom weavers had fallen to the point where widespread destitution was becoming apparent. In 1841 a visitor employed by the Guardians of the Poor visited a number of weavers and described what was found: 'Their principal food is oatmeal porridge, with either churned or sweet milk and potatoes stewed with a little water, salt and an onion or two for dinner. Rarely do they partake of animal food of any sort. Indeed they seldom procure a sufficient quantity of the coarse fare already

When the cotton trade was depressed thousands of the town's inhabitants found themselves out of work. Local schemes were sometimes set up to help some find temporary paid work; one such scheme was the building of Revidge Road which was cut out of the side of the hill in the 1820s. The road engineer in charge was the famous 'Blind' Jack Metcalfe, and this plaque commemorates the achievement and can still be seen today.

mentioned. Many were found without food whatsoever in their houses, and some were very nearly destitute. Their bedding is of the most wretched description, consisting generally of a coarse kind of sacking tick, very scantily supplied with chaff, and sometimes of bare straw. Their coverings are shreds of sheets, blankets, packing sheets and other scanty weaving apparel. In many instances there is only one bed of this description for six or seven individuals.'[8]

In Blackburn many handloom weavers prolonged their working life by obtaining employment in handloom sheds. These were owned by entrepreneurs, drawn from many walks of life including handloom weaving itself, and they represented the halfway stage between the true domestic system and the modern power-driven mill, employing weavers working on handlooms but outside their cottages and away from their families. The majority of such sheds employed 10–30 people but some accommodated as many as 100 weavers. These employees did not own the looms but worked regular hours under supervision.[9] They were usually younger people, as many older handloom weavers saw such work as beneath them, while employers found them difficult to train to factory rules. Such sheds were not immediately replaced by the mills and the demise of the handloom weaver was long and drawn out. The last handloom shop in Blackburn did not cease production until 1894, and the last former handloom weaver died as recently as 1921.[10]

*'Their principal food is oatmeal porridge, with either churned or sweet milk and potatoes stewed with a little water, salt and an onion or two for dinner.*

1841 REPORT ON
HANDLOOM WEAVERS

The steam-powered weaving mills which gradually eclipsed and superseded handloom weaving were destined to transform Blackburn beyond recognition. Richard Cartwright had invented a practicable power loom in 1785, but it is estimated that by 1820 there were still only 14,500 in the whole of Britain. Continuing technical difficulties inhibited its sales, but after the first commercially successful and technically efficient power loom (that of Roberts and Sharp) was marketed in 1822, their use grew very rapidly. In Blackburn the first mill to introduce powerlooms was Bannister Eccles' Dandy Mill at Grimshaw Park where, though it was originally built in 1820 for spinning, the owners installed new looms in 1825. In this part of the county the adoption of the new technology was relatively slow, for the first official census of power looms, made in 1835 by the newly appointed factory inspectors, showed that of 61,176 looms in Lancashire only 12,000 were in north Lancashire and just 3,200

James Sharples, who painted this internationally known painting between 1844 and 1847, began work as an apprentice at Blackburn's Yates Foundry, later known as Foster Yates & Thom, and based this picture on his experiences there. He always wanted to be an artist, and woke at 4 a.m. each morning to practise his drawing before going to work for 6 a.m. He then resumed his studies after work ended at 8 p.m. He died penniless, and is buried in Pleasington cemetery.

BLACKBURN MUSEUM

in Blackburn.[11] Other than the technical problems that had beset Cartwright's loom, and which made owners reluctant to commit themselves to the new methods, there were memories of early machine-breaking riots in Blackburn and – by no means unimportant – a still plentiful and cheap supply of handloom weavers. These factors meant that the main expansion of power looms in this town was delayed until after the mid-1840s.

The twenty years from 1850 to 1870 saw a dramatic acceleration of weaving in Blackburn with 68 new weaving-only mills built in the town and four combined mills. This followed the invention of the Kenworthy power loom, by a group of weaver engineers at the town's Brookhouse mill. The cloth that could be produced by this loom was of a far higher quality than had been possible before, on other power looms. Between 1870 and 1890 another eighteen weaving mills were built, but after 1890 the expansion was mainly in the size of the mills rather than in their number. The 48,000 looms in Blackburn in 1870 had increased to 88,770 by 1914.[12] Naturally, Blackburn had other industries, but cotton had become overwhelmingly important by the third quarter of the nineteenth century. The main secondary trade was engineering, though this was geared to the cotton trade and mainly produced textile machinery. It remained, however, quite small when compared with cotton. Thus, in 1881 engineering only employed 6 per cent of the total workforce of the town, while cotton accounted for 59.7 per cent, a proportion that had hardly altered by 1911.[13] In many other cotton towns the engineering trades were, comparatively, far larger. In Bolton and Rochdale, for example, the engineering workforce was about half the size of that in cotton, and in Oldham it was the same size. The only other significant industry in Blackburn was the building trade, as labourers and craftsmen busily erected not only the cotton mills but also the houses of the ever-growing numbers of cotton workers. Even in a county of cotton, Blackburn – like some other east Lancashire towns – was notable for its dependence upon the industry. In 1921 48.9 per cent of the workforce in Blackburn was in textiles. The proportion was even greater in Burnley (52.1 per cent) but rather more than in Rochdale (42.3 per cent) and Oldham (42.9 per cent). None of these, however, could match the astonishing figures for Nelson (68.3 per cent) and Padiham (73.7 per cent), where almost everyone depended, either directly or indirectly, on a single industry.

Since it was so heavily dependent on cotton anything that affected that trade had an immediate impact upon Blackburn. The result was a series of booms and slumps, which punctuated the general growth seen throughout the nineteenth century and up to 1914. Between 1800 and 1914 there were twelve major periods of between

During periods of high unemployment when the cotton trade was in recession local people and charitable institutions organised help for the town's populace through the opening of soup kitchens. Vouchers were given out to those deemed to be in most need and a meal of soup would be given in exchange. This one was issued during the great Cotton Famine of the early 1860s brought about by the American Civil War. Other vouchers were issued that could be exchanged for coal and bread.
BLACKBURN MUSEUM

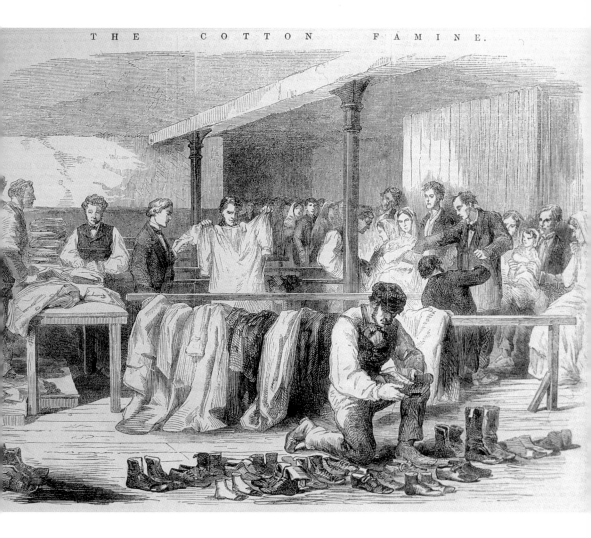

During the Cotton Famine of the 1860s national appeals led to parcels of unwanted clothing being sent to towns such as Blackburn. This illustration from the *Illustrated London News* shows unemployed workers choosing shoes and other items.

COTTON TOWN PROJECT

one and three years when the town, and Lancashire as a whole, experienced severe depression in the cotton trade, as well as the most notorious of all, the five-year Cotton Famine of 1861–65. All were painful for the employers but far more so for the ordinary working people of Blackburn. The slumps brought unemployment, short-time working and fewer looms per worker (which meant less pay) for those lucky enough still to be employed. Even in 1908 those in work found their earnings cut to 10*s*. (50p) per week compared with the normal 24*s*. (£1.20).[14] Nearly a century earlier, in 1826, workers were paying an even harsher price for a fall in the demand for cotton. A contemporary account reported that Blackburn was 'divided into sixteen districts, and Visitors appointed to call at every house, in order to ascertain the wants of the really necessitous poor. The task was a most arduous one to perform, and many were the heart-rending scenes of distress that they were compelled to witness. During the last nine weeks about fourteen thousand individuals (more than

half the population of the township) have been relieved weekly with food.'[15] During the slump of 1841–43 a soup kitchen was set up in the Old Square, while in 1847 the 'visitor' system was reintroduced and 12,000 people were supplied with food to help them survive the trade depression.[16] During the slump of 1908 there were 4,000 unemployed in Blackburn and 2,500 turned to the hastily constituted Distress Committee for relief.

But the largest, most famous and most distressing depression in Blackburn's history was the great Cotton Famine which caused immense hardship in the town between 1861 and 1865. Traditionally the blame for this catastrophe has been placed squarely upon the American Civil War, when, it was argued, the pro-union northern states blockaded the Confederate South and stopped supplies of raw cotton from reaching Lancashire. More recently, historians have suggested that a major factor was more coincidental and more local in origin. It is clear that cotton manufacturers in Lancashire had grossly overproduced cloth in the boom years of the late 1850s, so that there were huge stockpiles of unsold textiles by 1860–61. This meant that they cut back on production to avoid further accumulation of cloth and laid people off, creating an artificial

The opening of soup kitchens to help feed the unemployed was a common way of alleviating hunger during slumps in the cotton trade. This one was set up in Preston in 1862 during the Cotton Famine and would have been typical of those seen in Blackburn. Being cooked here in large vats was beef, barley, groats, peas, onions, carrots and turnip with salt and white pepper.

finally ended half-time working in 1918, though full implementation was phased in to allow mill-owners to adjust their work patterns. Children then had to be fourteen before they could work in full-time employment.

As was universally the case in the Lancashire cotton towns, women were another major source of labour in the mills since in terms of wages they too came cheap. In 1841, when the power looms were being established in Blackburn, there were 4,882 girls and women employed in the town's cotton trade compared with 2,821 boys and men. Many men in the first half of the nineteenth century remained in handloom weaving, while others obtained employment in engineering or as labourers in the building trade. As handloom weaving declined and the demand for labour within the mills increased, more men entered the cotton trade, but weaving remained a bastion of female labour through the nineteenth and into the middle of the twentieth centuries. In 1905 there were 16,604 females in the cotton industry in Blackburn, compared with 8,005 males.[26] The continued demand for female workers meant that in 1910 in Blackburn, 59 per cent of all women over the age of ten worked, 78 per cent of all unmarried women worked, and 44 per cent of all married women; among the highest percentages in any large town in the country. Outside cotton, some women worked in dress-making, others in shops and laundries, and a few were in domestic service, but the last category was, as in most working-class towns, a relatively small element in the female employment structure. Cotton was, for men and women, the dominant employer.[27] This also led to 'the textile unions [becoming] the pioneers of mixed unionism'.[28] Of the Blackburn Weavers Association's 17,000 members in 1908, 11,900 were women, and of the 1,862 members of the Card and Blowing Room Operatives Association, 1,489 were female. As will be seen in chapter 5, such a high proportion of women may have been one reason for the relative lack of militant trade unionism in Blackburn.[29]

Another consequence of the employment of so many women in weaving was that although equal pay was usual, so also were low wages. Just before the First World War four-loom weavers, who were the industry's elite, received between 22s. (£1.10) and 28s. (£1.40) per week. This can be compared with 36s. (£1.80) to 40s. (£2) for skilled men in the building trade during the summer months; 35s. (£1.75) to 38s. (£1.90) for skilled men in engineering; and 35s. (£1.75) to 43s. (£2.15) for spinners (who were predominantly male). In the furnishing trade the weekly wages were 34s. (£1.70) and in printing 32s. 6d. (£1.62). Skilled weavers' wages therefore only matched those of unskilled building labourers. Other workers within weaving received even poorer remuneration. Piecers, strippers, winders, warpers and three-loom weavers earned less than £1.[30] The

Table 2 *Female employment in Blackburn County Borough, 1911*

| Rank | Category | Total employed | % of total female employment | % of all females aged 10 and over |
|------|----------|---------------|------------------------------|-----------------------------------|
| 1 | textile manufacturing | 25913 | 74.4 | 44.0 |
| 2 | tailoring, dressmaking and millinery | 1944 | 5.6 | 3.3 |
| 3 | catering trades | 1940 | 5.6 | 3.3 |
| 4 | domestic service | 1755 | 5.0 | 3.0 |
| 5 | food and drink dealers | 1165 | 3.4 | 2.0 |
| 6 | teaching | 584 | 1.7 | 1.0 |
| 7 | charwomen | 392 | 1.1 | 0.7 |
| 8 | laundrywomen, washing, manglers | 309 | 0.9 | 0.5 |
| 9 | textile machinery making | 260 | 0.8 | 0.4 |
| 10 | midwives, nurses, attendants | 179 | 0.5 | 0.3 |
| 11 | paper-making and stationery | 169 | 0.5 | 0.3 |
| 12 | clothing dealers | 155 | 0.5 | 0.3 |
| 13 | clerks (commercial premises) | 122 | 0.4 | 0.2 |
| 14 | general shop keeping | 101 | 0.3 | 0.2 |
| 15 | local or national government | 90 | 0.3 | 0.2 |
| 16 | music, art and drama | 78 | 0.2 | |
| 17 | bread, biscuit, cake making | 74 | 0.2 | |
| 18 | hawkers and street sellers | 60 | 0.2 | |

(statistics reorganised from census tables: only groups with 50+ females are listed)

combination of such low wages for men in weaving, and the availability of relatively well-paid work for women, had far-reaching results for many families in Blackburn. With both husband and wife in work, and perhaps some of their children, it was estimated that in 1905 some households had a weekly income of between £4 and £6.[31] As will be seen in later chapters, such a relatively high total income influenced leisure activities and housing in the town. But when a family was reduced to just one wage earner through old age, unemployment, illness, accident or death, poverty was the almost inevitable result. The need for more than one wage earner in a family often required women to work throughout their pregnancies and to return within days of giving birth. As will be seen later, this was frequently considered by contemporaries to be a major factor behind serious public health problems and, especially, high levels of infant mortality. That women earned a wage appears to have done little in Blackburn to bring about any more general sense of the equality of the sexes. Though the gender division in the local economy and society may not have been so wide as in other communities, it was still there. Women far outnumbered men in weaving, but it was not until 1911 that the first two women were elected onto the committee of the Blackburn Weavers Association.[32] The inequality mainly showed itself in leisure pursuits, as will be seen in chapter 7, and within the home. Women returned from the mill to a second day's work in the evening and a subservient role. It was even claimed that 'In Blackburn . . . it is the usual thing for the husband, when he comes home late at night, to give his wife a kicking and beating. The women take it as part of the daily round and don't complain.'[33]

Blackburn's cotton workforce had a distinct age structure. Spinners had a working life of about twenty years, which meant that very few remained beyond the age of forty. In weaving the working life was only slightly longer. In 1892 60 per cent of the town's weavers were under 25 years of age.[34] When women eventually became too old to work they usually became full-time housewives. Men who left the mills often took on unskilled work or, if they had saved, became shopkeepers or publicans. It was the gathering pace of work, coupled with poor working conditions, which kept the workforce young. By the 1880s about 80 per cent of weavers had four looms under their control, and the machines were getting faster as technical improvements were continually made.

Pictures of mill girls are those usually seen, but it took a team of men to ensure all the machinery worked. Here, with their manager, are the power loom overlookers or 'tacklers' at Roe Lee Mill. Without their skill the weavers, who were on 'piece rates', could find their earnings reduced.
COTTON TOWN PROJECT, © LANCASHIRE EVENING TELEGRAPH

A HISTORY OF BLACKBURN

This is 'Nellie', a vertical steam engine built by George Rushton of Lodge Bank, Darwen, and installed at Sunnybank Mill, Darwen in 1872. It is a reminder of the ingenuity and engineering skills that were required to power the mills. Sadly, Blackburn itself has very few such examples of industrial monuments.

PHOTOGRAPH: CARNEGIE

Accidents were more numerous and more frequent, for faster looms meant, for example, a greater chance of losing an eye to a flying shuttle. Local opticians were renowned for their range of artificial eyes. But it was the practice of *steaming* which physically wore down the weavers the most. This was a form of artificial humidity, necessary to reduce breakages in the thread, which was created by injecting steam into the atmosphere. This procedure started in the 1860s, and by 1890 95 per cent of Blackburn's mills used such a system. The water used was often contaminated, which was itself hardly conducive to good health, but the main debilitating effect on the workers was caused by the severe drop in temperature experienced on leaving work, for ventilation within the mills was restricted in order for steaming to work effectively.[35]

One further aspect of the local economy that changed over the nineteenth century was the increasing size of the average mill. In 1860, 30 had fewer than 250 looms and 52 had fewer than 400. By 1895 the average weaving mill had 603, and by 1912 the number had risen to 822. In that year there were only two mills with under 300 looms, while 32 had over 1,000.[36] In comparison with other Lancashire cotton towns, Blackburn had always had some of the largest mills. As far back as 1841 Blackburn had an average of 281 workers to a mill, whereas Bolton had only 217, Bury 162 and Oldham 79.[37] This position changed significantly in the last decade of the nineteenth century and into the Edwardian period, when in Bolton and Oldham a new generation of massive red-brick mills was constructed. These had relatively little impact in the east Lancashire towns. From the 1860s onwards there were also numerous amalgamations among local cotton businesses, as the main family owned firms bought up any mill that came on to the market. In this way industrial concerns grew larger with minimal extra building. But a direct consequence of the increasing size of cotton firms was that a new managerial layer intervened between the workforce and the mill-owner. As we shall see, this had important social and political consequences for Blackburn.

During the nineteenth century, therefore, not only had cotton transformed

Table 3 *County borough of Blackburn, employment structure (1911 census)*

| Census category | total | male | female |
|---|---|---|---|
| General and local government | 622 | 532 | 90 |
| Defence | 27 | 27 | |
| Professional | 1,994 | 1,071 | 823 |
| Domestic service | 3,073 | 586 | 2,487 |
| Commercial | 2,415 | 2,269 | 146 |
| Conveyance (transport) | 3,574 | 3,527 | 47 |
| Agriculture | 567 | 506 | 61 |
| Fishing | | | |
| Mining and quarrying | 701 | 700 | 1 |
| Metals and manufacturing | 5,334 | 5,037 | 297 |
| Precious metals, jewellery etc. | 228 | 205 | 23 |
| Building and construction | 3,132 | 3,131 | 1 |
| Wood and furniture | 1,036 | 963 | 73 |
| Brick, cement, pottery and glass | 303 | 290 | 13 |
| Skins, leather, hair, feathers | 181 | 170 | 11 |
| Paper, printing, books, stationery | 1,051 | 821 | 230 |
| Textiles | 42,777 | 16,537 | 26,240 |
| Dress and clothing | 3,644 | 1,497 | 2,147 |
| Food, drink, tobacco, lodging | 5,465 | 3,525 | 1,940 |
| Gas, water, electricity, sanitation | 410 | 410 | |
| Other and undefined | 2,092 | 1902 | 190 |
| Without occupation or unoccupied | 29,566 | 5,457 | 24,109 |

*Note*: titles of categories have been modified from those used in the census tables themselves.

This table highlights the dominant position of cotton in Blackburn's employment structure. Even the 'metals and manufacturing' sector, the town's third largest employer, was heavily dependent on the production and maintenance of cotton machinery. The exceptional importance of cotton in terms of female employment is very clear.

Table 4 *Employment in textiles by sub-division, 1911*

| Sub-division | total | male | female |
|---|---|---|---|
| Cotton: carding and blowing-room processes | 1,707 | 427 | 1,280 |
| Cotton: spinning | 2,698 | 1,603 | 1,095 |
| Cotton: winding and warping processes | 6,708 | 1,766 | 4,942 |
| Cotton: weaving | 28,305 | 9,933 | 18,372 |
| Cotton: other processes | 1,182 | 1,138 | 44 |
| Cotton: undefined | 1,098 | 906 | 92 |
| Bleaching, printing and dyeing | 272 | 255 | 17 |
| Textile dealers (including drapers) | 696 | 386 | 310 |

*'In Blackburn they had only one string to their bow ... they might some day deeply regret it.'*

CHAMBER OF COMMERCE, 1890

Blackburn, but the cotton industry itself had undergone dramatic and far-reaching changes. The principle of the underlying technology was fundamentally the same in 1900 as it had been in 1800, but steam power was now universal and electricity was beginning to make its appearance and the scale, size and complexity of looms and spinning machinery had changed beyond recognition. But there were other changes, which with the benefit of hindsight seem very disturbing. Perhaps the most important of these was not the technology, or the labour force, or the source of power, but something even more basic – the market for the cotton produced in Blackburn and other Lancashire towns. There was a growing reliance not on the home market, huge though that was, but on the export markets of the Far East. Even during the boom period of 1849–1861 three-quarters of all the looms in Blackburn were producing cloth for the Indian market. By 1900, 90 per cent of all the town's cloth was exported to the Far East. But by 1914 India was beginning to manufacture her own plain coarse cloth, of the sort that had become Blackburn's staple product. Between 1905 and 1914 India doubled her loomage and increased her cloth production threefold. Blackburn had come to industrial and commercial maturity by 1914 on the foundations of an industry which was already in relative decline. Though cotton exports were still growing between 1890 and 1914, Britain's share of world consumption of raw cotton had fallen from 48.7 per cent in 1870 to just 20 per cent in 1913. Already foreign competition from Germany, the USA and India was squeezing Blackburn's products out of established markets. Blackburn's last cotton boom, just before the First World War, was based on the Chinese market, as the mill-owners desperately sought new outlets.[38] But, as the chamber of commerce had warned in 1890, 'In Blackburn they had only one string to their bow ... they might some day deeply regret it'. The interwar years saw this prediction come true. By then much of the town's character, in terms of its physical shape, the habits of its people and its social and political structure had already been moulded by the cotton industry of the eighteenth and nineteenth centuries.

A key to the industrial revolution was the transformation of the transport

infrastructure, a process which was both a consequence of expanding economic activity, but also a major contributor to that expansion. New modes of transport and new transport routes became central to the urban and industrial landscape and economy of Lancashire, and Blackburn, like the other cotton towns, bears the imprint of these changes to this day. There were three essential elements in the transport networks of the region by the middle of the nineteenth century: the turnpike roads, the canals and river navigations, and the developing railway system. In popular mythology these three modes of transport appeared and disappeared in sequence, as though one replaced the other, but the reality was that in Lancashire the different networks were overlaid, so that they interconnected and became mutually dependent. This gave an exceptionally intricate and complex transport infrastructure, inextricably associated with industrial location and the development of urban areas.

Turnpikes were toll roads, authorised by parliamentary act. A turnpike trust was formed to take over the management and upkeep of a defined stretch of road or, in the later eighteenth century and as late as the 1840s, to build a completely new section of road. The trusts were private non-profit-making bodies, usually comprising local businessmen, landowners, farmers and professional people, and they were empowered to charge tolls on traffic and to use the income for road maintenance and their own interest on loans. Lancashire was comparatively late to adopt the system – the county's first turnpike was

Local breweries also provided employment. This photograph shows various workers at Dutton's brewery in their distinctive working clothes in the last quarter of the nineteenth century. In the centre, hands on hips, is what appears to be the foreman while to his right is a worker holding a distinctive malt shovel. On the extreme right is a clerk with his ledger. Also to be seen are coopers who made the barrels and draymen who delivered to the public houses.
BY COURTESY OF LANCASHIRE EVENING TELEGRAPH

THE OLD TOLL BAR, BROOKHOUSE, BLACKBURN.    Nº 75

not authorised until 1725 and even by 1750 only 87 miles, all in the south and south-west of the county, had been approved. Then there was a major boom in turnpike development, and during the 1750s some 227 miles were authorised. The eventual total, up to 1842, was 754 miles. In the Blackburn district the first turnpike road to be established was in 1755, covering the route from Preston, via Higher Walton and Pleasington, to Blackburn and then on to Burnley, Colne, Skipton and Leeds. In 1769 the road from Knuzden to Haslingden, Todmorden and Bury was turnpiked, and this was followed in 1776 by the high-level road to Whalley via Bank Hey and York. By the 1780s the rapid growth of the town, and of the Lancashire textile districts, was under way, and schemes were prepared for new and improved roads focusing on Blackburn. In 1797 the main road south from Blackburn via Darwen to Bolton was taken over by a turnpike trust, and in 1810 the Haslingden Grane road to Helmshore and Livesey Branch Road were added to the network. Even more dramatic changes took place in the 1820s, radically reorientating the geography of the town itself. All the roads so far listed had been in existence before they became turnpikes – the trusts simply took them over and upgraded them to a greater or lesser extent, by resurfacing, draining, fencing, and similar comparatively modest works. By the 1820s there was a widespread feeling that fast inter-urban traffic, and the heavy goods wagons of the industrial age, needed easier gradients and superior alignments, so new roads were built which slashed across the grain of the countryside on carefully planned routes with substantial engineering

This photograph shows the junction between Cob Wall and Whalley New Road going out of Blackburn with the old Toll Bar in the centre (now replaced by a car showroom) to collect the monies for the turnpike trust which built the road. The road system is unchanged except for a mini-roundabout. The bay windows on the left of the picture belonged to the Craven Heifer public house which was demolished in the 1990s.
COTTON TOWN PROJECT

works. In the Blackburn area three such roads, each of them now a major traffic artery were constructed. The first, in 1818, was a new low-level road between Blackburn and Whalley, avoiding the steeply graded alignment of the old road through York. The very name, Whalley New Road, reveals its origins, just as the name Blackburn Old Road tells something of its predecessor. It was

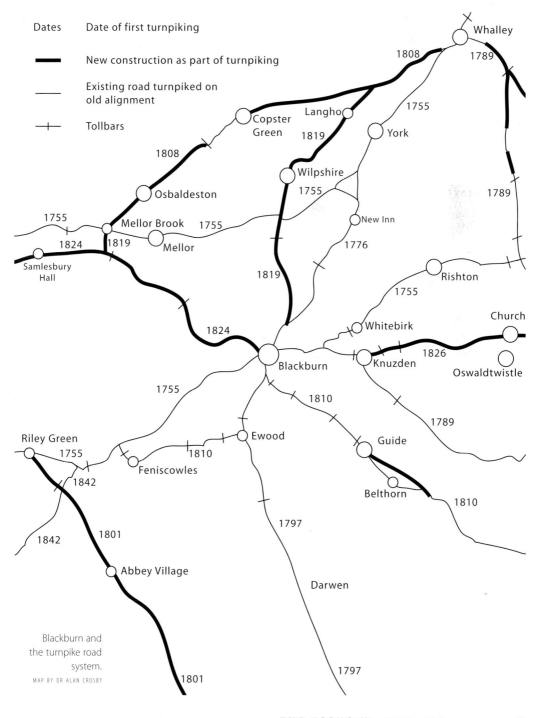

Dates — Date of first turnpiking

New construction as part of turnpiking

Existing road turnpiked on old alignment

Tollbars

Whalley
1808    1789
1755
Copster Green    Langho    York
1808    1819
Wilpshire    1755
1789
Osbaldeston
1755    New Inn
1824  1819  Mellor Brook   1755
Mellor    1776
Samlesbury Hall
1819    Rishton
1755
Church
Whitebirk
1824    1826
Blackburn    Knuzden    Oswaldtwistle
1755    1810
1789
Riley Green    Ewood    Guide
1755    1810
1842    Feniscowles
Belthorn
1842    1801    1810
1797
Abbey Village
Darwen
Blackburn and the turnpike road system.
MAP BY DR ALAN CROSBY
1801    1797

At midnight on 31 October 1890 the last three toll roads in Lancashire closed, to be taken over by Lancashire County Council. This picture was taken the following day at the old Shackerly Toll Bar near the Blackburn boundary on Preston New Road at Mellor. Tolls had been collected here since 1826.

followed in 1824 by the equally impressive Preston New Road, which climbed
out of the town on a series of long sweeping curves and then sliced through
the agricultural landscape of Samlesbury – the long wide straight stretches
past Samlesbury Hall and the *Windmill* betray its origins, contrasting with the
narrow winding lanes leading off on either side. Finally, in 1827, an entirely new
arterial road was built between Blackburn and Burnley, via Accrington. Again,
the long straights of Audley Range and Blackburn Road reveal its planned
origin. By 1830, therefore, Blackburn was a focal point on the regional road
network, with fast and well-aligned highways linking the town with neighbouring centres and carrying a heavy inter-urban passenger and freight traffic.

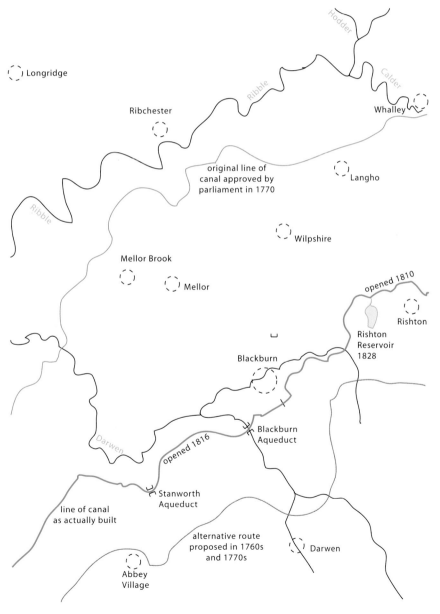

Blackburn and the
arrival of the canal.
This map highlights
the debate over the
local path that the
Leeds and Liverpool
Canal should take.
The successful plan
to route it through
what was then
the outskirts of
Blackburn was one
of three options. The
decision brought a
spate of industrial
expansion to the
town.
MAP BY DR ALAN CROSBY

Nine separate turnpike roads focused on the town, more than any other place in Lancashire apart from Bolton and Manchester. Though the turnpike trusts were wound up in the 1870s and 1880s, the network they had created remains the basis of the road system of the Blackburn area to this day – only the motorway and the 1920s bypass represent significant later additions.

Less than two decades after the first turnpike in the Blackburn area, work began on the great project to build a coast-to-coast waterway link, a canal from

A detail of the first edition Ordnance Survey map, showing mills clustered around the northern bank of the canal at Nova Scotia in 1848. Even by this date the mills close to the town centre had little or no room for expansion, something which is very clear from this 1:1056 plan. Even the millyards were awkward and very cramped, and it is not surprising that by the end of the century some of the smallest and oldest mills in these areas had already closed. The early terraced housing just to the north is at least provided with backyard privies, but the plan emphasises the exceptionally small yards, many of them (as on the south side of Commercial Street and Spring Street, extreme left) little more than narrow slots, or occupying only a couple of square yards. Note that both of the mills at this early date were combined spinning and weaving mills.

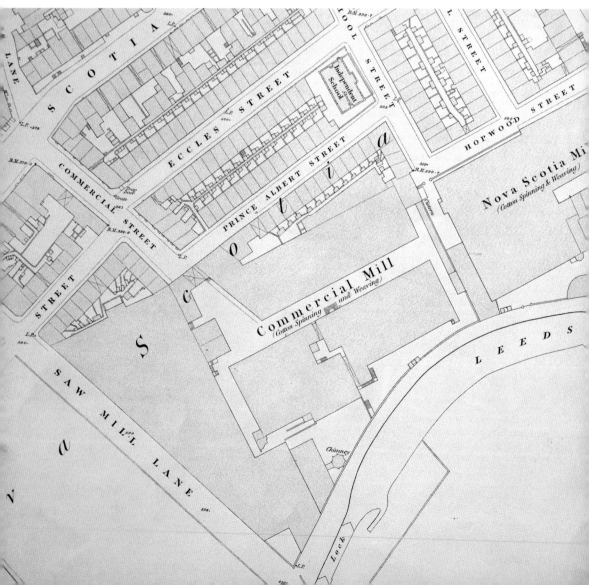

The Leeds and Liverpool Canal was a transport artery which brought many goods to and from the town. Though its late completion, allied to the advent of the railway age, meant that it role as the main transport provider was limited, it still played a role up until just after the Second World War. Here coal barges make their slow way to the local wharves.

the docks at Liverpool to the River Aire and thence to the Humber. The first detailed scheme for the Leeds and Liverpool Canal was drawn up in the mid-1760s, and the project was authorised by parliament in 1770. There had been much debate about the choice of route, and the balance to be struck between practical engineering and water supply considerations, and the need to serve centres of industry and population. The scheme approved in 1770 took a line from Parbold, on the river Douglas, via Lostock Hall, Samlesbury, Whalley and Padiham to Colne, bypassing Blackburn, Accrington and Burnley. By 1778 all the section from Leeds as far as Gargrave was open, but plans were already afoot to alter the route, initially to serve Wigan. Then the money ran out, and not until 1790 did work resume at Gargrave. Gradually, the canal inched forward, but it was realised that the route via Samlesbury and Whalley would not only serve none of the industrial towns but would also be extremely expensive. In 1794 the decision was taken to adopt a new alignment, via Blackburn and Burnley. The canal reached Foulridge in 1794, Colne in 1796, Henfield near Clayton-le-Moors in 1801, and at last, in 1810, the stretch thence to Blackburn. The *Blackburn Mail* recorded that:

> should the Corsican Tyrant [Napoleon] ever consent to peace, and free trade with the Continent, Blackburn may with facility send her manufactures by water to most of the sea ports of Germany. If a person who had been absent from this town for five years were to come to it from Burnley, he could hardly recognise that he had ever seen this place before ... the

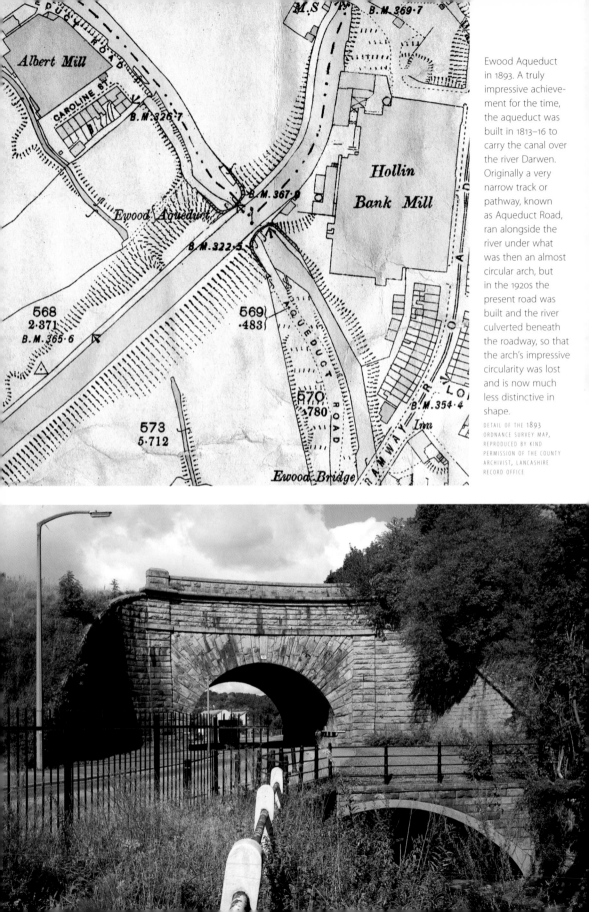

Ewood Aqueduct in 1893. A truly impressive achievement for the time, the aqueduct was built in 1813–16 to carry the canal over the river Darwen. Originally a very narrow track or pathway, known as Aqueduct Road, ran alongside the river under what was then an almost circular arch, but in the 1920s the present road was built and the river culverted beneath the roadway, so that the arch's impressive circularity was lost and is now much less distinctive in shape.

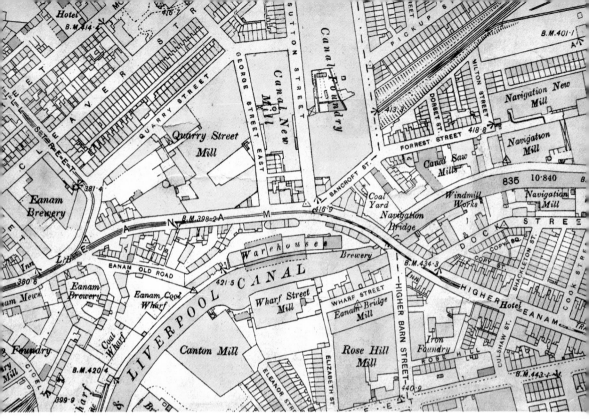

Eanam (1893): This was among the first areas of Blackburn to develop as an industrial zone (especially after the opening of the canal in 1816) and this is reflected in the small size of the cotton mills, their cramped and awkward sites, and the multitude of other industrial premises and wharves along the waterway. In the late 1840s the railway tunnel on the line to Burnley burrowed under Eanam, and most of the remaining open space was soon built over with congested, working-class housing. Note Eanam Old Road, all that was left of the narrow and twisting ancient highway after the widening and diversion of the road which was necessitated by the construction of the canal.

DETAIL OF THE 1893 ORDNANCE SURVEY MAP, REPRODUCED BY KIND PERMISSION OF THE COUNTY ARCHIVIST, LANCASHIRE RECORD OFFICE

canal has caused so great an alteration in the south-easterly part, where many new houses are erected.

A modern photograph from the south-east showing the river Darwen (*bottom right*) entering the 1920s culvert which now supports the road as it passes under the aqueduct. The canal is carried majestically above both river and road, though the aqueduct's arch is now of conventional shape.

PHOTOGRAPH: CARNEGIE

The final section of the canal, from Blackburn to Whittle-le-Woods, was opened to 19 October 1816, completing the longest canal in the country. The church bells of Blackburn rang out, and the town's business community celebrated. It is interesting to speculate about what might have happened if the original route had been opened. The canal had a major impact upon Blackburn, not only in terms of improving general accessibility, but also because much of the coal for new steam-powered textile mills was brought by barge, so it was logical for mills to be constructed on or very close to the canal banks, to minimise the problems of transhipment. Within two decades of its completion the canal, though Daisyfield, Eanam and Nova Scotia, was lined with cotton mills and other industrial premises. Blackburn would doubtless have been served by a less convenient branch canal, had the original route been followed, and mills would have congregated around the canal basin and terminus, but

The amount of traffic that still used the Leeds and Liverpool canal, even though the railways took the bulk of goods traffic, is shown here when forty barges were held up at Eanam Wharf in October 1919. The cause of the hold up was a drought that caused the water level to fall too far to cope with the drafts of fully laden barges.
COTTON TOWN PROJECT

where would that have been, and would the lack of a direct through waterway have restrained the growth of the town to some extent? The actual impact was clear. As well as the coal traffic, the canal, ideally suited to the transporting of bulk commodities, brought raw cotton from Liverpool docks and took away the finished cloth. Its competitive cheapness reduced the costs of industry and facilitated a substantial real reduction in the cost of cotton textiles, thus increasing demand and generating further business.

The Leeds and Liverpool Canal was completed as the railway age dawned. Here Blackburn was at something of a disadvantage because of its geographical position. Although tunnels, viaducts, cuttings and embankments could help to overcome the barriers of topography in a local sense, it was inevitable from the outset that the main trunk railway in north-west England would pass along the Lancashire plain, north–south through Lancaster, Preston, Wigan and Warrington, and that East Lancashire as a whole would be off that crucial axis. No matter how many lines were threaded through the valleys of Rossendale and over into Yorkshire, and no matter how many long-distance trains served the East Lancashire towns in the heyday of the rail network, the slight sense of being 'out on a branch' would always be apparent, a sense that was greatly exacerbated with the decline of the network in the 1950s.

The first line to serve the town was the Blackburn and Preston Railway, which received parliamentary approval in June 1844, was opened on 1 June 1846, and on 3 August 1846 was absorbed by the East Lancashire Railway, a

Blackburn railway
station, c.1900. The
original station was
built in 1846 behind
this new one that
was opened to
passengers in 1886.
Four times larger
than the former
station, this one
boasted a booking
hall and a clock that
was guaranteed not
to lose or gain five
seconds in a month.
Note the line of
horse cabs waiting
for custom and also
the cabbies' shelter
in the centre that
was a converted
railway carriage.

LANCASHIRE EVENING
TELEGRAPH

company in the process of expanding to form a sizeable local network. Another undertaking absorbed by the ELR was the Blackburn, Burnley, Accrington and Colne Extension Railway, authorised and taken over in the summer of 1845. The line to Accrington from Blackburn was opened on 19 June 1848. A third component of the ELR was the Blackburn, Darwen and Bolton Railway, which received parliamentary approval in June 1845 and was opened on 12 June 1848. By that time the little company had itself amalgamated with the Blackburn, Clitheroe and North Western Junction Railway, designed to head north up the Ribble valley to Ingleton and to form part of a new main line from Manchester to Carlisle. Its route from Blackburn to Whalley, Clitheroe and Chatburn opened on 20 June 1850, and the combined company (made up of the BD&BR and the BC&NWJR) was usually known as the Blackburn Railway. It did not have its own locomotives and rolling stock and instead was worked by the Lancashire and Yorkshire Railway. In 1856 its management alarmed the other, well-established companies in the area by proposing to build a completely independent line from Bolton into Manchester, and to extend from Chatburn northwards into the dales and beyond. The Lancashire & Yorkshire Railway promptly suppressed the idea by negotiating with the East Lancashire Railway to take over the Blackburn Railway jointly and, in 1859, the East Lancashire was itself taken over by the Lancashire and Yorkshire. These intricate and labyrinthine examples of railway politics was very characteristic, for none of

BLACKBURN STATION.

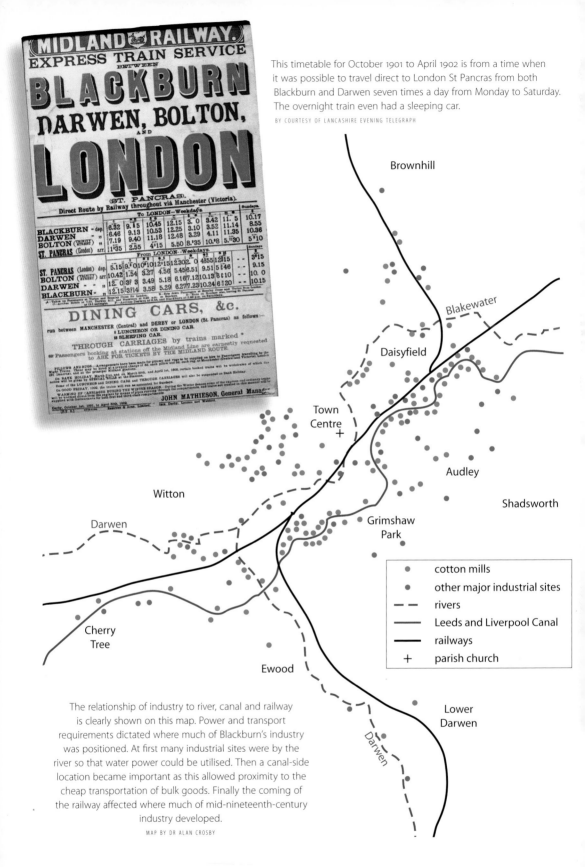

This timetable for October 1901 to April 1902 is from a time when it was possible to travel direct to London St Pancras from both Blackburn and Darwen seven times a day from Monday to Saturday. The overnight train even had a sleeping car.

BY COURTESY OF LANCASHIRE EVENING TELEGRAPH

Brownhill

Blakewater

Daisyfield

Town
Centre

Audley

Shadsworth

Witton

Darwen

Grimshaw
Park

| | cotton mills |
| | other major industrial sites |
| – – – | rivers |
| ——— | Leeds and Liverpool Canal |
| ▬▬▬ | railways |
| + | parish church |

Cherry
Tree

Ewood

Lower
Darwen

Darwen

The relationship of industry to river, canal and railway is clearly shown on this map. Power and transport requirements dictated where much of Blackburn's industry was positioned. At first many industrial sites were by the river so that water power could be utilised. Then a canal-side location became important as this allowed proximity to the cheap transportation of bulk goods. Finally the coming of the railway affected where much of mid-nineteenth-century industry developed.

MAP BY DR ALAN CROSBY

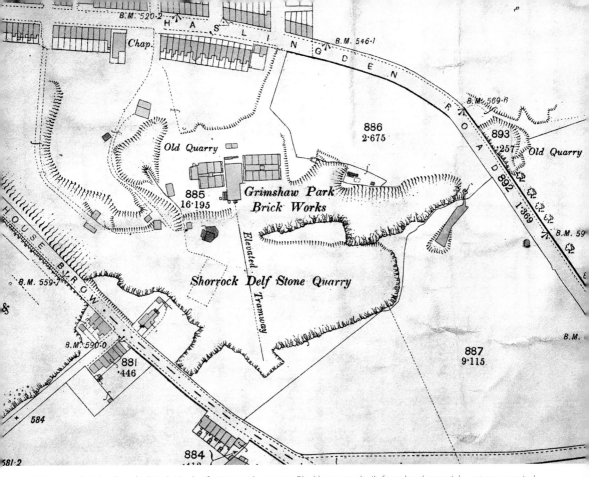

Grimshaw Park brickworks (1893). Much of nineteenth-century Blackburn was built from local materials – stone quarried on the hillsides to the south of the town or on the slopes of Revidge and Beardwood, or bricks which were made at a series of brickworks in the Grimshaw Park and Audley areas. That area was pockmarked with quarries and claypits, many of which were worked for only a short period. Indeed, some of them were opened simply to supply the material for a particular housing development, and were themselves later built over.

easy to assess. There is some evidence, for example, that mills clustered along railway lines, but this is perhaps not as obvious as their concentration close to the banks of the canal. In contrast to Oldham and Bolton, where the mills built in the 1880s and 1890s were often directly served by rail, with their own coal sidings, few Blackburn mills were so favoured – mainly because the land alongside the lines was densely built up at a much earlier date.

One obvious effect of transport improvements was the changing nature of the coal industry in the Blackburn area. A number of small pits had been worked in and around Blackburn since at least the seventeenth century, but the coming of the canal meant that coal could be brought from both the larger South Lancashire and Yorkshire coalfields and sold here at a lower price than the local output. Since the coal from the area around the town tended to be of inferior quality, and was much harder to work, being in thin, fractured and very wet seams the superior quality of coal from elsewhere was also readily

Coal was delivered around the town by horse and cart. This was still being done in 1920. The firm of Crook & Thompson had thirty-six horses at this time. It was the Second World War that saw most horses disappear, as feed for them was difficult to obtain and horsemeat was in demand as the usual cuts of meat were rationed. Note the young boy working. No doubt he is a 'half-timer', with a certificate allowing him off full-time education.

appreciated. In the week that the canal opened in 1810, 380 tons of coal were brought to Blackburn by barge. The hub of the trade in the eighteenth century had been the Northgate coalyard where virtually all the locally mined coal was brought and sold on. By 1814 the trade had been transferred to Eanam Wharf where imported coal brought by canal was unloaded. Within a few years many pits in the area had closed and the few that remained served only local needs. None of their output was taken and sold beyond the borough. But as the mining of coal contracted the rapid expansion of the town brought other work for the unemployed miners. Many pits became quarries for fireclay, which was used in brick, tile and earthenware manufacture. Quarries were still being opened at the beginning of the twentieth century, as at Messrs Whittaker's site on Coal Pit Moor, where new workings were started in 1900 and fireclay was extracted up to 50 feet below the original depth of the old coal workings. That quarry was filled in during the late 1960s and early 1970s with the rubble from the demolition of the old Blackburn market.

Some coal mining did continue to the end of the nineteenth century. Livesey

Colliery, beside the A674 at Cherry Tree was still working in 1879, a pit at Little Harwood operated as late as 1883, and the colliery at Whitebirk was only abandoned in 1895.[39] Only seven years before, that mine had employed 140 men and boys and its galleries extended for almost a mile from the shaft bottom. But it was a wet pit, with engines pumping out 500–600 gallons of water every minute. Relatively few of the miners employed in Blackburn pits after the 1830s came from the town, because employment in the mills was the preferred choice for local children. There, they could start working part-time two years earlier and the wages were higher. Instead, boys were obtained for the mines from schools in Liverpool.[40] Local coal pits had always utilised child labour, as at Little Harwood mine in 1841, when three of the thirteen people employed below ground were aged 10–12. Their job was to haul the coal from the face to the shaft bottom so that it could be hauled up. The tunnels were four feet high and tubs were hauled using a girdle and chain, a leather harness worn by the child to which a chain was attached. This ran between their legs and was hooked to a wheeled truck filled with coal.[41] Accidents were common. The area of the Little Harwood pit and the cottages alongside was known locally as Blow Up because of an explosion that occurred there in 1819.

> Last Thursday an inquest was held at Little Harwood on John Landlass, Thomas Pilling, John Tithrow and William Wood whose deaths were caused by the bursting of a boiler belonging to a steam engine of a coal mine there. The explosion was tremendous. Fragments of the boiler were carried to a considerable distance, and the building enclosing it was completely dispersed. One man was carried along with a portion of the boiler to a field some distance away, and another, who was working in the Engine Pit, was killed when the stones of the building fell in to it. Three other persons were badly injured.'[42]

Flooding was the result of an accident at the Higher Cunliffe pit near Bank Hey in 1836.

> Last Monday while several men were working in Mr. Clark's coal mine at Cunliffe near Blackburn, a large quantity of water suddenly broke in upon them and, before they had time to escape, they were immersed up to the neck. Fortunately there were no lives lost. Shortly after this, the earth above for a considerable distance sank about two yards and was instantly covered in water.[43]

Gas was also a constant danger. In 1885 an explosion of firedamp occurred at the Whitebirk colliery. One worker opened his safety lamp to light that of a fellow worker and the resultant explosion burnt the faces and bodies of both men.[44] Such accidents, and safety hazards, were of course ubiquitous in mining, and there is nothing to suggest that Blackburn was notably worse than anywhere else. East Lancashire pits as a whole had a relatively good safety record, compared with, for example, those of the Wigan area where major disasters were frequent but, as the examples above indicate, the pages of local newspapers are dotted with brief reports of small tragedies, each one a reflection of the harshness and danger of work in this vital, but largely unregulated, industry.

By 1914 the town's coal industry had departed and Blackburn was truly a cotton town though now a weaving one rather than spinning or even mixed. Much of the rest of the town's economy was also geared to cotton. In addition to the mills, other firms produced goods for the textile trade such as shuttles and looms. Even the town's transport infrastructure served mainly to bring spun cotton to the mills and to take away the woven cloth. In 1914 King Cotton ruled though revolutionary undercurrents could be discerned dangerously close to the surface.

This statue of William Henry Hornby, the first mayor of Blackburn, was originally erected in Limbrick in 1912. John Margerison, an employee who worked for over fifty years at the Brookhouse mills, left £3,000 in his will to cover the cost. It now stands close to the old town hall building.

PHOTOGRAPH: CARNEGIE

Whatever the industries that employed the workers of Blackburn, the weather ensured that umbrella makers were always needed. This is an early advertisement for Stanworth's umbrellas. Their shop was on Mill Street off Darwen Street and until quite recently umbrellas could still be purchased on the same premises. Sadly, but perhaps appropriately, some water damage has occurred to the photographic plate. The price too has been altered at one point perhaps indicating that this advert was used for some time.

J. HALSALL COLLECTION

# CHAPTER THREE

# Elites and political power before 1914

I T IS WIDELY ACCEPTED that British society is defined, to an unusual extent, by class distinctions and differentiations. These distinctions are not rigid or fixed, for the British version of the class structure has always allowed and tolerated a limited amount of upward or downward movement and, unlike the position in some European countries, was never formally defined in legal terms. The gradations of the British system have therefore changed over time. At certain times and in some historical periods the rate of change has been greater than others, and the industrial revolution was one such period. The social structure of industrialising and urbanising areas such as Blackburn altered very considerably during the phase of rapid and sustained industrial growth, because these developments generated new sources of wealth and drastically altered the population structure – the demographic composition – of the area.

The class structure altered to accommodate, first, the rise of a manufacturing and professional middle class; second, the appearance of the wage-earning working classes; and third, and finally, the relative decline of the landed classes. During the hundred years up to 1850 class mobility accelerated. Then the portals of advancement narrowed as class stability reasserted itself and fresh barriers were erected. Concomitant with this change in the class structure was a change in the wielding of power. A new elite began to mould a different type of political and economic control, one which reshaped and reoriented the direction of development within the town, for Blackburn was no exception to such change. In fact this area saw the decline of the landed classes long before the 1880s, the period from which most historians date its national decline.

The main basis of power and authority before the industrial period, in Blackburn as elsewhere, was land, and the main seat of power the position of lord of the manor. From the early eighteenth century the local aristocracy did not occupy this position, and this was to have important consequences for the town. We have already seen how the manor was split in two back in the twelfth century, but during the eighteenth century it began to come together again. In 1721 William Baldwin, Henry Feilden and William Sudell purchased the half that was held by Thomas Belasyse, 4th Viscount Fauconberg. The three men were local and they came from yeoman, rather than aristocratic, stock. It was not long before the full ownership was transferred to the Feilden family. Sudell's portion came to the Feildens by marriage, while Baldwin's third was purchased. Little is known of the Baldwin family after they were bought out, but the Feildens and the Sudells eventually moved fully into cotton, and there their real fortunes were made. Henry Sudell rose to become the greatest of the early Blackburn cotton merchants while William Feilden was, as members of his family had been since the seventeenth century, a putter-out and chapman supplying the handloom weavers and selling the woven cloth on. In addition

This is Joseph Feilden. From the early nineteenth century the Feilden family were the sole lords of the manor. It was the way this family either sold off or donated parcels of land that was partly responsible for the physical shape of present-day Blackburn.

it was he who, with his son Montague, helped to pioneer the factory system in Blackburn. Sudell bought a country estate just outside the town at Woodfold, Mellor, and there built a magnificent mansion, Woodfold Hall. He was reported to be a millionaire in 1820, but in July 1827 he was declared bankrupt with debts of £134,000 and assets of only £60,000, and later that year began the moves to sell a substantial part of his property. Unwise foreign investments had broken him, and he left Blackburn in shame and humiliation, never to set foot in the town again. Now, the Feildens of Witton Park reigned supreme.

In the meantime the Feilden family were steadily acquiring the other half of the land and title that made up the manor of Blackburn. This had been owned by the Church of England since the Reformation. The Feildens became tenants of part of this section of the manor during the eighteenth century and Henry and John Feilden subsequently purchased this portion. Then, in 1852, the Feildens bought the remainder for £20,000, with the exception of 467 acres which were kept by the Ecclesiastical Commissioners. By the mid nineteenth century, therefore, the Feildens owned virtually the entire original manor of Blackburn.[1]

By intermittently disposing of parcels of land, generations of Feildens now helped to form not only the geographical pattern of the town but also shaped its civic, educational and cultural growth. Land was sold by the family for, among many other purposes, Corporation Park, the market hall, the workhouse, the infirmary, the technical college and the grammar school. Nevertheless, in 1880 the Feilden family still owned 2,000 acres spread across the borough of Blackburn and drew rents from all parts of the town. By the mid-nineteenth century most senior members of this family no longer took an active part in the day-to-day running of their cotton mills. That was left to lesser relatives, or to managers, while the leading members of the family pursued military, political or business careers. With the death of Joseph Feilden in 1870, though, they also disappeared into the background of local politics in which they had previously been very prominent. Though they were still very influential socially, occasional appearances on the local magistrates bench and on Tory platforms at election times now sufficed. Others had taken their place.

Two main influences explain the emergence and character of the middle-class elite that controlled Blackburn from the 1850s to 1914. The first was the success of the early cotton merchants of the eighteenth century who controlled the domestic system of manufacture. Some of these went on to become the early factory masters. In addition to the Feildens and the Sudells, the main cotton merchants in the 1770s and 1780s were the Peels, Cardwells, Hornbys, Birleys, Chippendales, Maudes and Hindles.[2] Some of these were not originally Blackburn families, but had moved to the town to take advantage of the openings in the growing cotton trade. A good example is the Cardwell family who, like the lords of the manor, were of yeoman origin. They came from the Preston area in the early eighteenth century, but Richard Cardwell, born in Blackburn in 1749, was the true founder of the main family fortune. The Hornbys came from the Kirkham area in the Fylde, where they were local gentry. John

Witton Park (1893): the home of the Feilden family was built in 1800, a fine Georgian mansion set in a very extensive and beautifully-landscaped park. When the map was made it was at the end of its long period of grandeur, for after 1895 the family rarely lived there and the house began to fall into disrepair. In 1947 the entire estate was purchased by Blackburn Corporation and in 1952 the house was demolished. Today, almost no trace remains, although the stable block and outbuildings (north-west of the house) survive as the visitor centre and estate offices.
DETAIL OF THE 1893 ORDNANCE SURVEY MAP, REPRODUCED BY KIND PERMISSION OF THE COUNTY ARCHIVIST, LANCASHIRE RECORD OFFICE

Housing east of Corporation Park (1893). These large houses, all but a few of which are detached, were smaller-scale versions of the grand mansions higher up the hill to the west at Beardwood. They, too, have drives and shrubberies, and several also have hothouses and glasshouses (shown here by the distinctive cross-hatched symbol). The detail of the park landscape is well shown, including the ornamental pools, cascades, rocky stream, and extensive tree-planting which had softened what had been a bare slope less than half a century before.

DETAIL OF THE 1893 ORDNANCE SURVEY MAP, REPRODUCED BY KIND PERMISSION OF THE COUNTY ARCHIVIST, LANCASHIRE RECORD OFFICE

Hornby, born in 1763, settled in Blackburn as a cotton merchant and went into partnership with Richard Birley, the son of a West India merchant, also from the Kirkham area. The firm that they founded later built the Brookhouse cotton mills. The Peels, too, were originally yeoman farmers. They began in calico printing at Moorgate Fold in Livesey and at Church Brook.

These merchants, with a few newcomers such as the Glovers and Prymes, had the capital and cotton connection and so began the development and expansion of Blackburn's factory system. By 1851, however, only the Hornbys and the Feildens remained. Richard Birley's eldest son moved to mills in Manchester; all of Cardwell's sons made their careers outside Blackburn; and the Peels, tired of having their spinning machines wrecked by locals, packed up and moved to Bury and Burton-on-Trent. Even in those families which stayed, the older generation, having made their fortunes, left Blackburn to enjoy retirement in more congenial surroundings. Thus, John Hornby died at his seat at Raikes Hall near Blackpool. This pattern persisted throughout the nineteenth century and, as will be seen later, may partly account for Blackburn's lack of major public buildings or grand cultural heritage. Those who made money from the

This photograph, taken in 1854, shows the birthplace of the first Sir Robert Peel in Fish Lane. The Peel family were forced to flee Blackburn at the end of the eighteenth century after rioting spinners destroyed the spinning jennies which they had installed in their mill. They took their business to nearby Bury. A blue plaque at Cardwell Place now marks the site of their original home.

COTTON TOWN PROJECT

town left to enjoy and spend it elsewhere. The second influence to be noted is the relatively humble background of most of the leading families, another trait present up to 1914. With no local aristocracy to model themselves on, these families developed their own 'home-grown' social mores, more attuned to their new status and often based on an idealised but modest country gentry lifestyle. Again, this had far-reaching effects on Blackburn's social, political, educational and cultural development.

Blackburn's first steam-powered spinning mill was built at Wensley Fold in 1797 and others soon followed. In the late 1820s, with the introduction of the power loom to Blackburn, weaving mills were added to the already established weaving sheds. The family names of Eccles, Haworth, Pilkington, Ward, Birtwistle, Livesey and Hopwood now enter Blackburn's history. Most of these men came from even humbler backgrounds. Richard Haworth was originally a draper in Northgate. William Eccles had lowly working-class origins, but rose to be a solicitor and thereby accumulated the capital to advance as an entrepreneur. Henry Ward, born in Mellor village in 1813, was the son of a barber. His father's business was far from large: 'So slender an income did it yield that it took Ward senior all his time to clothe and feed his family'. Henry, too, became a barber for a short while but, with 'a bit of independent trading', by eighteen years of age had saved up the then tidy sum of £80, which he used to set himself up in the cotton trade.[3] William Birtwistle was brought up on a small farm near Great Harwood and raised his starting capital as a handloom weaver.[4] It was possible in the early nineteenth century to enter the cotton business with only a modest amount of capital, which allowed such men to rise fast up the economic and social scale: 'The reason that little initial capital was needed was that many of the early mills could be leased or even rented. Many were not purpose-built but were old warehouses. Yarn could be obtained on credit, worked up and sold before having to settle. In addition over half of those setting up in a new business began in partnership with one or more others. This meant that they only had to supply a part of the initial capital.'[5]

This sum could be raised in various ways. Many entrepreneurs used the profits accumulated in another business enterprise – for example, many cotton masters had previously been in business as shopkeepers, estate agents, builders or publicans. Others, such as Henry Ward, raised capital away from their daytime occupation by acting as middlemen and by doing some buying and selling on the side. Some made their capital while working in the cotton industry, and having climbed the employment ladder in the mill until they reached the status of manager, chose, instead of a salary, to receive a share of the profits. This allowed them the chance of accumulating capital, and eventually, all being well, enabled them to venture out on their own in an industry that they knew intimately. Some employers offered other managers a partnership, because of the business acumen that they showed. By the second half of the

'When a Blackburn Master gets on he often develops into a "swell" and though his father may have been a moulder, a blacksmith or a calico weaver, he talks about his ancestors, sends to the Herald's College for a crest and a coat of arms and buys an estate.

John Hornby (1763–1841) was the founder of the Hornby dynasty in Blackburn. These cotton masters dominated the local political scene throughout the nineteenth and early twentieth century. John Hornby came from a family of Kirkham merchants and arrived in Blackburn to make his fortune at the age of sixteen. After learning the trade he became a 'putter-out', supplying cotton thread to local handloom weavers and then collecting and selling the cloth. In 1828 he opened his first mill at Brookhouse. By the time he died his initial capital of £25 had risen to over £200,000.

nineteenth century, however, this type of progression was far more difficult: 'Not so many years ago it was the ambition of half the minor traders, the shop keeping classes of Lancashire, to get into the cotton trade. They assiduously saved up their profits until they had got a thousand pound, or perhaps two, when they at once proceeded to run up a weaving shed ... loom makers and machinists being quite ready to equip them with the plant, give them long credit and hoped for the ultimate payment of their accounts upon the profits that they might make.'[6]

In due course, the increasing cost of setting up a weaving shed prevented this form of access to the trade. Thus, in Blackburn, where the average size of mills had become larger, it had virtually ceased by 1860. In that year only 30 mills had fewer than 250 looms and only 52 under 400. By 1895 the average

weaving shed held 603 looms, a figure that rose to 822 by 1912. Thirty-two mills then held over 1,000 looms.[7] This meant that even before the mill-building boom in Blackburn that just preceded the outbreak of the American Civil War, the day of the self-made factory master was all but over. Class mobility via the cotton industry was becoming more unusual, though there was still an occasional exception. James Bead, who owned two mills in the 1880s, was the son of a spinner and had himself begun work in the Nova Scotia mills at the age of eleven, educating himself at evening classes. James Boothman, the son of a sailor, began as a weaver at one of Hopwood's mills in the 1850s. After working up to the status of manager he bought his first mill in 1874.[8] The mill-owning fraternity, however, was increasingly becoming a closed shop and, in order to keep it so, was becoming increasingly interbred. By the last quarter of the nineteenth century 60 per cent of the mill-owners in Blackburn had inherited the business from their father. Most others had succeeded into the business following marriage. Robert Hopwood Hutchinson's father had married the eldest daughter of Robert Hopwood. He inherited a fortune on his mother's death and, to keep the money in the family, used it to become a partner in Robert Hopwood & Son. By 1860 he was head of the firm and, as

Even before the age of the motor car, the town's elite did not have to walk. Many had their own carriages, but horse-drawn cabs were always available to them twenty-four hours a day. At the stables of the Old Bull Hotel grooms, ostlers and top-hatted drivers pose for a photograph with two of their horses and a bucket. The cabs can be seen behind them.

noted earlier, reputedly made £1 million by running the cotton blockade during the American Civil War.[9]

Blood or marriage ties increasingly joined together Blackburn's new middle-class elite. William Coddington (MP for Blackburn, 1880–1906) and Robert Hopwood Hutchinson were cousins. Joseph Dugdale, the main iron founder in the town, and Michael Birtwistle, head of the Birtwistle group of cotton mills, were brothers-in-law. The mill-owners Henry Shaw and James Pilkington were also brothers-in-law, while the mills of James Bead and John Lund, were also linked by marriage.[10] Another characteristic of this new elite was that they were virtually all local men. In 1880 70 per cent of them had been born in Blackburn itself while nearly all the remainder came from nearby villages. Very few outsiders had to be accommodated. Once the mill-owners began to close ranks, they also erected new class barriers to ensure that they remained the elite. The mid-Victorian period saw an exodus of mill-owners who, having made their fortunes in and from Blackburn, went elsewhere to enjoy it, but one consequence was the drawing up of a middle-class drawbridge. During the 1870s the town witnessed the departures of the Pilkingtons, Jacksons and Hopwood Hutchinsons, but their mills were sold to already established local mill-owners, not to newcomers. This encouraged the establishment of an exceptionally narrow plutocracy in Blackburn, and the town's leading mill-owners were unusually rich. For example, 24 per cent of Blackburn's leading late Victorian and Edwardian mill-owners left estates in excess of £100,000 at death compared with only 9 per cent in the neighbouring weaving town of Burnley.[11] But even within that elite there was a distinct pecking order. The Feilden and Hornby families led Blackburn's society, as the sole survivors of Blackburn's cotton industry of the late eighteenth and early nineteenth century. Below them were the relative newcomers, though by the second half of the nineteenth century they, too, were at least second-generation middle class and some had been around for three generations.

Unlike many other employers in the town, Daniel Thwaites was never popular. His only general election victory came in a by-election in 1875 after the death of one of the sitting MPs, a Feilden. In the next election in 1880 he came third behind the Liberal William Briggs and a fellow Conservative, William Coddington. For some reason Daniel Thwaites never had the common touch needed to win the support of his fellow townsmen.

Few others were able to penetrate the tightly controlled elite group of the town. The only major exceptions, at least in terms of wealth, political involvement and acquisition of estates, land and a fine house, were members of the Thwaites family. Their Eanam brewery opened in 1797 and the business gradually built up to become a source of major wealth. Daniel Thwaites was born in 1817 at the brewery in Eanam and dedicated his working life to the business, so that by the 1860s it had become the most important industrial concern in the area apart from the cotton mills, and was now one of Lancashire's leading breweries. Thwaites considered himself the leading citizen of the town, was active and influential in the politics of the new borough council, and served as MP for Blackburn from 1875 to 1880. When he died in 1888 he was the town's

This oil painting is of the laying of the foundation stone of the Cotton Exchange in 1863. Shortly after, the American Civil War led to a deep trade depression which meant that only one-half of the Exchange was ever built. The town's elite have turned out in force and ensured that their presence would be recorded for posterity by commissioning Vladimir Sherwood to record the occasion. The painting now hangs in the town museum, with the names faithfully recorded below. One lad (*top left*) has found a prominent, if precarious, vantage point, albeit probably in the artist's imagination.
BLACKBURN MUSEUM

richest man, but despite all this he was never at the very heart of Blackburn's social and political elite, which remained cotton-dominated, and his place in the magic inner circle was continually threatened by a Conservative caucus to which he never fully belonged. He wanted to establish himself as a country gentleman and, unlike Sudell, could take advantage of a ready-made estate and a large and impressive country house on the doorstep – indeed, he bought the Woodfold estate from his sister-in-law – for although Blackburn was expanding rapidly the property was far enough from the centre to be unaffected by industrial pollution or the visual intrusion of mills and chimneys. Thwaites was a great improver in the tradition of enlightened landowners, investing heavily in rebuilding farms and cottages, undertaking tree-planting, hedge-planting, road building and drainage throughout his estate, and adopting a paternal and benevolent attitude to his tenants which was often noted by contemporaries,

Two of the coats of arms on the ceiling of Holy Trinity church (see also page 248).

PHOTOGRAPHS: CARNEGIE

but it has to be noted that this influence was rural rather than urban. He also rarely lived at Woodfold, since he and his wife decided to hold the estate almost 'in trust' for their only child. On his death Woodfold, together with the many other properties which he had owned in Mellor, Samlesbury, Blackburn and Darwen, and the lordship of the manor of Mellor, passed to his young daughter, Elma Amy Thwaites, and her son was eventually raised to the peerage. It was a far cry from the baby born over the brewery down by the canal.

There was considerable scepticism about the arrival of the new elite, and cynics were wryly amused at their pretensions: 'When a Blackburn Master gets on he often develops into a "swell" and though his father may have been a moulder, a blacksmith or a calico weaver, he talks about his ancestors, sends to the Herald's College for a crest and a coat of arms and buys an estate.'[12] Though this may have been an unkind exaggeration there is an element of truth in it. The ceiling of Holy Trinity church, painted in 1848 with the newly acquired coats of arms of all the Blackburn families who were the major subscribers to the building costs, is testimony to this. Such an imagined past also meant the need for the new elite to participate in, or give patronage to, such organisations as the yeomanry or artillery volunteers and the Pendle Forest Hunt. This in turn moulded the way in which such disparate topics as law and order and leisure evolved in Blackburn.

Most of the new middle classes lived near each other in middle-class enclaves such as Preston New Road, on the exclusive high ground of the

From 1841 to 1910, with the exception of a handful of years, there was always a Hornby representing Blackburn in the House of Commons. None of this mill-owning family ever made any impact as regards government appointments or even legislation. In fact they very rarely spoke in the chamber. Members of Parliament in Blackburn were elected because of their local knowledge and influence, not national concerns.

BLACKBURN LIBRARY LOCAL HISTORY COLLECTION

western suburbs of the town. This growing desire for class segregation and the sense of being superior to the ordinary folk helped to mould the physical shape of Blackburn. This new middle class also sought to give their children a suitably exclusive education. At first the nonconformists among them sent their sons to Hoole's Academy, a commercial independent school, while many Anglicans sent their boys to Queen Elizabeth's Grammar School, an ancient foundation which in the mid-nineteenth century was virtually reborn on the strength of cotton money and social aspiration. As the public school movement reformed itself and expanded in the 1850s and 1860s many of these same families packed their offspring off to boarding schools in Yorkshire, Cheshire, Manchester and Liverpool. The crème de la crème of Blackburn's elite were different again. That group sent their sons to the top public schools further south. Young Hornbys and Jacksons went to Harrow, while boys of the Briggs and Baynes families were sent to Rugby.

As Blackburn's elite created a new class structure, and with it much of the character of Blackburn itself, they also began to achieve their ambition of taking control of the reins of political power. As a class, their grasp on Blackburn's representation at Westminster and on the town council was tightened, even when they fought out among themselves the secondary party political battle. Blackburn had become a two-member parliamentary borough under the Great Reform Act of 1832. From the start the town's MPs came from the ruling elite

In 1888 the future Edward VII and Queen Alexandra visited the town. The then Prince and Princess of Wales came to open the new Technical College. After alighting by train at Cherry Tree station they can be seen arriving at Witton House, the home of the Feilden family who played host during their visit. The 400-acre estate was purchased by the town council in 1947 although the house, built in 1800, was demolished in 1954 after falling prey to dry rot.

COTTON TOWN PROJECT, © LANCASHIRE EVENING TELEGRAPH

and from the cotton industry. With only isolated and temporary exceptions, such as Daniel Thwaites' period as MP from 1875 to 1880, cotton dominated. Within that circle, two families – the Feildens and the Hornbys – held most of the reins of power. William Feilden served as one of Blackburn's MPs from 1832 until his retirement in 1847. His youngest son Montague Feilden followed his father and was elected in 1854. Joseph Feilden was MP from 1865 to 1869. His son Henry immediately took over what was virtually the family seat and held it until his death in 1875. The Hornby family began their parliamentary career in 1841 with the election of John Hornby, the fourth son of the original John Hornby who founded the Brookhouse mills. He was MP until 1852. In 1857 his elder brother William was elected, and served as MP until 1869 when he handed over what was then apparently a family property to his second son Edward, who kept it until 1874. William Hornby's fourth son, Harry, recovered the seat for the family in 1886, retaining it until 1910. Between 1832 and 1910 the Hornby family had contested fourteen election contests and was defeated only twice.

*'If nothing more ... [Blackburn] has sent to the House as many, if not more, speechless members than any constituency in the country.'*

In terms of party politics, the Conservative party usually won control of the borough's parliamentary seats. The town became the 'Gibraltar of Toryism' in mainly Liberal Lancashire, especially after the 1867 Reform Act when the franchise was extended. The Liberals were represented by James Pilkington between 1847 and 1865, and by William Briggs between 1874 and 1885, but thereafter the Conservatives had total control until the middle of the Edwardian period. The party's share of the vote shows the deep trouble in which the Liberal party found themselves: at the 1880 election the Conservatives won 51 per cent to the Liberals 49 per cent, but in 1892 the shares were 57 per cent to 43 per cent, and in 1895 73 per cent to 27 per cent. At the 'Khaki' election of 1900 the Liberals did not even field a candidate. But whoever was MP for Blackburn, and from whichever party, their desire for political power was purely local and not national. It is claimed that none of the Feildens ever spoke in Parliament and Pilkington was similarly silent for the entire eighteen years that he sat in the House of Commons. Harry Hornby went even better, allegedly never uttering a single word from the backbenches in a twenty-three-year career. Edward Hornby, in comparison, was garrulous. He spoke twice, which probably accounts for the fact that he never managed a second term of office. Blackburn could proudly boast that 'if nothing more ... it has sent to the House as many, if not more, speechless members than any constituency in the country'.[13] What this emphasises is that becoming a member of parliament for Blackburn was primarily a matter of achieving and cementing local status.

The struggle for power at council level followed a similar pattern. Blackburn had had a form of modern local government – the Police Commissioners and the Improvement Commissioners – since the early nineteenth century, but the need for a fully fledged town council was apparent after 1835, when the

Municipal Corporations Act made it possible for communities to seek incorporation by the grant of a borough charter. In Blackburn, the decision to seek incorporation as a borough was taken in the Assembly Rooms in King Street, at what was known as 'The Hotel'. Built in 1804, this had become the social, commercial and political hub of the town. As well as having rooms in which to hold meetings, play billiards or read newspapers, it had 25 bedrooms, seven eating rooms, a coffee room and stabling for twenty horses. It was also the main departure point for stagecoaches. The idea of incorporation and the construction of a town hall were first raised at a leypayers meeting here as early as 1836, the procedure for the grant of a borough charter having been revised by the legislation of 1835. Deliberations were slow and complex, but finally in 1850 a petition for a charter of incorporation was drawn up in the same rooms. The queen, via the privy council, accepted the petition and Blackburn was incorporated on 10 November 1851. Under the terms of the charter the town was to have a mayor, twelve aldermen and 36 councillors. The borough was divided into six wards each with six councillors: St Mary's, St John's, Trinity, Park, St Peter's and St Paul's. Here, too, cotton dominated from the beginning. Twenty-one of the 48 inaugural councillors and aldermen were textile manufacturers and two others, classed as gentlemen, had a cotton background. Since the charter of

This is one of the earliest photographs of Blackburn, taken in the early 1850s. It shows the laying of the foundation stone of the town hall by Joseph Feilden, the lord of the manor, surrounded by the dignitaries of the day, many of whom appear to be wearing masonic aprons. For the town's elite, membership of a masonic lodge was almost obligatory. Note also how the women are seated separately.

COTTON TOWN PROJECT

This painting, by an unknown artist, is of a general, perhaps county, election in the town. Blackburn was quite infamous as regards bribery, corruption and violence at elections throughout most of the nineteenth century. This picture shows an excitable crowd of all classes. The building in the background, under the church tower, is the Old Bull Inn, the traditional headquarters of the Tory faction at the time. Free alcohol for voters and supporters was often liberally available and many in the crowd appear to have enjoyed this largesse.

in 1900 it was said that 'it is notorious that the Blackburn Tory party wins its elections by means of the beer barrel'.[17] In some areas the political struggle intensified. Registration battles took on a new lease of life. The court which adjudicated on challenges to voter registration took just three hours in 1864 to judge on the eighty cases brought before it. In 1868 it took seven days to plough through 2,000 objections. There had originally been 6,000 but behind the scenes bargaining had reduced that figure. In 1873 4,000 objections had to be adjudicated and a further 2,000 in 1878.

The Conservative party was very willing to use local levers, to good effect, to consolidate its hold on Blackburn. For example, it was prepared to exploit the anti-Irish sentiment widely felt in mid- to late-Victorian Lancashire. Fuelled by both racial and religious hatred, the issue of home rule for Ireland was often in the forefront of election campaigns from the 1880s, though the Irish question was never as important in Blackburn as it was in Liverpool, Preston, Manchester or St Helens (where Irish immigration was much more substantial). By 1901 Blackburn only had about 2,500 Irish-born residents, mainly concentrated in the Penny Street area. The Orange movement was strong, however, claiming 1,200 members in seventeen lodges and led by the brewers Thwaites and Rutherford and the cotton manufacturer Thompson. Militant Anglicanism in various forms also helped the Conservative party. The Conservatives were the party of the established Church and the established Church was dominant in Blackburn. In addition to the Orange Movement, Blackburn had a Church of England National Protection League with 900 members, and in 1885 a Church Defence League was formed. The Church of England fought hard for the control of the hearts and minds of Blackburn's population and was reasonably successful in warding off the spread of Nonconformism, the religious rock of Liberalism. The way in which the Church of England won the battle to educate the borough's youth is yet further evidence of its power, and such influence could readily be transferred into political authority for the Conservative party.

The Conservatives also put up candidates who epitomised what Blackburn's electorate apparently looked for in their leaders. The people of Blackburn felt a 'traditional dislike to strangers as their candidate'.[18] Between 1832 and 1859 not one 'stranger' won an election, and between 1865 and 1906 Sir Robert Peel in 1885 was the only exception and he had an historic connection. And local really meant local. In the 1860s J. G. Potter, a paper manufacturer from Darwen, unsuccessfully stood three times. Although coming from a town virtually on the doorstep he was still seen as 'a stranger without any substantial interests in the borough'.[19] Blackburn had a very strong community sense bred in its self-imposed isolation from neighbouring communities. Blackburn's people felt different from their neighbours and were proud of the fact. The actual birthplace of candidates was not of crucial importance. What counted was a strong stake in the community and an abiding interest in local affairs. The failure of John Morley, one of the most distinguished of Blackburn's parliamentary candidates and one who had been born in the borough, typifies this. On his return he was regarded as 'a London scribe'.

On the other hand, Harry Hornby, the town's MP for 23 years up to his retirement in 1910, typifies the kind of man that the people of Blackburn admired. He was known locally as 'Mr Harry', the 'owd 'un' or 'the gam' cock'. He personified the qualities most respected in Blackburn society. He had little knowledge of affairs outside the borough and little interest in the evolving

Harry Hornby MP was known locally as 'Mr Harry', the 'owd 'un' or 'the gam cock'. He successfully carried on the Blackburn MPs' tradition of silence by not speaking once at Westminster throughout his entire 23-year-term of office which ended on his retirement in 1910. Although he was a staunch Conservative, he had little interest in affairs outside the borough, a trait apparently much admired by the town's parochial electorate.

policies of his party. His outlook was basically apolitical yet when necessary he knew just what he stood for and stuck to his beliefs. Outside political change merely washed over him. Hornby remained a staunch believer in free trade even though eventually the majority in the Conservative party did not. Though a cotton man, the image he assiduously portrayed was that of a gentleman land-owner and amateur politician. Blackburn's elite copied this image. Hunting, horse breeding, greyhound racing, coursing and cricket were far more impor-tant than politics. John Rutherford proudly kept a successful racehorse, while William Briggs, the only successful Liberal candidate in the late nineteenth century, gave humorous speeches in local dialect and constantly paraded his prize-winning greyhound on the election hustings. The abrupt shortness of Daniel Thwaites' political career was put down to his failure to match up to this image of 'Hornbyism'. Thwaites was considered to be too arrogant, and too concerned in displaying his wealth and too aloof from local affairs to be seen as a 'real' gentleman.

*'It is notorious that the Blackburn Tory party wins its elections by means of the beer barrel.'*

The key to the success of Blackburn's elite, be they Conservative or Liberal, was that they won the respect, devotion and loyalty of Blackburn's working classes. Part of that loyalty was based on the fact that the town's workers accepted a hierarchical society. They did not ape the middle classes, merely admired them and dutifully accepted their place in the social order. Most

In the early years of the camera it was the fashion to have your portrait taken at a local photographer's studio. David Johnson, who had a studio at 3 Corporation Street, took these photographs of anonymous middle class ladies. The name of the gentleman is known. He was Eli Pickup, who was one of a family of coal dealers and carters. He lived at 45 Thomas Street, which had been built by his grandfather in 1823.

COTTON TOWN PROJECT

loyalty, however, was based on the mill and was akin in many ways to present-day loyalty to the local football team. Employers noted this and tended to stand for election in the ward in which their mills stood rather than the one in which they lived. As a contemporary observed in 1868, 'Each individual operative comes to identify with the mill at which he works, and if he be not troubled with convictions of his own readily accepts its political shibboleths.'[20]

Political colours were sported at election time in the mills, with workers even attaching them to their looms. When someone stood out against the rest, factory ejections took place and employers rarely had to become involved. Their employees did their work for them, often violently. The result of this tribal instinct was that streets loyally voted according to the political persuasion of the owner of the local mill.[21] Examples of this have already been given. Others are numerous. In Park ward, in the 1868 general election, the streets surrounding the mills of the Pilkington Brothers, Eli Heyworth and Briggs returned 626 votes for both Liberal candidates and only 312 for the two Conservatives. In the same ward in the streets encircling the mills of Harrison, Hopwood and James Thompson, all of whom were known Conservatives, only 212 voted for the Liberal candidates while 466 voted for the two Conservatives. And it was not just mill workers who loyally voted. In St John's ward where Hornby's Brookhouse mills were situated, the landlords of all seventeen public houses

The Royal Infirmary photographed in 1865 the year in which it was opened with a total of thirty-five beds. It is an example of local philanthropy being a gift to the town from the cotton magnate James Pilkington. It was badly needed since most in the town had no access to medical care. Those with serious illnesses or injuries often had to travel to Manchester for treatment.
COTTON TOWN PROJECT, © LANCASHIRE EVENING TELEGRAPH

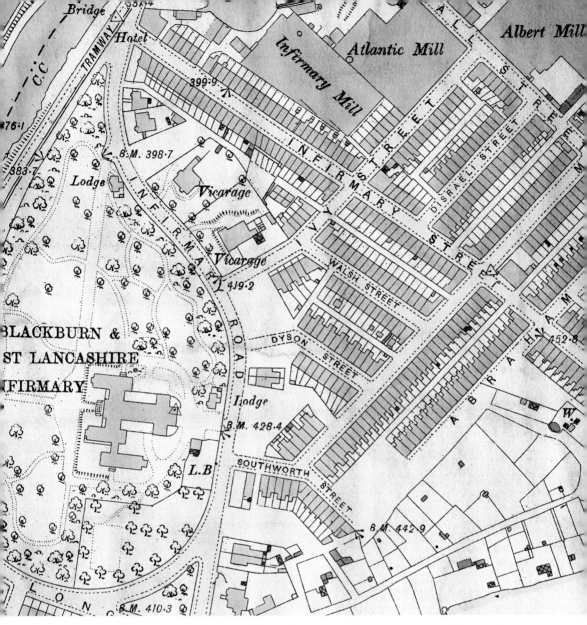

Blackburn and East Lancashire Infirmary (1893). The infirmary, opened in the early 1860s, was (like many Victorian institutions) set in attractively landscaped grounds. When it was built it stood outside the town, although by the early twentieth century closely packed terraced housing had covered much of the surrounding land. The infirmary was extended in 1897, just after this map was produced, by the construction of the new Victoria Wing, commemorating the queen's diamond jubilee.

DETAIL OF THE 1893 ORDNANCE SURVEY MAP, REPRODUCED BY KIND PERMISSION OF THE COUNTY ARCHIVIST, LANCASHIRE RECORD OFFICE

voted Conservative as well as the owners of 20 of the 25 beer shops. Loyalty to the Conservative cause was also partly won within Blackburn because leading members of the party actively supported policies that were close to the heart of the town's populace. These included support for factory reform and holding out against the introduction of the New Poor Law.

By careful and psychologically effective manipulation of working-class support, Blackburn's elite won loyalty. Support followed philanthropy and paternalism. Back in the early 1800s, in times of hardship, Henry Sudell often provided vegetables at below market prices, and it was his annual custom to provide an ox for roasting in the market square at Christmas. The Pilkingtons founded Blackburn Infirmary in 1858. Many of the elite financed the building of schools and subscribed to church building. In addition to building workers' housing, some also built public houses to serve them. Employers might forego rents in bad times and charge low rents in good. Hornby's even allowed old ex-employees to remain living in the houses rent free in the same manner as country gentry might look after old and faithful servants or tenants. During the Cotton Famine in the 1860s factory inspectors reported that half of the town's employers ran their mills on short time at a loss and also gave 'unobtrusive assistance' to their workers.[22] Turner provided almshouses and Eli Heywood provided a crèche for nursing mothers as well as a canteen at his Audley mill.[23] As a result, Blackburn's elite had a greater hold on the electoral support of the people after 1867, with the addition of new voters. The franchise was extended to encompass a growing number of the working classes, and thereby the political dividend of their social control could be collected. Nevertheless, as towards the end of the nineteenth century the dominant Conservative faction, having seen off the challenge of their Liberal counterparts, encountered a new challenge. New political allegiances began to emerge from below as some members of the working class began to search for their own voice, and even flirted with socialism.

Working-class movements had always been weak in Blackburn. Though spontaneous violent outbursts were relatively common, the working classes, in the intervening periods and most of the time, were quiescent. Chartism was always weak, and other possible foci of working-class concern, such as the anti-Poor Law movement and agitation for factory reform, were success-fully controlled by the town's employers. Trade unionism, though widespread, was very conservative. Once the 'standard list' had been established in 1853, giving agreed piece rates of pay for the job across all the mills in Blackburn, the concern of the unions was mainly that of defending the status quo, not actively pursuing radical change. By the last quarter of the last century, however, some local unions did feel it was time that they had a more powerful voice in the town's political dialogue. Therefore, the textile unions persuaded James Boothman to stand for parliament in the general election of 1885 under the auspices of the Labour Representation League. Their choice of candidate is telling, for they picked a wealthy local cotton master. Equally significant, perhaps, is that he came bottom of the poll.

The trade unions also resurrected the Trades Council. Originally formed in the 1860s, and a supporter of the Liberal Party in the 1868 elections, this had been the first attempt at giving the unions a single voice, but it soon

*'Each individual operative comes to identify with the mill at which he works, and if he be not troubled with convictions of his own readily accepts its political shibboleths.'*

disintegrated. It was resuscitated in 1884 to help James Boothman's election campaign, but had no permanent organisation until 1889. Even then, in the true spirit of Blackburn's working classes, it was far from being a radical organisation. The ruling body of the Trades Council was opposed to what it viewed as extreme politics, and in accordance with 'Lib/Lab' tradition it expelled a member in 1896 for 'trying to force down the throats of the executive his own socialist ideals'.[24] The fear, within the Trades Council, of what it saw as extreme political views was governed by the conservatism of Blackburn's trade unions. At this time the Blackburn branch of the Weavers' Association shunned socialism. It was worried about keeping its members. The Weavers' Protection Society was set up in 1885 as a breakaway organisation from the main union. By 1900 this group, which openly supported the Conservative Party, had 3000 members. In addition the Conservative Working Men's Vigilance Committee

This, in 1906, was the annual old folks' treat, paid for out of the mayor's fund, another example of local philanthropy. At a time before old age pensions were introduced advancing years, especially for widows, often brought poverty. Hundreds attended free meals such as this. Nearly all the guests wear mourning clothes, made fashionable by Queen Victoria. For the poor such dress was worn even after the designated mourning period as clothes were not thrown away until totally worn out.

was founded in the town in 1894 to fight any form of radicalism in the local trade union movement. The result was that in order to retain support, Blackburn's trade union leaders had to tread warily in their search for a more vocal political voice. The success of Blackburn's middle classes in ensuring a conservative workforce proved a formidable barrier in delaying any movement to the political left in the town's working-class organisations.

But radical politics did begin to appear in the town at the end of the nineteenth century, from an unexpected quarter – women mill workers. The electoral franchise denied all women the right to vote in parliamentary elections, or to stand as a candidate. In the late nineteenth century women began to organise themselves to demand democratic rights, and in 1897 the North of England Society for Women's Suffrage came into existence. Three years later, Esther Roper, Eva Gore-Booth, Sarah Reddish and Sarah Dickenson, the first two of whom were from middle-class or aristocratic backgrounds and the second two having nearly forty years of factory and mill experience, decided to raise a petition calling for female enfranchisement. This was to be signed by female Lancashire mill workers. Blackburn, with its sixteen thousand women mill workers, was chosen as the place for the public launch of the petition, and this took place at an open air meeting on 1 May. Sadly the *Blackburn Times* felt that the event was not newsworthy. Some sympathetic mill-owners, however, allowed the organisers to pass the petition around their workers, while others allowed them to set up tables in mill yards, though most signatures were collected door to door after work ended. The final petition, with just under 30,000 signatures, was handed in at Westminster by a deputation of fifteen Lancashire mill workers in March 1901.[25]

The campaign carried on in the years that followed, although the more famous suffragette movement, headed by the Pankhurst family, did not take a serious hold in Blackburn. Most women involved in the movement believed

This garden party held at Pleasington Hall in September 1906 portrays some middle-class ladies of Blackburn in part of their social round. The rather formidable lady in her invalid chair is probably the hostess. Such events were often held to raise money for local charities or political fighting funds. Even though women could not yet vote in general elections many still took part in the political process.

The Votes for Women campaign was certainly a talking point in the town: Richard Jackson, complete with bowler hat, stands with his son Fred outside his newsagent and stationers shop at 25 Johnston Street. The hoardings outside refer to suffragist or suffragette 'outrages', although Blackburn itself saw very few.

in pursuing their aims within the law, but even so they did not have an easy time. Giving public speeches in the market place, to a crowd that did not differentiate between the various suffrage organisations, meant that one young Blackburn mother of three had to have a bodyguard of helpers to protect her against the crowd.[26] Other suffragists in Blackburn spoilt their case by linking their own pet concerns with the vote question. Ethel Snowden, whose husband, Philip Snowden, was in 1906 elected as Blackburn's first socialist MP, was a member of the suffragist temperance campaign and called for the abolition of barmaids on the grounds that they were being sexually exploited to attract men into public houses. Her plea was far from popular with the working men of the town.[27] There were other attempts to encourage the working classes to travel down more radical political avenues. Fresh attempts to form socialist and labour organisations were instigated in Blackburn and some were even modestly successful. A local branch of the Social Democratic Federation was formed in 1884. This occurred soon after Henry Hyndman and William Morris, the national leaders, came to speak in Blackburn during the weavers' strike of 1883–84. By 1900 the branch had one hundred members. These were not cotton workers, however, but mainly self-employed men such as shopkeepers, barbers and tailors. Their power base was therefore weak. And when compared with the membership of one thousand in neighbouring Burnley the extent of socialist penetration is seen in its true perspective.

The weakness of socialism in Blackburn is also apparent in the chequered history of the town's Fabian Society. A local branch was founded in March 1892. It was dissolved within a year, and did not re-emerge until 1912. From its initial demise, however, arose a branch of the Independent Labour Party. Even this was never strong in terms of membership (by 1903 only two hundred people had joined) but it proved more successful than most of other radical organisations in the town. Perhaps the difficulties encountered by local socialists in converting the people of Blackburn to their political philosophy were summed up by Tom Stephenson, who explained that: 'It was very often the case of talking to a couple of men and a dog and a couple of kids'.[28] After Boothman's dismal failure in the general election of 1895 the next attempt to put up a candidate to represent explicitly the working classes of Blackburn was in 1900. The young Philip Snowden, who a quarter of a century later would be the first Labour chancellor of the exchequer, stood as the Labour and Socialist candidate. This title was chosen specifically so as not to offend any single organisation. With no Liberal opposition, which allowed a straight run against the Conservative candidates, Snowden polled 7,096, or 25.5 per cent of the vote. It was not enough. In 1906, when the Liberals again gave him an unopposed run at the Conservatives, Snowden succeeded. His 10,282 votes sent him to Westminster, beside the long-standing Conservative MP Henry Hornby. The shock proved too much for Henry, and he never stood for Parliament again, but the result was not totally out of line with Blackburn's political past. With the Conservative Party in 1906 very badly split over tariff reform, the wonder was that Blackburn still returned at least one Conservative MP. The constituency was one of the very few in the entire northwest to do so.

It is interesting to note how Snowden chose to fight his election campaigns. He copied the tactics honed so successfully by generations of Hornbys and the remainder of Blackburn's elite. Policies took a back seat, as did the King's English. Snowden's successful 1906 election campaign poster cried out; 'We

*'We want a gam' cock that con feight. Snowden con. He's o'reight.'*

It is ironic that though Blackburn was predominantly a Conservative bastion throughout the nineteenth century, it was the great Liberal Prime Minister William Ewart Gladstone who had a statue erected. This photograph, taken in 1922 of the Boulevard, shows the statue of Gladstone in the foreground in one of its many previous positions. That of Queen Victoria has managed to remain in place. In the background behind the now sadly demolished domed Palace Theatre can be seen the cooling tower and 250ft chimney of the town's electricity works. This has also disappeared but with greater public approval.

COTTON TOWN PROJECT, © LANCASHIRE EVENING TELEGRAPH

want a gam' cock that con feight. Snowden con. He's o'reight.' This was a fitting acknowledgement of the psychological hold that Blackburn's middle-class elite had on the minds of the workers of the town. But Snowden's electoral success cannot be brushed aside. Cracks were beginning to appear in the working-class Toryism of Blackburn by the beginning of the twentieth century. It was being undermined as amalgamations and takeovers among the cotton mills diminished the number of cotton masters. Moreover, family firms were becoming limited public companies, and the growth of a deeper managerial layer in the enlarged firms and the rise of directors and shareholders led to a widening division between the workers and the remaining cotton kings. With their growing isolation, the old values of paternalism and the common touch grew weaker. Some workers, in the absence of a Liberal centre, crossed directly over to the left of politics. Nevertheless, as the political history of interwar Blackburn showed, the loss of Tory support among the working class was not terminal. That it did not prove fatal is yet another tribute to the success of the town's nineteenth-century elite in securing control of Blackburn. Not only did they carve out for themselves a dominant and all-powerful place in the town's social structure, with its own distinctive social mores based on an imagined semi-rural squirearchy, they also won political dominance. Blackburn was not unique in this experience, for other mill towns in Lancashire and Yorkshire showed the same tendencies, but in this town the extent of control by a few was particularly marked, and notably long-lasting. Few towns as large as Blackburn, anywhere in Britain, had such a conservative political and social structure in the years preceding the First World War.

Great Tacket

Blacow Moor

48

Middle Tacket

48

27 25

29

30

Part of

earer

raven

Croft

North Gate

68

36

35

34

33

26 Croft

26

12.a

31

23 Fish Lane

12.a

23

Little Tacket

Preston

Water Street

7

37 38 39 37

40

41

37

40

1

Part of the Barn Meadow

67

63

22

22

Back Lane

Church Street

37

VICARAGE

20

20

Part of the Mill Field

19 2 20

16 17

13

12 b

12

10

11

Mrs Meadows

13 c Gardens

Part of the Lower Stoncy Butts

Part of the Meadow by the Brook

# CHAPTER FOUR

# Townscape and society,
# 1750–1914

BETWEEN 1750 AND 1914 Blackburn developed from a market town with fewer than 5,000 inhabitants, though with an expanding textile trade, into the self-proclaimed weaving capital of the world with a population of over 130,000. Such an expansion was by no means untypical of the developing industrial centres of Georgian and Victorian England, many of which showed comparable or even greater rates of growth, but here, as almost everywhere else, it brought about far-reaching and dramatic changes in the physical shape, visual appearance and social character of the town. In analysing the ways in which Blackburn evolved over that period of 175 years, we have to consider such factors as the patterns of landownership, the changing transport networks, the locations favoured for industrial development, the class divisions within local society, and the extent and impact of civic intervention in the form of local government action. It is the mix of such influences that determines the individual shape of each town, rather than one factor acting alone, and in Blackburn, as elsewhere, there is a complex story to be told.

The statistics of growth and change are clear. From 1801 onwards the census, taken every ten years, gives us reliable evidence for the size of population, while from 1841 the detailed individual returns of the census give a vast amount of information about individual households, streets, districts and people. The trend of expansion can be correlated with changing social and economic conditions and circumstances. The highest percentage increase in a single decade was during the period 1811–21, when the steam-powered spinning mills were

A detail from the 1759 survey of the lands held by the Archbishop of Canterbury within Blackburn: this map is of exceptional interest, as it is one of the earliest really detailed portrayals of any Lancashire town. The finely drawn pictures of individual properties owned by the Church tell us a great deal about the architecture and appearance of the town. For example, some of the houses in Church Street (now Darwen Street) and Northgate are only single-storeyed, as are most of those in Fish Lane and Blakey Moor. The small size of the town is very apparent, on the eve of the Industrial Revolution (compare with map on page 99, drawn 65 years later).

Table 5 *Population statistics for Blackburn, 1780–1931*

| Year | population | % change | absolute change |
|------|-----------|----------|-----------------|
| 1780 | 5000 (est.) | | |
| 1801 | 11,980 | | |
| 1811 | 15,083 | 26.0 | 3103 |
| 1821 | 21,940 | 45.7 | 6857 |
| 1831 | 27,091 | 23.5 | 5151 |
| 1841 | 36,614 | 32.9 | 8909 |
| 1851 | 46,538 | 29.3 | 10538 |
| 1861 | 63,126 | 35.6 | 16588 |
| 1871 | 76,339 | 20.9 | 13213 |
| 1881 | 104,012 | 36.3 | 27673 |
| 1891 | 120,064 | 15.4 | 16052 |
| 1901 | 129,216 | 7.6 | 9152 |
| 1911 | 133,052 | 3.0 | 3836 |
| 1921 | 129,400 | −2.7 | −3652 |
| 1931 | 122,971 | −5.0 | −6429 |

opening up, and at the same time handloom weaving was enjoying its 'golden age'. The 1820s, beset by a series of industrial and commercial crises and depressions, saw a slackening of growth, as did the 1840s, when trade was again disrupted by economic turbulence and upheaval. By 1851, however, Blackburn, with over 46,000 people, had tripled in size since 1811, an extraordinary rate of growth though one paralleled by the experience of some other Lancashire towns. During the 1860s the protracted crisis in the textile business (the Cotton Famine) sharply checked growth rates, though there was still a significant increase, but the recovery from the end of the decade was dramatic. During the 1870s the population growth of almost 28,000 was not only the second greatest in percentage terms, but also by far the greatest numerically. In just ten years the equivalent to a major town was added to the population of Blackburn. Such rates could not be sustained, and growth fell very sharply from the early 1890s onwards to the eve of the First World War. Blackburn's peak population, of just over 133,000, was recorded in 1911. Between the wars decline set in, and in the period from 1911 to 1931 the town lost over 7 per cent of its population. The great age of growth and expansion was well and truly at an end.

As already noted, Blackburn had developed as a market town which was centred on the road junction where Darwen Street, King Street and Church Street met near a crossing over the river Blakewater. Around this focus centuries of gradual piecemeal development had produced a small town characterised by narrow streets and yards, and varied and architecturally unambitious housing and shops. A visitor described Blackburn quite succinctly in the 1790s: 'The town itself consists of several streets, irregularly laid out, but intermixed with good houses, the consequence of commercial wealth.'[1] A year after this description, the vicar of Blackburn, the Reverend Thomas Starkie, leased out

The Gillies map of 1822 was privately produced for the Reverend Whittaker after his appointment as vicar of Blackburn.
It clearly shows that the town grew up on the river Blakewater and was centred on the crossroads where Darwen Street,
Church Street, King Street and Northgate intersected. The industrial colonies of Grimshaw Park and Nova Scotia can be
clearly seen to the south-west of the old centre of the town. It was the birth of such colonies that helped shape the
development of Blackburn.

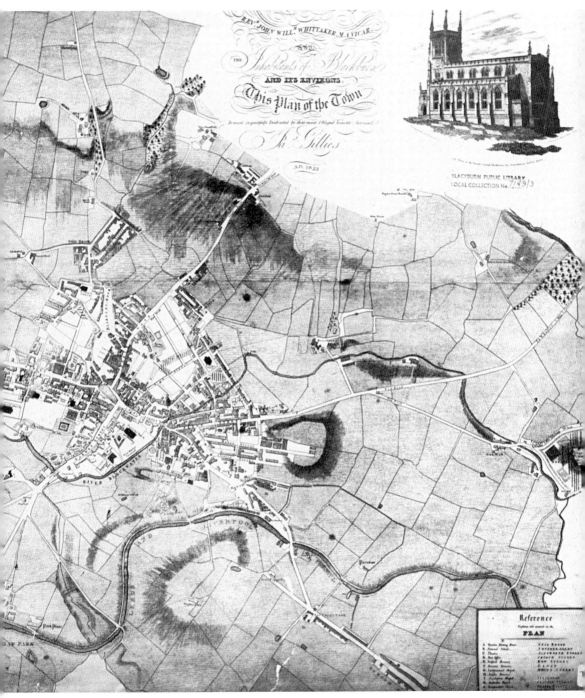

the glebe land of St Mary's church for building on a 999-year lease.[2] This land, totalling 70 acres to the east of the parish church, was used for farming or for laying out bleached cloth to dry but, as it was now available for development, it was soon covered with mills, foundries, breweries and workshops. The expansion of the town was therefore well under way by 1800, a process which was spurred on by the rapid growth of the cotton industry and its growing demand for new and larger premises and transport facilities. The shape of this industry's growth was always an important factor in the direction the town's expansion took. As we have seen, the cotton merchants who provided the spinners and handloom weavers with their raw materials, and who collected the woven cloth for sale and distribution, began to dominate the town's trade and commerce in the second half of the eighteenth century. These merchants worked from warehouses which were mainly situated along King Street and Ainsworth Street. In order to receive the raw cotton and then distribute the finished cloth these merchants needed a better road system, and so were active and vigorous in promoting and financing the turnpike network which is discussed in chapter 1. The routes to Preston and Burnley were improved as early as 1754–55 and that northwards into the Ribble Valley, along Whalley Old Road, in 1776. In

*'The town itself consists of several streets, irregularly laid out, but intermixed with good houses, the consequence of commercial wealth.'*

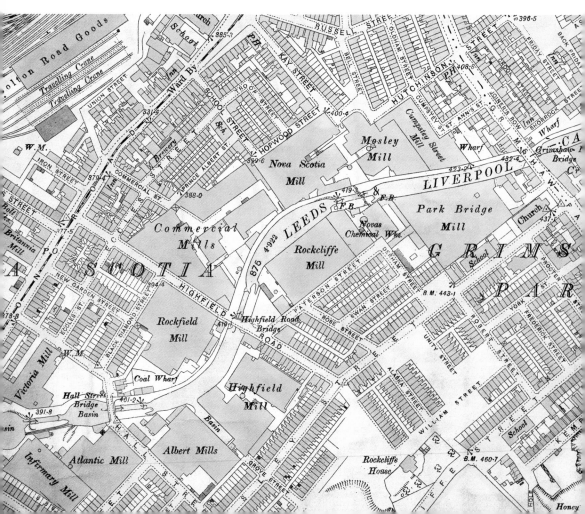

the 1820s came the major expansion of the network via newly built routes to Whalley, Preston and Accrington. These various trunk roads provided the framework within which the new areas of the town developed, supplemented by the Leeds and Liverpool Canal and, from the early 1840s, the emergent railway network.

Transport was one of the keys to the location of industry, but the first generation of cotton mills as well as many other industrial sites also needed water as a power-source and for production processes. The first generation of water-powered cotton mills was therefore built along the banks of the river Blakewater and the river Darwen. As steam superseded water power, the canal provided the means of transporting the large supplies of coal which were required, as well as allowing the easy movement of raw materials and finished products. In 1867, as a consequence of the locational pressures and requirements, 35 mills and weaving sheds could be counted along the banks of the river Blakewater, 34 alongside the river Darwen, and a further 39 by the side of the canal. Their powerful influence in determining the pattern of industrial location was very clear. During the next great mill-building boom, of 1850–70, the railway provided a far quicker and more efficient service in the movement of coal which, increasingly, came from further afield, beyond the Blackburn area or adjacent parts of the east Lancashire coalfield. Industrialists could now exploit sites away

Nova Scotia (1893). As this map extract reveals, the Leeds and Liverpool Canal (completed in 1816) exerted a powerful influence upon the location of industry in the growing town of the mid-nineteenth century. It provided relatively cheap and easy transport of coal and other bulk products, and by 1900 was lined, along its entire length through Blackburn, by cotton mills and factories. Hemmed in by the canal and the adjacent high-density terraced housing, these had no room for expansion, so the last generation of cotton mills were built further out, on green-field sites.

DETAIL OF THE 1893 ORDNANCE SURVEY MAP, REPRODUCED BY KIND PERMISSION OF THE COUNTY ARCHIVIST, LANCASHIRE RECORD OFFICE

These houses on Cleaver Street were typical handloom weavers' dwellings. They were erected around 1800. They were purposely built raised above street level, which necessitated the steps up to the front door, in order to allow light into the workrooms below. These windows at pavement level had been bricked up by the time this photograph was taken.

COTTON TOWN PROJECT

from a riverside or canal, although the since the main line of the railway from Pleasington through central Blackburn to Rishton roughly paralleled the canal route the same general areas were chosen for industrial development. The impact of the railway was less than in some other towns for example at Bolton, where it made a major difference to the location of later industrial expansion. Plotting the sites of Victorian industry on a map therefore shows a reasonably close correlation with waterways and transport arteries, as belts of mills and other factories and workshops emerged stretching outwards along these axes from the town centre. But to visualise the shape of Blackburn's industrial growth solely as expanding ribbon development is misleading, for the process went hand in hand with the development of mill colonies, the areas where the workers lived, so that the spaces in between the 'fingers' of transport routes were rapidly, and usually completely, filled up with housing.

Three main areas of industrial housing, or mill colonies, coloured the development and shape of Blackburn: those at Brookhouse (north of the town centre), Nova Scotia (to the south) and Grimshaw Park (to the south-east). All began their life in the 1820s, and they were the earliest major areas specifically given over to industrial housing. The reason for their location outside the old town centre was partly that the land there was cheaper and partly that buildings ripe for conversion and extension as factory premises already existed. These were old bleaching and dyeing works, which in the past had needed extensive open spaces in which to lie out the cloth to dry and bleach in the sun and rain. Robert Hopwood at Nova Scotia and John Hornby at Brookhouse both took over such premises and there developed new cotton mills in existing premises.[3]

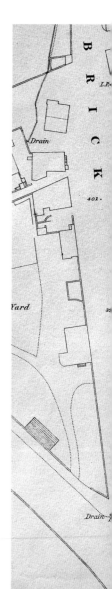

Richmond Terrace and Kirkham Lane (1848). This small area of the town showed remarkable contrasts in housing styles. The impressive Richmond Terrace of the early 1830s (completed in 1838) was designed as a prestigious residential development and, although it later fell on hard times, its recent restoration and renovation (albeit as offices) has given it a new lease of life as one of the town's 'heritage' features. The name of Tontine Street recalls the widespread use of the 'tontine' a form of annuity scheme widely used among small investors in the eighteenth and nineteenth centuries. On Kirkham Lane can be seen a group of handloom weavers' cottages, identifiable by the characteristic front steps, which are marked, and which indicate that there was a large half-lit cellar below street level.

DETAIL OF THE 1848 ORDNANCE SURVEY MAP, REPRODUCED BY KIND PERMISSION OF THE COUNTY ARCHIVIST, LANCASHIRE RECORD OFFICE

These mills needed workers and since most workers had to live within a few streets of their workplace, so that they could walk to work as quickly as possible, housing had to be provided nearby. Streets of small dwellings appeared, and continued to appear, as the mills expanded and fresh ones were constructed. Churches and schools followed, or sometimes were provided from the outset, with the result that self-contained colonies, almost entirely populated by cotton workers, grew up. By 1847 the colonies of Brookhouse, Nova Scotia and Grimshaw Park contained the largest mills in Blackburn, which between them employed one-third of all the cotton operatives in the town – in 1852, for example, William Eccles employed 1,900 workers at his Nova Scotia mills. Smaller colonies were also being formed. In the 1850s the Daisyfield area experienced rapid expansion, Audley grew very quickly between 1870 and 1900 around the mills belonging to Eli Heywood, and at the same time the Mill Hill area developed between the railway and the canal around the Cardwell Mill of

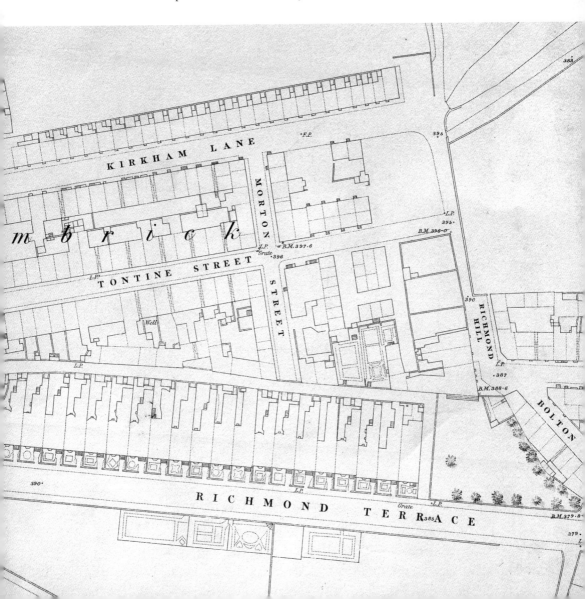

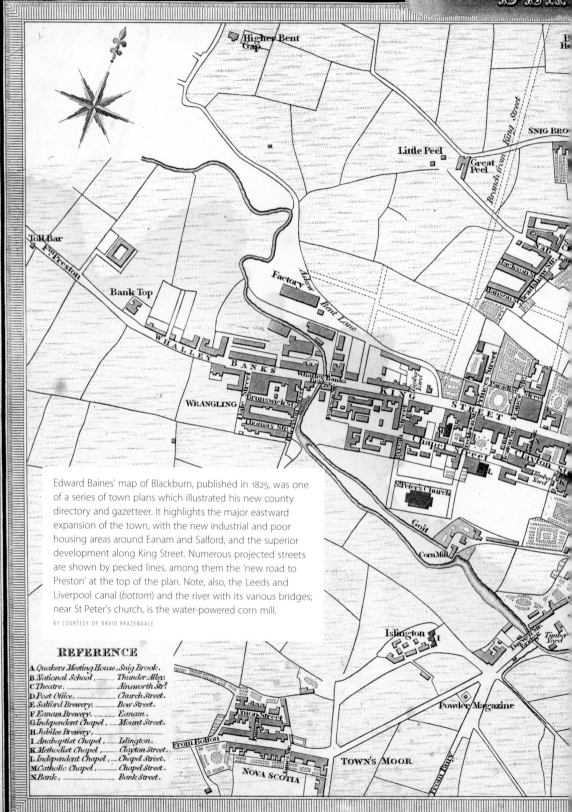

BLA

Higher Bent Gap

Little Peel

Great Peel

SNIG BRO

Branch from King Street

Toll Bar

Fm Preston

Bank Top

Factory

Aclew

Bent Lane

Jackson St Bradshaw St

Benson St

WHALLEY

BANKS

Whalley Banks

KING

STREET

Princes Street

Paradise

WRANGLING

Brunswick St.

Thomas St.

Byron Street

Chapel Street

Clayton St

St Peter's Church

Timber Yard

Goit

Corn Mill

Islington

Day's St Bridge

Timber Yard

Powder Magazine

Edward Baines' map of Blackburn, published in 1825, was one of a series of town plans which illustrated his new county directory and gazetteer. It highlights the major eastward expansion of the town, with the new industrial and poor housing areas around Eanam and Salford, and the superior development along King Street. Numerous projected streets are shown by pecked lines, among them the 'new road to Preston' at the top of the plan. Note, also, the Leeds and Liverpool canal (*bottom*) and the river with its various bridges; near St Peter's church, is the water-powered corn mill.

BY COURTESY OF DAVID BRAZENDALE

## REFERENCE

A *Quakers Meeting House*, *Snig Brook*.
B *National School*, *Thunder Alley*.
C *Theatre*, *Ainsworth Str*.
D *Post Office*, *Church Street*.
E *Salford Brewery*, *Bow Street*.
F *Eanam Brewery*, *Eanam*.
G *Independent Chapel*, *Mount Street*.
H *Jubilee Brewery*,
I *Anabaptist Chapel*, *Islington*.
K *Methodist Chapel*, *Clayton Street*.
L *Independent Chapel*, *Chapel Street*.
M *Catholic Chapel*, *Chapel Street*.
N *Bank*, *Bank Street*.

Union Street

From Bolton

NOVA SCOTIA

From Bury

TOWN'S MOOR

Surveyed by Jas. Gilhes.

Salford Bridge and brewery (1848). The confusion of industrial buildings, houses, streets and yards around Salford Bridge was gradually reduced, later in the nineteenth century, as urban redevelopment got under way – most notably, perhaps, the culverting of the Blakewater and the reconstruction of the bridge itself in the 1880s. North of Starkie Street can be seen back-to-back houses (some of the relatively few in the town) which were occupied by handloom weavers, while west of Penny Street the foetid back courts, approached by narrow tunnel entries, and some with pumps which were the only drinking water supply, are all too obvious.

DETAIL OF THE 1848 ORDNANCE SURVEY MAP, REPRODUCED BY KIND PERMISSION OF THE COUNTY ARCHIVIST, LANCASHIRE RECORD OFFICE

church and the Feilden family. The leases were usually for 999 years, which amounted to a form of freehold possession, and the builders financed their ventures by raising short-term credit through limited-life mortgages negotiated via a local solicitor, insurance company or building society. The mortgage would be repaid when the houses were built and sold. Most of those who built speculative working-class housing were small concerns, often a couple of men who built only a handful of houses at a time, and quite often just one or two. The purchasers of the completed houses were nearly always local people looking for a safe long-term investment for their capital, one on which they could keep a close eye. Generally, therefore, the purchasers were intending from the outset to let the properties to working families and to derive rent income from the investment. The bulk of such people owned fewer than ten houses each. They were small investors, normally of lower middle-class or even superior working-class social status. This 'shopocracy', the petty bourgeois of Blackburn, looked for a safe regular return on their hard-earned savings while their capital remained secure in the shape of bricks and mortar.[8]

Some building in Blackburn was undertaken through the device of the 'building club'. These were cooperative ventures in which individuals formed a group for the building of houses, each members contributing financially and with a promise of the opportunity to purchase as the houses were constructed. It meant economies of scale, and also allowed the initial start-up capital to be raised whereas a single individual was unlikely to be in a position to do so. For

Lund Street is another example of early nineteenth-century working-class housing. Many were now being built of brick but these were still made of stone. They were also still standing and inhabited 150 years later in the 1960s.

The interior of one of the houses on Lund Street in 1963. The old man is sitting in front of the kitchen range that not only provided heat but was also the used for cooking, heating the kettle and, in addition, to dry the washing. The fire was nearly always kept in twenty-four hours a day and was 'banked up' at night to keep it alight.

example, in 1822 the Blackburn Friendly Union was formed for this purpose, and others followed suit. Members paid in an agreed sum per week. With this, land was purchased and building carried out. The order in which members took possession of the new houses was usually determined by drawing lots. Other people or small groups might raise mortgages from building societies or through local solicitors, but in Blackburn owner-occupation was limited. By 1914 it was still under 10 per cent, a remarkably low figure, whereas in Burnley, the influence of the well-established, pioneering and highly successful Burnley Building Society meant that owner occupation already exceeded 35 per cent, and in some working-class districts approached 50 per cent.[9]

During the 1850s the rate of housing construction in Blackburn accelerated dramatically. Between 1840 and 1849, for part of which time there was a very serious commercial and industrial slump, a total of 1,433 houses were built. In contrast, over 1,000 new homes were constructed in the year 1851 alone.[10]

This 1881–82 photograph shows the start of Penny Street on the other side of the Mason's Arms seen jutting out onto the pavement on the left. On the far right is the chemists and druggists Kenyon & Son. Next door, plastered with posters, is Richard Arkwright's newspaper and stationer's shop. Next to that is a clothiers that appears to be shared by W. Hirst and George Green, who was also a pawnbroker. His sign of three brass balls can be seen above the door. Then comes the shop of saddler John Irvin (Irwin?) and then Miss E. Hacking's draper's store.

COTTON TOWN PROJECT, © LANCASHIRE EVENING TELEGRAPH

Housing expansion also accelerated after the end of the Cotton Famine in 1865. Between then and 1879, with the exception of a limited slump in 1874–76, an average of 400 new houses a year was built. In 1877–78 the total reached 1,500. By 1879 Blackburn had 19,042 houses, compared with 6,648 in 1841 and 12,952 in 1865. A map of the town produced in 1852 shows new building in progress at numerous locations on the fringe of the built-up area and on open ground between the 'tentacles' of transport routes – among them were St Alban's, Brookhouse, Copy Nook, Cob Wall, Nova Scotia, Grimshaw Park, Bank Top, Witton, Daisyfield, Strawberry Bank, Limbrick, Shear Brow, New Branch Road, Eanam, Bridge Street and Salford. But whereas until this time almost all building had taken place on low-lying ground, from the early 1850s the bricks and mortar of working-class housing gradually but steadily crept up the slopes of the surrounding hills, occupying sites which were more agreeable, breezy and, it was confidently hoped, healthier. Those being built at Strawberry

This photograph shows the short length of street between Penny Street and Salford Bridge. The shop of R. Worden dominates the scene with almost certainly the proprietor standing in his doorway. The large pole protruding from the wall beside his door shows that as well as a tobacconist he was also a barber. To the shop's right is the three-storey Mason's Arms and to the left the shuttered premises of provision dealer James Stanley.

COTTON TOWN PROJECT, © LANCASHIRE EVENING TELEGRAPH

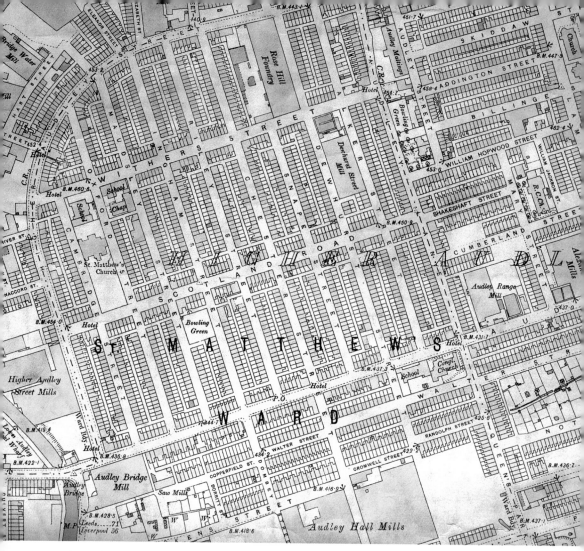

Higher Audley (1893). Lying on the south side of the canal away from the town centre, this area was developed during the later nineteenth century, in the period when Blackburn's cotton industry underwent a further (and, as it turned out, final) massive expansion. The new housing areas were laid out after the introduction of bye-laws and building regulations, giving rise to the rigid geometry which is such a striking feature of this map extract. The streets were of standard width, the houses of standard size. The name of the Alexandra mills, at the junction of Audley Range and Lambeth Street, helps to date the area: Princess Alexandra of Denmark married the Prince of Wales in 1863.

DETAIL OF THE 1893 ORDNANCE SURVEY MAP, REPRODUCED BY KIND PERMISSION OF THE COUNTY ARCHIVIST, LANCASHIRE RECORD OFFICE

Bank, for example, were seen at the time as model housing, described as being 'airy, salubrious and well built, and delightful domiciles. They are a pleasant retreat from the busy hustle and bustle of the town for those who enjoy them.'[11] The new housing was, in terms of the mid-nineteenth century, of reasonable quality, even though it fell a very long way short of later minimum standards, but the older housing in the town – that built in the later eighteenth century and first forty years of the nineteenth – was now giving rise to serious concern. Awareness of public health and sanitation issues had grown sharply in the 1840s, as scientific and medical evidence became available for the direct link

Hollin Bank (1893). Although bye-laws now ensured that streets were laid out in a planned fashion, building was still piecemeal alongside roads that often remained unmade for many months. The reason for this was that numerous small builders were involved, each constructing a handful of houses at a time on his own small patch of ground. By this date the cotton mills along the canal and river bank were larger than the earlier ones because with greater investment in the trade they were purpose-built on open land..

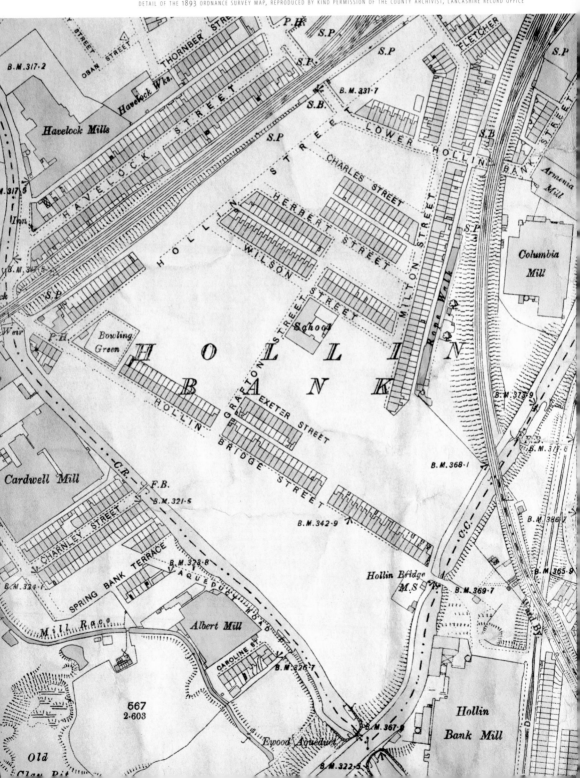

This 1910 photograph of Salford near the junction with Railway Road shows the old alongside the new. The late-eighteenth- or early nineteenth-century window of Boyles House Furnishers with its small panes of coarse glass contrasts with the larger and more confident windows of the late-nineteenth-century Saddler's shop of Leeming and Yates next door.
COTTON TOWN PROJECT

This photograph of a ginnel running behind the terraced houses at the Croft, Ewood, was taken as evidence to support the Blackburn Improvement Bill of 1879. The accumulated waste, often several feet deep, is mainly ash from the fire grates but among the detritus are many oyster shells. This highlights the fact that a dish that is now seen as somewhat of a luxury was staple fare for the working classes of industrial towns such as Blackburn before over-fishing depleted stocks.
BLACKBURN LIBRARY LOCAL HISTORY COLLECTION

between insanitary conditions and the ravages of epidemic diseases such as cholera. In many towns, and Blackburn was no exception, it was becoming apparent that filthy and overcrowded housing represented a really serious problem for the community as a whole.

The first stage in meeting this challenge was, as so often is the case, to undertake a survey. In 1852 John Withers, the newly appointed borough surveyor, wrote a report in which he listed the town's glaring defects and proposed a range of possible solutions.[12] With regard to housing, one of the issues which he raised was the absence of even the most basic sanitation in many areas of Blackburn. Very large numbers of houses had no lavatory or privy provision of any sort, not even a tub that was emptied by the nightsoil men. Numerous properties had shared privies, where several families or households used a communal facility in a yard or court. A lot of these shared privies were not even on the pail system, and nobody had any formal responsibility for emptying or maintaining them. They were filthy and malodorous and a dangerous health hazard, unless someone took the accumulated human excrement away. In all, Withers listed 53 streets which he believed to be the worst examples. Some are given below:

| Street | No. of houses | No. of privies |
| --- | --- | --- |
| Ainsworth Street | 10 | 1 |
| Blakey Moor | 2 | 4 |
| Duke Street | 14 | 2 |
| Eccles Street | 38 | 7 |
| Livesey Row | 30 | 10 |
| Penny Street | 71 | 20 |
| Water Street | 31 | 3 |

Despite the subsequent strenuous efforts to rectify this appalling situation, there were still 4,611 old-style privies remaining in 1890. By 1900 most had been removed, or were emptiable on the tub system. By that time many privies and lavatories emptied directly into the main sewer, which seems sensible, except that the waste was not flushed down with water and so there was a tendency for the excrement to pile up, harden and eventually block the sewer pipes.[13]

The typical working-class house built in the second half of the nineteenth century was terraced and had four rooms. In the earlier ones, built before the end of the 1880s, the downstairs front room, opening directly onto the street, was the living room and kitchen and measured approximately 13 feet × 14 feet. The downstairs back room was generally used as a scullery and wash-house and measured about 10 feet × 11 feet. Between these rooms was a stairway leading up to the two bedrooms, which were exactly the same size as the two rooms below. The back door led to a yard which was paved or flagged and contained the lavatory, most of which employed the 'water carriage' system, using either waste or clean water and with an ashpit. This yard in turn opened onto a paved back street about 12 feet wide. From about 1890 onwards an improved type of worker's house was often built, though it followed the same general arrangement as the previous design. In some the front room was now separated from the street by a small lobby, and a small scullery only 6 or 7 feet square, with a slopstone and sometimes a washing boiler, was added onto the back room. The back room, now that its washing and scullery functions were moved elsewhere, could become a kitchen and living room, which freed the front room to serve as the parlour. The front room was provided with a drawing room grate, while in the back room was a kitchen grate with an oven on one side and a hot water boiler on the other. There was also a small unventilated pantry under the stairs. Upstairs, taking advantage of the scullery extension, a tiny third bedroom or, much less frequently, a bathroom were added. Of 20,000 working-class homes inspected in the town in 1908, 16,000 were two-bedroomed and only 182 had bathrooms.[14] The rarity of the latter perhaps explains the initial attitude of children at Regent Street Special School, when faced with the prospect of being bathed: 'At first many of the children were afraid of the bath, and had to be coaxed to watch the performance before submitting to the bath themselves.'[15]

As for the infamous back-to-back houses, very few were ever built in Blackburn and almost all those that were, mainly near the town centre, had

The quality of working-class housing improved as the nineteenth century progressed. Here in Infirmary Street, looking up towards Rockcliffe Street, the four chimney pots show that each room in these two-up two-down houses had heating. However, the uniform appearance of the terraced housing, where the front doors opened directly onto the street, had altered very little from those built earlier in the century.

COTTON TOWN PROJECT

This is Salford in the late 1870s, looking west just before an improvement scheme to raise the quality of both the streets and the pavements. In an age before health laws were strictly enforced note the hams hanging up outside the corner shop. On the other side of the road a delivery is taking place and the sacks are being winched up to storerooms on the first and second floors.

been demolished in improvement schemes before 1914. Although the account above highlights the negative aspects, it is also unmistakeably apparent that working-class housing in Blackburn was of a higher quality than that available in many neighbouring towns, in terms of space, sanitation and ventilation. This was largely due to a local act of parliament, promoted by the new town council and passed in 1854. This forward-looking legislation, unusually progressive for the period, gave the council powers to control certain aspects of development – a sort of emergent planning role – and it was possible to ban the construction of back-to-back housing and to set down minimum requirements regarding the area, height and ventilation of rooms. This was something, at least, of which Blackburn could justifiably be proud.

Who lived in these houses? The population growth in nineteenth-century Blackburn was partly due to the increased birth rate and, once health and sanitation improvements began to produce results, the decreasing death rate. But the town also grew because of in-migration from local villages and further afield. In the early years this migration often took place as a result of considerable pressure in the home communities of those moving. Historians and geographers recognise two primary motives for migration: the 'push'

This is Salford in 1882, after the completion of an improvement scheme. The entrance to the Bull's Head Vaults is on the left. Although the road surface and pavements had been improved, it was still an uncomfortable and bumpy ride in light carriages such as that shown parked at the corner.

COTTON TOWN PROJECT, © LANCASHIRE EVENING TELEGRAPH

factors, forcing people more or less unwillingly to move, and the 'pull' factors, drawing people more or less willingly to a new location. It is a convenient division, though all researchers recognise that in reality migration is an immensely complex process. We can, however, identify various of these 'push' and 'pull' factors in the case of Blackburn. For example, in the early nineteenth century some mill-owners bought up cottages in nearby hamlets in times of depression and then evicted the weavers, while offering them alternative employment in their Blackburn mills. As one local mill-owner explained to a government committee in 1838, 'villages from 2–6 miles distant were being depopulated, the inhabitants being encouraged by the manufacturers to be nearer the factories.'[16] A study of migration into Blackburn between 1850 and 1870 has shown that the tendency was for whole families to move into the town, rather than just the young men and women, and that the average distance travelled was five miles per generation. Thus, most of those who migrated into Blackburn came from nearby rural handloom-weaving settlements such as Mellor, Wilpshire, Pleasington and Tockholes. The reasons behind migration differed. They ranged from unemployment, through the desire to increase family income yet remain in the same trade (which could mean the father sacrificing his own work as a handloom weaver in order for his children to find work as mill workers), to a change of trade, whereby a weaver sought to become perhaps a shopkeeper or publican.[17]

Notwithstanding the constant population growth, Blackburn does not seem to have suffered a real housing shortage at any time during the nineteenth century. Admittedly in 1871 some 23 per cent of all households in the town contained at least one relative other than husband, wife or child, but that had more to do with the responsibilities of the extended family than a housing shortage. A similar percentage of households also had lodgers, who were mainly single or widowed unskilled males, unmarried mothers and their children, or travelling salesmen.[18] This familiar element of the working-class domestic economy provided extra income so families could pay the rent, and did not betoken a shortage of rented accommodation. However, in the early years of the twentieth century a shortage of housing does seem to have become a limited problem, primarily because the rate of house-construction fell very sharply indeed, sometime only reaching ten or twelve per year. This problem was not confined to Blackburn, but was found nationally. The main reason was that the pool of small investors, willing to put their savings into property in

LARKHILL, BLACKBURN.                    No 88

return for rent income, was fast drying up. Rising building costs meant that in order to obtain a decent return on capital, rents would have to rise to a level unaffordable by most tenants. In addition, with far more companies offering company shares on the market, both at home and abroad, attractive alternative investment opportunities presented themselves. Whether such a change in investment habits by the 'shopocracy' was permanent or not is still debated by historians, but no reversal had been seen by 1914.[19]

Partly because Blackburn did not suffer a housing shortage until just before the First World War, there was a high turnover of tenants in many houses. Frequent moves within particular areas, from street to street, are a familiar theme in working-class popular history, and this phenomenon is supported by the evidence of academic research. In a town such as Blackburn, where the housing market was free and open, it was possible for families to move relatively easily according to the fluctuations in their income. An extra sixpence or shilling wages might permit a move to a slightly better house, or to a slightly superior street. This produced a high level of population mobility. For example, between 1845 and 1851 in New Mill Street nine of the 19 houses (45 per cent) saw a change of tenant, while in Old Mill Street the tenancy changed in 18 out of 28 houses (64 per cent). This can be compared with Union Street and Pump Street in Nova Scotia, which saw turnovers of 66 per cent and 57 per cent during the same period.[20] Since some houses may have seen more than two tenants over this period the figures may in fact underestimate the real levels of

Other areas of the town have remained virtually intact. This turn of the twentieth century postcard is wrongly annotated as the Bull's Head, Wilpshire. In fact the photographer stood outside that hotel to take this view. Except for the smithy on the left of the picture, with the farm labourer taking his scythe for sharpening, all the buildings shown still exist, including the Rising Sun public house that was originally a beer-house. This, I am glad to say, is also mainly unaltered inside.

COTTON TOWN PROJECT

BASTWELL, BLACKBURN. 158.

This view, taken in about 1900, is of Bastwell looking down towards Brownhill. Bastwell Hotel can be seen on the left. Open until the 1990s, it is now a kebab house. Of especial interest in this picture is the horse-drawn milk float on the right. Milk was then delivered direct to the door in churns and your jug filled using a measuring ladle.

family mobility. The high rate of turnover in working-class areas does not seem to have diminished as the century wore on. Over 30 years later, of a sample of 1,170 residents in 28 streets listed in the 1881 census, only 47 per cent were in the same house five years later and only 21.5 per cent ten years later.[21] A further reason for such high working-class mobility is that families moved on changing jobs, to be nearer their place of work. Such job changes were frequent in a town such as Blackburn.

Another consequence of the nineteenth-century working-class pattern of living within a few streets of the workplace was a lack of status division among workers. Contemporaries could claim that such distinctions were not as marked in Blackburn as they were elsewhere, although such opinions tend to be anecdotal and many towns probably showed comparable levels of 'togetherness'. One Blackburn worker felt that, 'Although the labourer did regard the craftsman as a little above him I don't think there was any hostility. They worked together, they lived together, they drank together in the pubs and their children married each other.'[22] This observation certainly seems to be supported by the evidence of the census returns, which gives us information about the occupations of neighbours. For example, in 1871 in Moor Street, a run-down working-class area near the canal, there lived nineteen skilled workers, 31 weavers and labourers and eight clerical workers and shopkeepers. Across the town in Cambridge Street, Audley, which had been built up relatively recently, there were 24 skilled workers, 33 weavers and labourers and four clerical workers

With a growing lower middle class moving into newly built small villas on the roads radiating from the town there arose a demand for skilled tradesmen. Here, in 1904, is the workforce of Fielding & McCarthy, painters and decorators who had premises at 92 Cleaver Street. Becoming apprenticed in such a firm meant years of training in such skills such as marbling and wood graining with paint as well as sign-writing. Becoming a skilled man was one way of rising up the social ladder.

In an age before the motor car, trams provided the main form of transport to the outer reaches of the town. The lack of traffic at Witton Stocks, around 1910, is shown by the fact that the two men appear so at ease walking in the road. On the other side can be seen the traditional barber's red and white striped pole standing out proudly from the shop front. In the left foreground a young boy strides in anticipation towards the confectioner's shop.

and shopkeepers.[23] Working-class residential divisions certainly appear to have been blurred and, in the case of the shopkeepers and clerical workers, such areas included people who had aspirations to a higher status and were on the margin between the 'workers' and the 'petty bourgeois'.

The advent of the tram, popularly known as the 'gondola of the people', made little real difference to mobility rates, and had a relatively modest impact upon the residential location of the working classes.[24] The first tramway

The uniformed drivers and conductors were the usual human face of the trams, but what tends to be forgotten is that in order to keep the trams going many mechanics were needed. Here, at Intack Tram Depot, such men in their oil-stained working clothes, complete with obligatory flat caps, pose for a group picture in the Edwardian years.
J. HALSALL COLLECTION

route in Blackburn was opened by the Blackburn & Over Darwen Tramways Company in 1881, a steam-operated line from St Peter Street in the town centre to the Angel Inn, Darwen. From 1886 a network of routes was opened by the Blackburn Corporation Tramways Company, which despite its name was a private undertaking although the Corporation owned the tracks and leased them to the operator. Steam-trams, clanking hissing monsters, operated the route to the Commercial Inn at Church where they connected with the Accrington tramways and along Whalley New Road to the cemetery, while horse-trams were used on the routes to Preston New Road (Billinge)

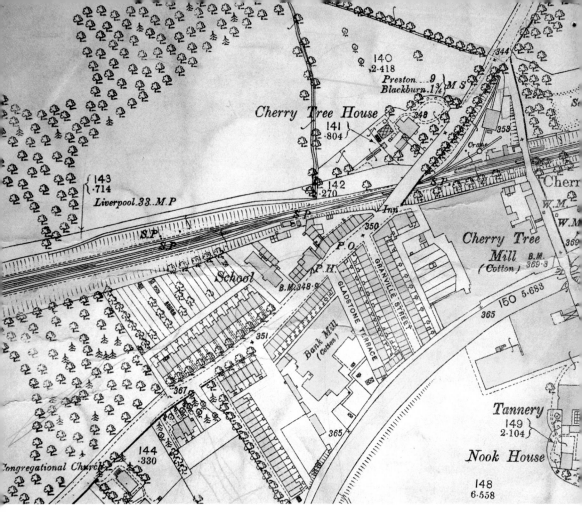

Cherry Tree (1893). Cherry Tree was a self-contained mill community, relatively remote from the rest of Blackburn. The Cherry Tree spinning mill was opened at the end of the 1840s and the Bank Mill in the early 1860s, but even though the railway was opened in 1846 neither mill had a rail connection, and both used the canal for transport well into the twentieth century. This was a company village: from 1869 onwards both mills were owned first by the Cherry Tree Mill Company and then by John Dugdale & Sons, cotton spinners, and some of the housing was built by these firms for their workers.

DETAIL OF THE 1893 ORDNANCE SURVEY MAP, REPRODUCED BY KIND PERMISSION OF THE COUNTY ARCHIVIST, LANCASHIRE RECORD OFFICE

and to Cherry Tree. In 1899 the network was taken over by the Corporation, and between then and 1902 it was electrified, and extended to Wilpshire and Audley. The building of the original tramway network followed the redevelopment of Salford, which in the late 1870s and early 1880s was 'improved' by major road-widening, the partial culverting of the river Blakewater, and other street works. On the insistence of the Corporation at least two early morning and evening trams had to be provided on each route for workers, but these were so little used that in 1891 the tramway company asked for permission to withdraw them, and they were still under-patronised in 1901. The reasons are clear. Not only were fares too high, but with the exception of the route to Audley the tram routes tended to serve expanding middle-class suburban areas, rather than

working-class districts – Billinge, Cherry Tree and Wilpshire were all favoured by the new lower middle classes. Thus, although it encouraged suburban ribbon development, the tramway network had little direct impact on the geography of Blackburn. In contrast to the larger cities, such as Liverpool and Manchester, no new roads were built specifically for tram routes.

Contradicting these relatively comfortable and close-knit images of the working-class community, one specific group – the immigrant Irish – experienced major disadvantages and a strong degree of racial segregation, as they did in every town of any size in north-west England.[25] Irish immigration to England was centuries old but the main influx began in the second half of the

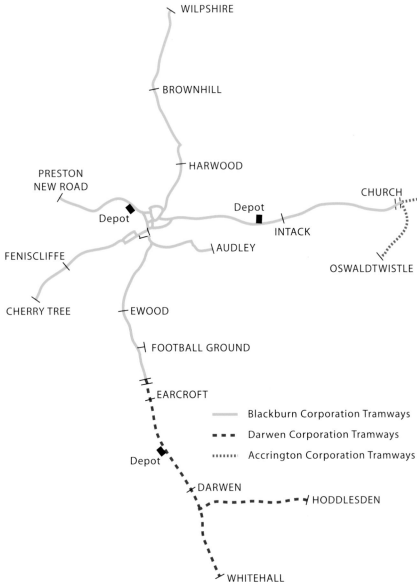

The tram routes of Blackburn.
MAP BY DR ALAN CROSBY

WILPSHIRE.

eighteenth century, prompted by a series of famines and food crises in the 1770s and subsequently encouraged by Wolfe Tone's failed rebellion of 1798, the economic depressions of the early nineteenth century, and the political union of Great Britain and Ireland in 1801 which facilitated easier movement between the two islands. As well as permanent migration, there was a long-standing tradition of seasonal movement of agricultural workers from Ireland to work in the harvest and crop-picking in northern and midland England. The proportion of Irish-born among the population grew steadily, with a substantial new influx in the 1820s, but settlement was still confined largely to Liverpool and Manchester. In 1841 only 9 per cent of the Irish-born population of Lancashire lived outside those two cities. This state of affairs was dramatically altered by the massive acceleration in Irish immigration during and after the catastrophic

The Wilpshire Hotel has hardly altered over the years. Note the amount of horse dung on the road: most photographers went to the trouble of deleting such blemishes.
COTTON TOWN PROJECT

The Corporation Tramways also employed uniformed parcel delivery boys. He stands in the Griffin area just before the First World War. The Griffin Hotel, at the junction of Griffin Street and Redlam still stands today but the shops on the right and the Redlam Inn have gone. In the distance a tramcar makes its way over Redlam brow to Witton.
COTTON TOWN PROJECT, © LANCASHIRE EVENING TELEGRAPH

At the end of the nineteenth century house building extended along the main roads into Blackburn as many of the town's lower middle classes left the older terraced streets to live in new, larger villas away from the mills and to travel to work on the trams. Here, on Whalley New Road at Brownhill, respectable couples and mothers with prams go for a leisurely stroll.

J. HALSALL COLLECTION

and tragic famine of 1845–48. The census figures demonstrate how the Irish community in Blackburn grew with astonishing speed through the 1850s. In 1851 Blackburn had 2,505 Irish-born inhabitants, making up 2.8 per cent of the population, but in 1861 the figures were 6,378 and 5.3 per cent. These statistics actually underestimate the proportions in Blackburn town, since they are based on registration districts which included outlying villages with few Irish, and neither do they allow for children born locally to recent Irish migrants. The true proportion for the Irish population of the town of Blackburn in 1861 is probably nearer 10 per cent.

The lack of skills of the majority of these immigrants, and their readiness to accept very low wages since anything was better than starvation, pushed

Preston Old Road at Feniscowles with yet more new villas with small front gardens. Trees and open spaces ensured a semi-rural atmosphere even by the Edwardian years.

COTTON TOWN PROJECT

them into menial jobs. There was a racial, cultural and religious clash between Lancashire-born industrial workers, whether Protestant or Catholic, on the one hand, and rural Irish Catholics, usually illiterate or semi-literate and adrift in an unfamiliar world. They were looked upon as an inferior race and they were, from the outset, isolated culturally, socially and physically. Crammed into the oldest and poorest housing, such as that in the Penny Street area, the Irish frequented their own clubs, public houses and friendly societies, all under the watchful eye of the priest. Hostility was widespread, from negative and pejorative official views down to individual prejudice. Thus, in 1852 a report which commented on the cellar dwellings that were still inhabited, contrary to the new bye-laws, claimed that they were 'principally occupied by the lower class of Irish ... [and] ... many of these are exceedingly unwholesome: cooking, sleeping, sick and healthy, male and female beds etc all being in one apartment.'[26] These Irish communities often suffered violence at the hands of their fellow townsfolk, which we saw in the previous chapter and will see again in chapter eight.

Blackburn's middle class were also socially distinct, but their geographical and residential segregation was entirely voluntary and the consequence of being able to exercise freedom of choice. During the first half of the nineteenth century the merchants and business people, with relatively few exceptions, lived in large houses in or close to the centre of the town, often with warehouses attached to the rear where those who were in the cotton trade conducted their business. Sudell Street, which was renamed King Street in 1815 after the victory at Waterloo, was the most fashionable and popular residential location for Blackburn's elite in the Regency period, and it was thus the social, commercial

This barber stands proudly outside his shop on Victoria Street together with his son or apprentice. Here you could be shaved with a cut-throat razor after having your face prepared with hot towels or have your hair and moustache trimmed and oiled. The window to the right appears to be filled with glamour postcards of the music hall artistes of the day, perhaps a profitable sideline for the proprietor.
J. HALSALL COLLECTION

and restrictive clauses in leases and title deeds, preventing the building of public houses or industrial premises anywhere in the vicinity. Between 1860 and 1914 this area had the most superior social tone in the town proper. Of the 184 heads of household along Preston New Road in 1881, 113 were mill-owners, professional men or 'gentlemen'. The remainder were mainly high-class tradesmen or widows with private incomes. Little had changed by 1912 when 108 of the 191 household heads were from this limited and exclusive group.[27] The great majority of the subscribers to the new telephone system were also in this area, a sure sign of affluence before 1914. The typical middle-class villa was set back from the road, with its own carriage drive, and it had twelve to fifteen rooms,

This aerial view shows that Montague Street has changed greatly in recent times. In the early nineteenth century it was a middle-class residential area, but its residents moved to escape encroaching industry and working-class neighbours. Barbara Castle Way now ends halfway up the road and nearly all the buildings, including those on both sides of the lower end, have gone. That includes the Trinity Methodist Church with its distinctive domed tower. The trees at the top of the picture, behind Preston New Road, show the start of what became a new middle-class district of the town in the second half of the nineteenth century.
COTTON TOWN PROJECT

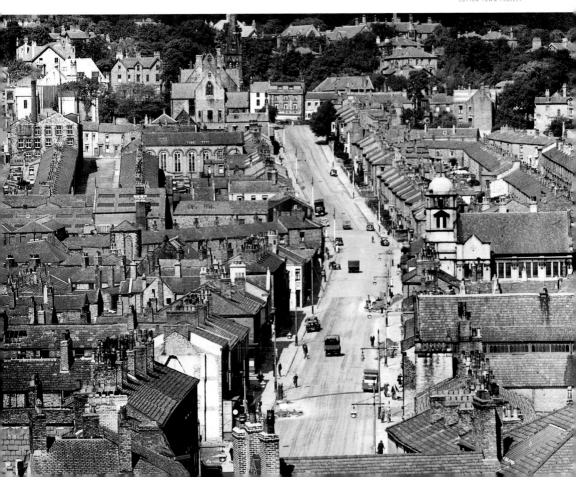

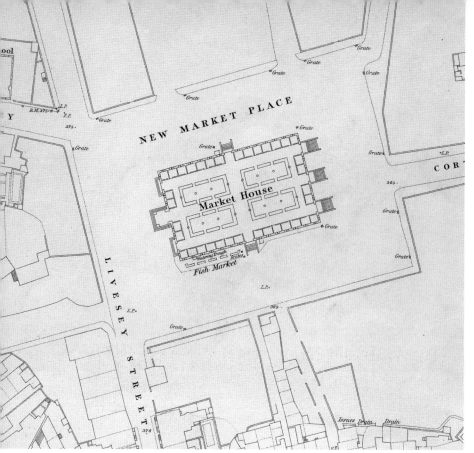

NEW MARKET PLACE

Market House

Fish Market

LIVESEY STREET

some of which accommodated the servants, of whom there were usually two. Some villas included a billiard room and had a lawn tennis court in the garden. The lower middle classes, people such as clerks and salesmen, also tended to live in distinct areas of the town, such as Mill Hill, where they occupied small villa-type houses, or superior terraces, with a small front garden and architecturally with some decorative elements such as terracotta mouldings, leaded lights and stained glass. However, the geographical and social dividing lines between this group and the working classes were fainter and more blurred than those between the lower middle class and the professional and employer class.

Blackburn's wealthy middle class also shaped the town's physical appearance by their major role in the erection of public buildings. Some of these were the result of philanthropy from wealthy citizens, and some were developed by public bodies on which the wealthy men sat and voted the expenditure. A market house in early Italian palazzo style, with an interior measuring 186 feet by 109 feet, was built in 1848 at a cost of £9000. It stood at the end of King William Street on a site formerly known as Sudell's Croft. The framework and roof supports were entirely of iron and the roof was divided into three spans, supported by walls and two rows of iron columns, eight in each. Ornate decorations to the columns and ironwork were picked out and painted in bronze. There

This south view of the market place in 1860 shows the new buildings in the centre of the town erected as the town grew wealthier. Both the market house in the Italian palazzo style, built in 1848, and the new town hall of 1856 are drawn in detail. However, the picture gives a somewhat idealised view as regards human activity. A few well-dressed ladies window-shopping, a gentleman out riding and a few workmen unloading carts is all that can be seen at 11.08 a.m.

were eight arched doors, three at each end and one in each side. Over the central door stood a clock tower on four pillars with arches twelve feet wide. The whole building was illuminated by gas, and was claimed at the time to be without equal in Lancashire. In 1853 the new borough council enlarged the market place, by demolishing properties on the south side of the old market square, and in 1870–72 a second, though less impressive, market house, originally destined to be a fish market, was built.[28] In 1852 the new councillors decided to build a handsome new town hall in the Italian renaissance style. Erected next to the market, it was finished in 1856 at a cost of £35,000. Still looking to the Italian peninsula for architectural inspiration, the town's worthies then authorised a new courthouse and police station in King Street, built in Venetian gothic style and completed in 1872. In 1888 the Prince of Wales laid the foundation stone of Blackburn Technical College, at Blakey Moor, built in brick to a High Victorian gothic design. For the first half of the nineteenth century Blackburn lacked a cotton exchange, an institution which many regarded as essential in a place so central to the global cotton industry. On Wednesday afternoons a weekly cotton yarn market was held at the Old Bull Inn, and after incorporation in 1851 the council discussed building an exchange on the site of the old market cross where Lloyds TSB Bank now stands. This, too, was abortive, and

More or less the same view as on page 139. An 18-foot mast holding a copper ball topped the Market Hall's tower. At noon each day it began to rise up the pole, reaching the top an hour later at which point it dropped as a signal for the firing of the town's one o'clock gun, which was heard up to 1931. This photograph was apparently taken shortly after 1903, when the mechanism broke, not to be mended until 1924. Also of interest in the picture is the tar boiler: it appears that chesty children were made to breathe the fumes from such boilers in the belief that it did them good.
COTTON TOWN PROJECT

The old town hall, photographed in summer 2006.
PHOTOGRAPH: CARNEGIE

This 1909 view shows the half-completed cotton exchange. Today its heavily disguised entrance admits you to a cinema, and the one wing that was completed houses an Italian restaurant. The District Bank building later became a bar, and is now an office block but, paradoxically, the draper's shop on the opposite corner has been demolished and replaced by a bank.

COTTON TOWN PROJECT

One of the elaborate friezes on the outside of Blackburn Museum.

PHOTOGRAPH: CARNEGIE

finally the mill-owners formed a company to build an exchange. The foundation stone was laid in 1860. As originally envisaged, the building would have had two wings, one facing the town hall and one on King William Street, with a central tower and an exchange measuring 140 feet by 53 feet. However, the timing was unfortunate, since work began just as the Cotton Famine began to have its effect. Although the tower and the King William Street wing were built at a cost of around £9,000, the second wing was never completed.

By the end of the nineteenth century, therefore, thanks to the efforts of the council and the elite in society Blackburn had a town hall, courthouse, market hall, technical college, and half a cotton exchange. All were connected with either the pursuit of money or, like the workhouse considered below, social control. Other than in architectural style none had any connection with culture in the accepted sense. The only exception made to this prevailing utilitarian view was in 1871 when the council purchased a site on the corner of Richmond Terrace and what was formerly known as Frances Street for a library and museum. Here, at a cost of £10,000, was constructed a building in decorated gothic style. It was unambitious. Although sculpted exterior panels were paid for by local dignitaries, the building pales into insignificance when contrasted with the museums and libraries in many other northern towns of comparable size. As for an art gallery, often seen in the late nineteenth century as an essential element in the task of bringing culture to the workers, Blackburn is still waiting. Just before the First World War a public hall to seat 3,000 was

Built in 1871 in Gothic style, the Free Library and Museum was decorated with sculpted friezes paid for by individual benefactors. Notwithstanding this largesse, it is far smaller than comparable buildings in other northern industrial towns and cities, reflecting the relative dearth of ornate public buildings in Blackburn. Today the building houses the town's museum, while the public library has moved.
COTTON TOWN PROJECT

planned for the same slum clearance site upon which the technical school was built. It would also be provided with 1,000-seat assembly hall and a lecture hall, but the war intervened and the complex was not finished until 1921. Why was there so little emphasis upon culture, in contrast to the experience of, for example, Preston? In 1852 one contemporary commented that, 'Blackburn has been, perhaps justly, stigmatised by neighbouring towns as a place where the love of trade and pecuniary profit seems to have entirely absorbed every feeling for the enjoyment of the intellectual luxuries and ornaments of life; and the utter neglect which the fine arts have hitherto experienced, has been repeated in support of the allegations.'[29] The reason is perhaps that the town's elite aped the narrow interests of an imagined squirearchy, rather than performing the role of cultural patron associated with the aristocracy. For them, to breed and own a prize-winning horse or greyhound was culture enough. Blackburn has suffered from this legacy ever since.

Perhaps the most imposing public building erected in the town in the nineteenth century, one which sat high above Blackburn in isolated splendour, brooding daily over the town's populace, was the workhouse. The 1834 Poor Law Amendment Act required that the old system, whereby individual

The first union workhouse (1848). This large-scale plan of 1848 gives fine detail of the layout of the first workhouse of the Blackburn Poor Law Union, which had been built in the early years of the century by the township of Blackburn and taken over by the newly established Board of Guardians in 1837. It could allegedly accommodate 500 paupers, although the usual number was well below that figure. It had a school for pauper children, exercise yards, and a weaving shop where handloom weavers could ply their trade and offset the costs of the institution, although by 1848 the long, steady decline of the handloom weaving trade was well under way.

DETAIL OF THE 1848 ORDNANCE SURVEY MAP, REPRODUCED BY KIND PERMISSION OF THE COUNTY ARCHIVIST, LANCASHIRE RECORD OFFICE

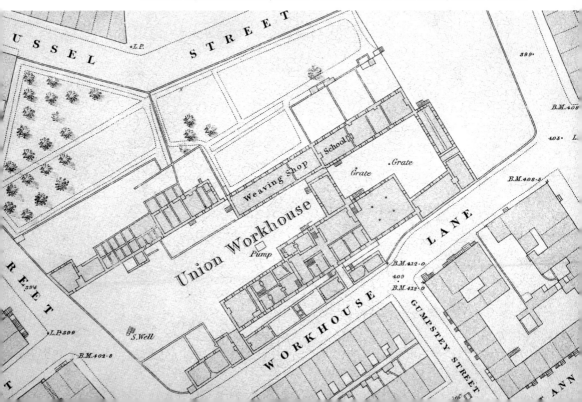

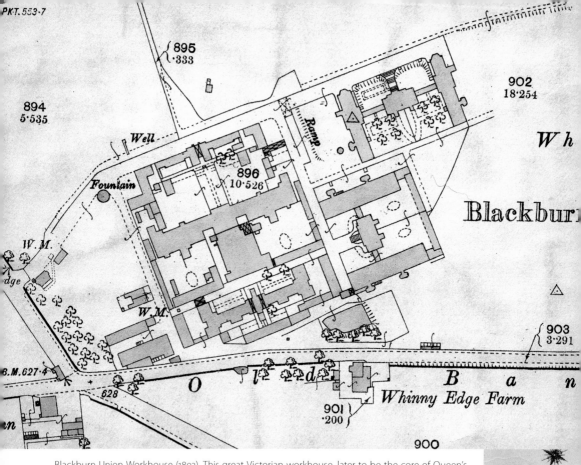

Blackburn Union Workhouse (1893). This great Victorian workhouse, later to be the core of Queen's Park Hospital, was built on a windswept site at Whinny Edge between 1861 and 1864 to replace the five smaller ones which had served Blackburn and the surrounding villages. Based on the 1834 Poor Law Act, it was designed to ensure that no-one would choose to go there unless as a last resort. Men, women and children were housed separately, and inmates had to perform arduous menial tasks. After extensions were opened in the late 1880s some 1,500 paupers, twice the original number, could be accommodated in its vast, forbidding buildings in which, as government policy dictated, males and females were strictly segregated, as were adults and children, the sick and the able-bodied, and the young and the elderly.
DETAIL OF THE 1893 ORDNANCE SURVEY MAP, REPRODUCED BY KIND PERMISSION OF THE COUNTY ARCHIVIST, LANCASHIRE RECORD OFFICE

parishes or, in northern England, townships had responsibility for their own poor, should be swept away and replaced by district-wide Poor Law authorities, known as Poor Law Unions. These were to be administered by Boards of Guardians of the poor, elected by ratepayers, and they were to be centred on a market town. Each union was to build a new central workhouse, capable of accommodating large numbers of paupers, and local workhouses were to be closed. The principle underlying all this was that the poor were expected to help themselves and 'stand on their own two feet'. In contrast to the old procedures, they would not be given financial support if they lived in their own dwellings, and applicants for assistance would be rigorously checked and assessed. Anyone who was incapable of supporting himself or herself would be sent to the workhouse, which would be spartan, strictly regimented and uncongenial. In

established in 1854 and purchased 45 acres of land on the edge of the borough at Bank Hey in Little Harwood for use as a public cemetery. It was walled, landscaped and three mortuary chapels were built at a total cost of £19,000. The cemetery opened in July 1857 and within a few years there was an average of 2,500 burials a year. In 1893 the Corporation took over full responsibility for the cemetery. Refuse disposal was another problem created by rapid and uncontrolled urbanisation. At the time of incorporation most refuse was simply thrown into the nearest ash pits or watercourse, or dumped on a nearby piece of empty or waste ground. The new council quickly took steps to tackle this major problem, which was not only unsightly but posed a very serious threat to public health. By the end of the nineteenth century the council had provided four disposal plants and seven tips, and kept 60 horses to pull the refuse carts which now carried out collections. In 1908 the corporation also obtained parliamentary powers to compel local residents to provide galvanised iron dustbins, though this was not enforced until 1924. Blackburn's first public waterworks was opened in 1772. Before that time, ancient wells and pumps had sufficed. The original reservoir was sited in Pemberton Clough, to the north of the old town centre, and it was turned into ornamental lakes when the area became Corporation Park later in the nineteenth century. The Blackburn Waterworks

This view looks up Church Street from Salford around 1905. In the centre can be seen the entrance to the underground public conveniences which were sealed off in 1962 and unearthed in 2004 during pedestrianisation of the area before being covered over once again. The buildings on the left are largely the same today whilst those on the right, including the ivy-covered home of Dr W. R. Pollard, The Royal Commercial Hotel, Cowburn's umbrella manufacturers, Seller's fishmongers, the Golden Lion public house and Parker's boot dealers have slowly disappeared due to the passing of time and various modernisation and redevelopment schemes.

COTTON TOWN PROJECT, © LANCASHIRE EVENING TELEGRAPH

Blackburn.                                                                                                          Church Street.

Company was formed in 1844 to provide a more adequate supply from new reservoirs constructed at Guide and Pickup Bank. In 1875 the Corporation bought out the water company and sought more copious and reliable supplies from further afield. Eventually, in the early 1880s, sources at Whitendale in the Forest of Bowland were tapped and piped via new trunk mains to new storage reservoirs at Guide and above Corporation Park.

Such improvements to the basic essentials of urban existence gradually had an impact upon public health. Life expectancy in Blackburn began to increase, though until well into the twentieth century the town still had figures which were worse than the national average. In the mid-1880s the death rates for Blackburn, Burnley and England and Wales respectively were 1000 people was 21.3, 21.6 and 19.5 per 1000 people, but in 1914 the corresponding figures were 15.0, 16.3, and 13.8.[34] Death rates also varied greatly, throughout the nine-teenth-century, between different parts of the town, for levels of mortality were

This is a section of Church Street, in the last quarter of the nineteenth century, with proprietors and workers lined up on the pavement. Pickering's the brushmakers is flanked to the left by the premises of Joseph Constantine described as a small ware dealer and the Blackburn office of the *Preston Herald*. The differing size of buildings, styles of architecture and uneven depth of frontage show how the town centre grew slowly in an unplanned manner over the years.
COTTON TOWN PROJECT

With the town's churchyards full Blackburn cemetery was opened in 1857. This central carriageway from the main entrance took the horse-drawn hearses to the three mortuary chapels, one of which can be seen in the background. One chapel was for Church of England services, one catered for those of the Catholic faith while the third was for Nonconformists. Burial then took place in the relevant segregated area of the cemetery. This photograph was probably taken in the 1870s, since the lodge house was covered in ivy by the 1890s. The gentleman in the foreground is probably the lodge keeper.

closely related to social and economic circumstances, even after major attention had been given to public health improvements.[35] Between 1900 and 1909 the average death rate was 24.6 in St Mary's ward, a central working-class district, and was 40.0 in some canalside slum areas. Yet in the middle-class wards the death rate was 17.0 per 1000 and in the St Silas ward, covering Preston New Road with its expensive housing, the rate was only 12.8. Infant mortality was also at its greatest in the central working-class areas of Blackburn. Poverty caused by low wages, rather than poor physical conditions, appears to have been primarily to blame. The Medical Officer of Health put down the high infant mortality rate in certain areas to the under-nourishment of pregnant women, many of whom worked right up to the last stages of pregnancy, and to the poor feeding of babies on dinner scraps and contaminated milk. The daily fare of older children can be discerned from the reaction of children in 1907 when offered school meals that could include stew with vegetables, fish, Yorkshire pudding, stewed fruit, suet, rice or sago puddings: 'At first many of the children hesitated to make a good meal from the above dietary, and expressed a wish for Hot Peas, (tinned) Salmon, Chips, Bloater, and a Cup of Tea'.[36] A survey of 10,000 Blackburn children in 1911 reported that 94 per cent showed some signs of under-nourishment and 16 per cent were actually malnourished. Of the pupils at St Gabriel's School, 30 per cent were diagnosed as having rickets caused by a deficiency of vitamin D.[37] Worries were also being expressed about the town's birth rate. In his 1903 annual report the Medical Officer of Health remarked, with regret, 'that the birth rate is still decreasing'. In 1871 there had been 41.2 births per thousand of the population compared with an average for the largest 70 towns, including Blackburn, of 31.0, but by 1882 this had fallen to 38.4 and by 1889 to 34.3. By 1914 it had fallen further to 20.8 compared with the national figure of 23.6. One reason for this, and for the fall nationally, was a greater awareness of contraceptive techniques, but that does not explain why Blackburn's birth rate, once higher than the national average, was now lower. That young women increasingly delayed marriage in order to carry on working may be one factor, while another could be the relatively low wages of men in the mills, which may have delayed their decision to wed. Like the death rates, birth rates differed according to class: in 1903 in the working-class wards of St Mark's and St Luke's the rate was 30.0, but that in St Silas ward was one-third lower (20.3).[38]

Ordinary health care in Blackburn was largely non-existent for the bulk of the population until the second half of the nineteenth century. A 'General Parochial Dispensary' was opened in 1793 to offer free health care to the sick poor of the parish and, financed as a charity by the wealthy families of the

Death was a constant companion, and had its own customs. This is the junction of St Peter's Street with Back Lane (now Mincing Lane). A hearse, complete with ornate black plumes, stands outside the Wheat Sheaf Hotel awaiting the undertaker and his assistants who have, no doubt, been invited to the funeral tea being held inside. In the distance is a steam tram sitting on a short siding off Darwen Street.

Blackburn Orphanage was originally housed in two buildings at Wilpshire and the nearer one still stands. It was founded in 1886 by a Scotsman, James Dixon, with his life savings of £50 after finding six boys sleeping rough in the doorway of a Blackburn warehouse.

town, it treated just over one thousand people a year by 1810. The dispensary employed a doctor who helped with difficult births, stitched gashes and mended fractures as well as attempting to cure the sick, but with the rapid growth of population its services and facilities were overwhelmed. By the early 1820s it was quite unable to cope, and in 1824 a Blackburn General Dispensary was opened at 58 King Street. It was mainly funded by the overseers of the poor, at a cost of £235 per annum. In addition, subscriptions were sought and the town's wealthy ratepayers were allowed to 'recommend' or send one patient for treatment for every pound that they gave in annual subscription. The patient would be given a letter from the subscriber, which authorised admittance or treatment. Employers often gave such letters to their workers. Shortly after the opening of the new dispensary a fund was begun in order to raise money for an infirmary in the town, but progress was exceptionally

This young orphan was one of the first to be admitted to the Blackburn orphanage. He was photographed in a studio, perhaps to raise awareness of the plight of such children and to encourage donations to this worthy cause. Studies by Booth in London and by Rowntree in York showed that in the 1890s some 30 per cent of the population lived below the poverty line, but the circumstances of the thin, ragged and dirty pauper orphans were particularly hard.

These two boys in the kitchen of Blackburn orphanage are spreading jam spooned out from the large storage pot on to the slices of bread piled high on the table. This would be to provide early evening tea for the rest of the children. Note the adage 'Waste not Want Not' carved into the stonework above the cooking range.

Just over fifty young orphan boys of various ages are lined up for their photograph. All have cropped hair; this was done to aid against any recurrence of infestations of lice that many had when they were their admitted.

slow and Blackburn lagged far behind other industrial towns such as Preston, Bolton and Salford. The dispensary treated between 3,000 and 4,000 people annually, and did good work, but in 1838 it was forced to close when the new Poor Law Guardians withdrew the annual subsidy since under the Poor Law Amendment Act of 1834 medical provision for the poor could only be given in the workhouse.[39]

In the years that followed many inhabitants of the town had no access to health care. A few mills set up sick clubs, linked to a specific doctor, but these were few in number and catered for only a minority of the workers. Some doctors willingly gave free help to those who could not afford to pay for their services, but it was never enough. The 1840s and 1850s were notably bad decades for health in the town, with the position being in real terms far inferior to that of 1800–35. Only in the late 1850s, over thirty years after the idea was first seriously proposed, was the infirmary project revived. Money was collected from the town's elite, especially the Pilkington family, and in 1858 the mayor, James Pilkington, laid the foundation stone. Though building work was delayed by the impact of the Cotton Famine, the 32-bed infirmary was eventually opened in 1865. By 1891 it had been enlarged to 90 beds and the new Victoria wing was begun in the jubilee year of 1897 and opened in 1901. By the early 1890s Blackburn infirmary was treating nearly 2,000 in-patients a year and just over 6,000 out-patients.[40] Intermittent epidemics of contagious diseases during the nineteenth century led to a different type of medical provision. During a smallpox outbreak in 1888 an isolation hospital was opened at Finnington, 3½ miles from Blackburn in an old ammonia works. The hospital was retained and after further alterations in 1895 it could accommodate between 50 and 60 patients. In 1894 a fever hospital was built on 10 acres of land at Longshaw, with three main sections: one for scarlet fever, one for typhoid and an isolation block.[41]

Yet despite all the many improvements, the numerous new public buildings, and amenities, and the general sense of progress and development over the

In an age before the discovery of antibiotics diseases such as scarlet fever, diphtheria and tuberculosis were killers. This picture of the fever hospital in 1904, now Park Lee Hospital, shows mothers visiting their sick children. Because such children were then kept in isolation parents could only see and talk to them through the windows. This heartbreaking scene was repeated until as late as the 1950s.

COTTON TOWN PROJECT,
© LANCASHIRE EVENING
TELEGRAPH

second half of the nineteenth century, in 1914 life for most people in Blackburn was still hard. The town was one of Britain's greatest industrial communities, a sprawling urban area dominated by mills which loomed over endless streets of terraced housing. A group of public buildings stood conspicuously in the centre of the town. The employers and the middle-class professionals lived in their own enclaves on the higher ground to the northwest, but the majority of the working classes clustered on the lower land, some looking over their shoulder with anxious concern and apprehension to the workhouse on the ridge opposite. The canal and the railway line bisected and dissected the town, and tramlines criss-crossed its main streets. The shape of Blackburn for generations to come had been set, for good or ill, and the town's elite, in their dual role of employers and civic leaders, had been the main factor which had determined that shape and character.

Blackburn market was the focal point for shopping for the bulk of the people for many years. The almost total lack of men in this picture shows that it was probably taken on a weekday, though it is still busy even at 4.45 in the afternoon. The open-air market in Blackburn has gone. It was amalgamated with the indoor one in new premises in the 1970s.

COTTON TOWN PROJECT, © LANCASHIRE EVENING TELEGRAPH

# CHAPTER FIVE

# Law and order, popular protest and crime, 1750–1914

I N A SMALL COMMUNITY, according to received wisdom, everyone knows everyone else, and nobody's business is truly private. In such circumstances, when anything illegal occurs suspicion is quickly focuses on certain individuals, perhaps those who do not entirely fit into the expected norms of the community – for example, those from outside, those whose behaviour is eccentric, or those who wilfully flout the conventions and customs of the time. Within such a community it is more difficult to commit a crime and remain undetected, but to balance this apparently comfortable state of affairs were other, less palatable, facts. Most conspicuously, nowhere in Britain had a police force in the modern sense until the late 1820s, and all communities had to rely on voluntary unpaid constables whose role, powers and function were radically different from those of a present-day police constable. Furthermore, crime was endemic and lawlessness was a major problem at particular periods in the past. We should not be too sentimental about life in the past, or imagine that human nature was any different. During the eighteenth century, in areas of Britain which were beginning to urbanise and industrialise, a new range of problems and pressures appeared. Organised crime against property became more widespread; the sheer numbers of people made old methods of community action against criminals ever less effective; and new types of crime or lawlessness (as they were perceived at the time) such as industrial unrest and grassroots popular protest, started to emerge. This meant that new structures of law and order and social control had to be created, in the late eighteenth and early nineteenth centuries, to tackle the problems of a world which had changed beyond recognition.

In Blackburn, as everywhere else, the main agency of administration in the medieval period was the manor, with its decisions, and its efforts at maintaining social control and order, enacted and enforced through the mechanism of the manor court. The lord of the manor exercised authority through what were technically two separate courts. The 'court baron' was a private court, which had jurisdiction over internal matters such as tenancies and management of the manorial and communal lands, while the 'court leet' was a public court which enforced social control and regulation, punishing manorial tenants and others for petty crimes and for infringing what would now be called the bye-laws. For more serious crimes the assizes, which emerged from the Anglo-Saxon and post-Conquest courts, met at Lancaster twice a year, and in the thirteenth and fourteenth centuries the government introduced and refined the office of justice of the peace, whereby the local gentry in each county took on responsibilities for law and order as magistrates. During the sixteenth century national governments began to transfer further tasks to the magistrates, who emerged not only as the mainstay of law and order and defence in the localities, but also as the main mechanism by which counties were administered for civil purposes.

The role of the manor courts gradually diminished, so that they continued to have jurisdiction over the manorial business but their community role was steadily reduced. Furthermore, in each township or parish the ratepayers began to exercise a more significant role, meeting annually or more frequently and electing a series of officers who dealt with particular aspects of local government: the church-wardens, the overseer of the poor, the surveyor of the highways and the constable. Ratepayers meetings were usually known as the 'vestry', because originally they met in the church,

Dressed in his livery this is John Balshaw appointed in 1848 as town crier. His other main job was as bill-poster putting up various official posters all over the town to inform the public of civic meetings or events or to ensure all knew of the penalties that could be incurred if certain misdemeanours took place.
COTTON TOWN PROJECT

Shopping on seven days a week may be allowed now, but it is a relatively modern law. This poster, put up in 1815 on the orders of the annually elected Constable of Blackburn, reminds the local populace of the Sunday trading laws. It was felt that they were being flouted at the time. It also explains that informers would be financially rewarded and that if fines were not paid offenders would be placed in the stocks.

# PROFANATION
## OF THE
# Lord's Day.

The several Offences hereinafter mentioned, having been long practised in this Town and Neighbourhood, and the Penalties and Punishments thereby incurred being little known, it has been thought proper thus to make public the Laws in these respects, that no one may plead ignorance, in case an Information be laid against him; and all persons interested are hereby required to take warning.

By the 1. James, c. 22.—No SHOEMAKER shall shew, to the Intent to put to sale, any Shoes, Boots or Slippers upon the SUNDAY, on pain of 3s. 4d. a pair ; and the Value thereof.

By the 3. Charles, c. 1.—No CARRIER, Waggoner, Carter, or DROVER with Cattle shall, by themselves or any other, travel on the LORD'S DAY on pain of 20s.—Or, if any BUTCHER by himself or any other for him, with his privity and consent, shall kill or sell any Victual on the LORD'S DAY, he shall forfeit 6s. 8d.—The Conviction to be in six months.

By the 29th Charles II. c. 7.—No DROVER, HORSECOURSER, WAGGONER, BUTCHER, HIGLER, or any of their Servants, shall travel or come to his Inn or Lodgings on the LORD'S DAY on pain of 20s. And no TRADESMAN, ARTIFICER, WORKMAN, LABOURER, OR OTHER PERSON shall do or exercise any worldly Labour, Business, or Work of their ordinary calling on the Lord's Day, (except Works of Necessity and Charity, &c.) on pain of every Offender above 14 Years of Age forfeiting 5s. And no Person shall publicly cry, shew forth, or expose to sale any Wares, Merchandize, Fruit, Herbs, Goods, or Chattels whatsoever on the LORD'S DAY, (except selling of Milk before 9 in the Morning, and after 4 in the Afternoon) on pain of forfeiting the same. And no Person shall use, employ, or travel on the LORD'S DAY, with any BOAT OR BARGE (unless allowed by a Justice of the Peace on extraordinary occasions), on pain of any sum not exceeding one third part of the Penalty.

In default of Payment or Distress, the Offender is to be set publicly in the Stocks two Hours.

All Goods cried, shewed forth, or put to sale on the Sunday, are declared by the mentioned Act, to be forfeited to the use of the Poor, and the Constables and Churchwardens may seize and sell the same.

### T. H. CARDWELL
Constable of Blackburn

9th February 1815.

T. Rogerson, Printer, Market-Place, Blackburn.

although latterly an inn or tavern was a more likely venue. This group of prominent citizens normally included the vicar and his curate. The constable's job was unpaid and for a one-year term of office, and he had no training and few powers. In country communities the constable was normally a dogsbody, who carried out a range of routine and often uncomfortable tasks (he was, for example, the man who had to collect the rates, which was never congenial) but in towns the volume of work was such that a paid deputy constable was appointed on a longer-term salaried basis. In Blackburn the position of deputy constable was only a part-time post and was limited to looking after the town during daylight hours, but because a good deputy constable might well be kept on by a new parish constable a degree of continuity existed.

As the town grew, this very modest provision was manifestly inadequate, so in 1794 a regular watch was instituted to provide police protection during the hours of darkness. This was expanded further in 1803 when, following a local Act of Parliament, the Police Commissioners took over the responsibility of appointing the parish constable, in addition to their other duties which included seeing to the upkeep and cleansing of the streets. Almost immediately the commissioners decided on change. From 1805 it was decided that Blackburn would have a full-time paid constable, and the job was given to the then deputy constable, a butcher named John Kay. He remained in office for 25 years and also had two full-time deputies. The night watch was formally disbanded in 1827, because it had been exposed as an inadequate anachronism: the two workmen employed in 1825 were found in a drunken stupor while on duty. Their responsibilities were transferred to the new constable and his deputies, helped for a time by a bellman who alerted citizens to such matters as lost children. Thus, the range and scope of law and order agencies increased, but only in a piecemeal and haphazard fashion, and it was apparent here, as in many other places, that more radical and far-reaching reforms were long overdue.

In 1829 the Metropolitan Police were created, and this provided an example which could be applied to other areas of England and Wales. The result was the County Constabularies Act of 1839, which made it possible, but not yet compulsory, for modern-style police forces to be established under the auspices of county magistrates. Lancashire adopted the Act and created its own constabulary, and in 1841 a police station was opened in Blackburn in a building in King Street. The parish constables now passed into history, replaced by a superintendent, Edward Shepherd, with a local force of four sergeants and twenty constables which made one officer for every 1,440 inhabitants. Incorporated boroughs had the power to operate their own town forces, separate from the county constabularies, so as soon as Blackburn received its charter of incorporation the leading ratepayers and councillors determined to adopt those powers. In 1852 the Blackburn Borough Police Force was established, with Mr Laverty as the first chief constable. This was partly for reasons of local pride, partly to give local ratepayers greater control over policing in the borough, and partly to save money, for it was claimed that the cost to the town had increased eight-fold with the coming of the county force in 1841.[1] The borough force took over a building further down King Street, backing on to Clayton Street. It had one superintendent, one sergeant and a reduced number of just ten constables. Dressed in tall beaver hats, long-tailed blue coats and white trousers, each was armed with a truncheon and equipped with a rattle until whistles were introduced later in the century. The force totalled 35 by 1863, 89 by 1879 and 112 by 1885. This then gave a ratio of one policeman to every 1,000 inhabitants.

It is interesting to analyse the social and economic backgrounds of these men. Though records only exist for appointments after 1889 there is no reason to suppose that recruitment patterns had changed dramatically from the position twenty or thirty years earlier. About two-thirds of the new constables were local, their average age on recruitment was about 25, and approximately half of them were married. Blackburn was predominantly a cotton town by the 1890s, but fewer than one third of the recruits had such a background. The remainder tended to be unskilled labourers or carters, interspersed with a sprinkling of tradesmen such as butchers, joiners, plumbers and tailors. One-third had had some form of military experience, mainly those from outside the area. All were Lancashire men, people who had applied to forces in their home county on leaving the colours.[2] Women did not enter the borough police force until 1947 and Blackburn was one of the very last forces in the country to appoint them. A town which was Conservative in politics also employed a very conservative police force. As this local force grew up to 1914, its premises expanded. From King Street the headquarters moved first to the rear of the newly built town hall and then in 1913 to a purpose-built station in Northgate. In the meantime,

*'In Blackburn ... it is the usual thing for the husband, when he comes home late at night, to give his wife a kicking and beating. The women take it as part of the daily round and don't complain.'*

J. CORIN, 1810

a local presence had been established, with small police stations, under the command of sergeants, at Copy Nook (also covering the Brookhouse area), Revidge and Livesey. Local police now patrolled their local area. The force also expanded in other ways to cope with the new problems that urbanisation brought. A part-time mounted section of nine men, seven of them being ex-cavalrymen, was recruited in 1892 and by 1912 had increased to thirteen.

The system of courts and justice also had to change as population grew and urbanisation accelerated. At the beginning of the nineteenth century there was no sitting of the magistrates in Blackburn, although a number of prominent magistrates lived in the area. The pattern of quarter sessions, whereby the magistrates met four times a year, had for three centuries been based on sessions at Lancaster, Preston, Wigan, Ormskirk and Manchester, and so cases for this part of the county were normally heard at Preston, with occasional meetings at Burnley or Whalley.[3] If, as happened from time to time, a special sitting of magistrates was held in Blackburn, they met in the parlour of an inn or, later, in the town's assembly rooms. When the town became a borough, however, it was granted the right to hold its own quarter sessions, with the mayor and

Blackburn Borough Police, Duckworth Street section, around 1912. Blackburn's police force comprised mainly local men, although very few had a background in the cotton industry. Over half of the recruits were taken from the armed forces, used to discipline and able to take care of themselves when violence flared, which in an age of strong drink was quite often.
COTTON TOWN PROJECT

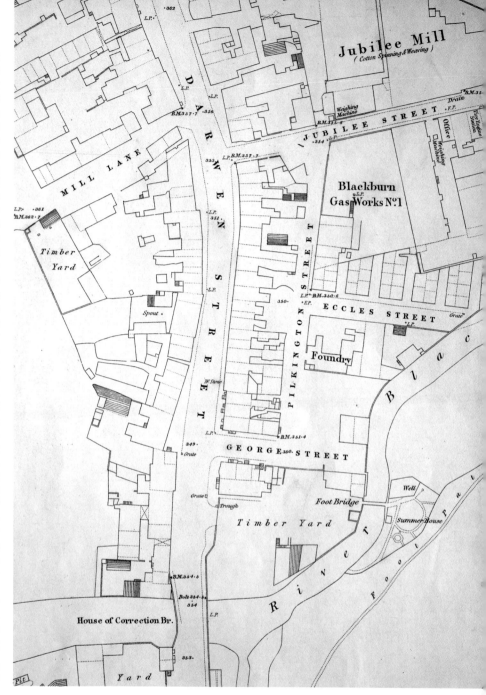

Darwen Street (1848). The House of Correction, after which the bridge over the Blakewater (*bottom*) was named, was a rather grand title for the cellar of the building on the south end of the bridge, which had been used for many decades as a temporary lock-up by the town's night watch. It was only intended for 'passing trade' – any serious criminals who were apprehended were sent to the proper House of Correction (from 1832, the jail) in Preston or to Lancaster Castle. The plan also shows the town's first gasworks, opened in 1837 and, somewhat incongruously, the gardens and summerhouse on the banks of the river (which was surely heavily polluted by this time) – its site is now occupied by the southern end of Blackburn railway station.

DETAIL OF THE 1848 ORDNANCE SURVEY MAP, REPRODUCED BY KIND PERMISSION OF THE COUNTY ARCHIVIST, LANCASHIRE RECORD OFFICE

aldermen serving as the twelve magistrates, and in 1852 a Sessions House was opened in King Street. Subsequently, the court moved to larger and more suitable premises until in 1913 it finally settled in its present home in Northgate in 1913. The town had for many decades had a small lockup, the cellar of a building used by the night-watch, next to the bridge over the Blakewater in Darwen Street. As more room was required, the cellars of public houses were rented, but

not until the opening of the police station were proper cells provided. Prisoners accused of more serious crimes could be sent to the House of Correction in Preston which opened in the early seventeenth century, to Lancaster Castle or, from 1789, to Preston Gaol. During some periods of unrest and discontent, such as the 1790s and the years after Waterloo when all of Lancashire was under suspicion of potential revolution, the maintenance of law and order was also the responsibility of the troops – the cavalry and the militia – ordered in by the government.[4] In 1829 this was deemed so necessary for the preservation of law and order that the leading inhabitants of the town, the bulk of whom were mill-owners, wanted a barracks built on church land near the canal backing on to Bolton Road.[5] As late as 1838 there was still active encouragement for a plan to build a barracks holding up to 800.

Though the property owners were unsuccessful in their strategies of bringing the army in permanently, here as everywhere else they were successful in keeping law and order under their control. From 1817 the vestry was reconstituted as a 'select vestry', under legislation of that year. This procedure, widely adopted throughout England and Wales, meant that direct influence was taken away from the ratepayers en masse, though they continued to attend an annual meeting, and instead was concentrated in the hands of a small inner group. In Blackburn this numbered between from nine and 24 members, all of them among the main freeholders and manufacturers. For the rest of the century the leading landowners, industrialists and merchants kept strict control of the reins of law and order in Blackburn as such groups did in most towns. An analysis

This is a print of the old prison or house of correction in Darwen Street. In the late eighteenth century a cellar was used under this small building by the bridge over the river Blakewater to hold those arrested before they appeared in court. In the nineteenth century the building was being used as a barber's and umbrella repair shop. The proprietor, who can be seen standing in the doorway, was a Mr Croasdale. He had a large family and his youngest son, Ainsworth, was born there in 1850.
COTTON TOWN PROJECT

of fifty of Blackburn's elite in the last quarter of the nineteenth century shows that forty of them were justices of the peace at some point in their careers.[6] Their grip on law and order appeared necessary, because as working people came together in towns like Blackburn, for the first time in large numbers, they began to realise that they could speak with a collective voice. The seductive power of that voice, allied to action in the form of demonstrations, strikes and even riots, was directed at many social and political issues. To the middle class these activities seemed to threaten the status quo. That status quo was not necessarily sacrosanct, but if it *was* to be altered the changes had to be those of which the urban ruling class approved. Their hold on the forces of law and order would help to ensure this.

Early stirrings of community action were seen during the Napoleonic wars. The shortage of food brought about by the dislocation of trade and especially the high price of corn was the cause. In 1800, when the price of wheat rose to 118s. 3d. (£5.91) a quarter, attacks were made on farmers in order to seize their produce. The Riot Act was read, and the cavalry and infantry of Blackburn's Loyal Local Association of Volunteers were mustered under its officers, members of the Sudell, Birley, Feilden, Cardwell and Hornby families. This 'who's who' of Blackburn's elite galloped to restore order. In 1808 a crowd attacked provision shops in Darwen Street. Four ringleaders were arrested, tried and convicted. Over fifty years, later in 1862, during the hunger brought about by the Cotton Famine, a Blackburn mob tried to rescue four men who had been convicted of poaching in order to feed their families. The police,

who were jostled and stoned, retreated to the town hall for safety. The crowd followed, smashing its windows and then damaging property along Northgate, King Street, Montague Street and Preston New Road. Again, the Riot Act was read, two hundred special constables were sworn in, and a troop of the 5th Lancers sent for. Prison sentences of up to three years were meted out to those apprehended and convicted.

As class tensions developed in the late eighteenth and early nineteenth centuries, industrial relations became ever more troubled. The first riots witnessed by industrial Blackburn were motivated by trade grievances. In 1768 handloom

The Victorian version
of the Bay Horse
Inn lasted less than
one hundred years.
Here it can be seen
being demolished in
1963 as the people
of Blackburn get on
with their everyday
business.
COTTON TOWN PROJECT

weavers from Darwen, Mellor, Tockholes and Oswaldtwistle converged on Blackburn and joined forces with local spinners. Their aim, which was successfully achieved, was to destroy the cottage of James Hargreaves, the man who had invented the spinning jenny, and to ransack Peel's Mill at Brookside, which had installed the new machinery. Their fear, understandably enough, was that this invention would harm their livelihoods. Machine-breaking riots broke out again in 1779 during a trade depression. By this time all forms of machines were a target, including carding machines as well as jennies. Only jennies with fewer than 24 spindles were spared. The machines from Peel's mill at Altham were thrown into the river and another mill at Wensley Fold was attacked and machines destroyed. It has been suggested that the merchant 'putters out', fearing that mechanisation could undercut their prices, encouraged the rioters in their destruction and that some magistrates may even have protected rioters from punishment.[7] Perhaps in some circumstances machine-breaking could be tolerated, if it was felt to be in the interests of those in authority, but for other leaders of local society, such as Robert Peel, these events were intolerable. He left the town and never returned.

Although in the early years of the nineteenth century there was widespread hardship because of the Napoleonic Wars, food shortages and rapid inflation, industrial relations in Blackburn were relatively peaceful. Luddism, the spate of machine-breaking in the years around 1812, came no nearer than Bolton. In 1818 some 4,000 cotton workers paraded through Blackburn with a tricolour at their head, protesting not at political issues but at low wages. They headed for the home of the main employer Henry Sudell of Woodfold, but his timely grant of a 5 per cent wage increase defused the situation and the marchers soon dispersed peacefully. However, trade union activity did grow during this period. In 1794 the town had at least 24 combinations of workers, most of them based on local inns. The anti-combination laws of 1799 and 1800 forced them underground or compelled them to convert, at least on the surface, to friendly societies. When the Golden Ball Inn on Blakey Moor was demolished in the early twentieth century a secret room was found which, it is believed, was a relic of illegal trade union activity. After the Napoleonic Wars a new disguise adopted by trade unions was that of scientific and botanical societies, which grew rapidly in number and also met at local inns.[8]

The final, and greatest, episode of machine-breaking was in 1826, a year of exceptionally high unemployment caused by a sequence of bank and manufacturing failures and a severe trade depression. The crisis coincided with the introduction of the power loom to Blackburn's mills, with its inevitable impact upon the employment of handloom weavers. In April 1826, out of an estimated 10,686 weavers in the town and immediately adjacent areas, 6,412 were unemployed and a further 1,467 only worked part-time, while 14,000 people in Blackburn (from a population of 26,000) were receiving some form of poor relief and the number was increasing daily. The wages of those who were in work were being cut: 'The very real evil about Blackburn ... is the number of weavers who, having become small manufacturers [are] obliged to sell at any price they can obtain and to make up their losses by reducing the wages of their weavers.'[9] The power looms seemed to be a cause of much of the distress, and they were therefore the target for the mob. There were limited outbreaks of violence as early as March 1826 when, for example, the home of the clerk to the justices of the peace was attacked and the coaches taking mill-owners to and from Manchester were stoned.[10] The main violence and destruction started on Enfield Moor near Oswaldtwistle, where the roads from Blackburn, Burnley, Whalley, Clitheroe, Haslingden and Accrington converged. Five hundred weavers gathered there armed with home-made pikes, sledgehammers and a few guns. After an orgy of machine-breaking at Accrington, Wood Nook and Rough Hey they descended on Blackburn around midday, their numbers swollen to between 5,000 and 6,000. A troop of dragoons which attempted to halt them was swept aside and the power looms in Bannister Eccles and Co.'s Dandy Mill off Darwen Street were wrecked. Soldiers attempting to stop the crowd were stoned and shots were fired. The Riot Act was read, but though the mill was surrounded by soldiers most of the mob escaped and split up to search for more power looms. A large group entered the mill of Feilden, Throp & Townley in King Street but left when they found that the power looms had not yet arrived. Another group marched on Houghton Mill at Grimshaw Park and destroyed the 25 power looms installed there. Shooting broke out as the soldiers vainly attempted to defend the mill and several rioters were killed. By evening there were 10,000 people on the streets and all the power looms in Blackburn had been destroyed. Apart from the power looms, nothing was touched – spinning machines were respected and hurt to individuals avoided. Even the mill-owners and the military held back as much as possible, for despite the mayhem and occasional shooting, casualties were in single figures. When the crowd was finally dispersed from the streets the dragoons used only the flats of their swords.

The aftermath was also relatively low-key. Only 42 rioters were convicted in the courts and although ten received the death sentence the penalty was later commuted to transportation, while the remainder were merely imprisoned for between six and fifteen months. Perhaps this was because the magistrates, many of whom, as we have seen, were closely connected with the textile trades, regarded this not as the harbinger of a new and terrifying wave of industrial protest, but rather as the dying spasm of the old industry. The employers were confident for the future: by 1830 the mills of Hopwood, Hornby, Eccles, Turner, Howarth, Feilden, Briggs and Rodgett had all installed fresh power looms and together they now employed 3,500 power loom operatives. From this time onwards, though, organised trade unionism began to exert a greater and more

*'The very real evil about Blackburn ... is the number of weavers who, having become small manufacturers [are] obliged to sell at any price they can obtain and to make up their losses by reducing the wages of their weavers.'*

powerful influence. This, too, might have been construed as dangerous to the interests of the employers, but Blackburn's trade unionists were essentially conservative in outlook, and did not have a radical, disruptive agenda. The power loom weavers were unionised in 1840 and from the start they concentrated largely on practical industrial issues, not political and social agitation. Their first major strike was at Hopwood's Nova Scotia Mill in 1847, and it fizzled out when arbitrators found that wages were fair and reasonable. In 1853 an attempt to secure the restoration of a previous 10 per cent wage cut was settled without widespread confrontation, in very marked contrast to the experience of nearby Preston where there was a protracted lock-out, bitter antagonism and sporadic violence. In Blackburn the mill-owner Hornby persuaded his fellow employers to accede to the demands of the employees, and a victory parade was held by the workers. But it was a pyrrhic victory, for the defeat of the Preston workers meant that the wage cut could be reintroduced. Clever timing by the employers had kept industrial peace, yet still maintained the low wages. Though strikes were not uncommon, it was not until 1878 that intense, violent industrial trouble once again disturbed Blackburn's mill-owners.[11]

A 10 per cent cut in wages in that year brought out weavers all over north-east Lancashire, with 20,000 striking in Blackburn alone. The dispute reached its height 14–15 May, when hopes had been high that a settlement could be reached. The employers and the unions were meeting in Manchester in an attempt to find

Clayton Grange, Wilpshire, gutted by fire during the riots of 1878, was for many days an attraction not only for sightseers but also a photo opportunity for the local police. Colonel Robert Raynsford Jackson and his family escaped by minutes. Many of the rioters did not, and retribution soon followed in the form of up to fifteen years' imprisonment.

COTTON TOWN PROJECT, © LANCASHIRE EVENING TELEGRAPH

Once the Riot Act was read civil liberties were suspended and the local forces of law and order could clamp down on all unrest. John Fowden Hindle was the county magistrate who was in charge of the police and army during the Chartist Plug Plot riots of 1842. It was he who read the Riot Act a number of times during the violent disturbances in Blackburn. In 1844, probably partly as a reward for his actions then, he was appointed High Sheriff of Lancashire. Initially he lived on King Street but then moved to Woodfold Hall near Mellor, once the home of Henry Sudell who went bankrupt in 1827.

BLACKBURN MUSEUM

a solution, and the weavers' union offered to accept a 5 per cent wage cut. The employers would not move. A large crowd gathered in Blackburn awaiting news, and when it was learned that the talks in Manchester had broken down many workers lost patience. There was a large and noisy meeting on Blakey Moor that evening and this erupted in an orgy of destruction. Mills and the houses of mill-owners were targeted and hundreds of windows smashed. The chairman of the employers' side was a local man, Colonel Robert Raynsford Jackson who owned four mills in the town and employed 1,500. He lived at Clayton Manor in Wilpshire, and a crowd of as many as 5,000 people marched on his house. Jackson managed to force his way through to reach home before the crowd, hastily remove his wife and child to safety at a friend's house, and then return to Blackburn by a different route. When the mob arrived they broke into the lodge and burnt it, then forced entry into Clayton Manor itself. Finding paraffin in the cellar, they doused the furniture and walls and set it alight. The house was burned to the ground, and the rioters even rung the necks of the colonel's chickens. Returning to the town, they dragged with them one of Jackson's carriages, complete with effigy, which they burnt together and then began attacking more mills. On the morning of 15 May a crowd, estimated by the chief constable to number up to 30,000, gathered outside the town hall and small groups began another bout of window-smashing. Martial law was proclaimed and 120 cavalry, 250 infantry and 800 special constables dispersed a rampaging crowd of perhaps 6,000 in the Preston New Road district where many mill-owners lived. The military gradually regained control of the streets. With relatively small exceptions the damage was confined to the property, both commercial and private, of the mill-owners. A bakery was set on fire because the mob were not satisfied with the amount of free bread distributed to them and the landlord of the Oddfellow Hall Inn on King Street was blinded in one eye when vitriol was hurled in his face because he refused free beer to a group of strikers, but cotton was the real target. The law came down hard. Of the forty Blackburn men and women put on trial, two received sentences of fifteen years, one of ten years, three of seven years and one of five years. Many others also received prison terms. All was in any case in vain, for a month after the riot the strike was broken.

The events of 1878 can be viewed as an aberration, albeit a notably dramatic one. There were many further strikes, but none was marked by such levels of violence. In 1880 30,000 workers came out to try to win back the pay cuts

This mug commemorates the riots of May 1878. One side depicts the burning of Colonel Robert Raynsford Jackson's home in Wilpshire, while the other shows the second day of unrest when a mob rampaged along Preston New Road breaking the windows of the houses of the town's middle classes. Though the mug illustrates the riot itself, it really records the successful crushing of it, and the tight control of the working classes, by Blackburn's middle-class elite.
BLACKBURN MUSEUM

imposed two years earlier, and there was another six week strike in the winter of 1883–1884 against yet more wage cuts. Compared with its neighbours, though, Blackburn had a reputation as one of the most peaceful of weaving towns. The ability of the town's mill-owners to know (usually, at least) just when to bend helped bring this about. Thus, the introduction of the 'standard list' in 1853 typified their ability to control the workers by meeting them part-way. The list established an agreed rate of pay for a defined piece of work throughout all the mills in Blackburn. Since wage rates were the primary issue for the unions, disagreement was reduced to a minimum and industrial peace generally maintained. The skill of the owners in manipulating the support of the working classes and channelling their energies down less destructive paths can also be discerned in other areas. Factory reform was one such. Mill workers formed a Short Time Committee in 1825 to press for the eleven-hour working day. At first it failed, but was reconstituted in 1836 and then, partly because of growing national publicity for the issue, the town's employers began to take note of it and, at the same time, to seek to control and restrain the campaign. The Factory Act of 1833, which had limited the working hours of children, was supported by the majority of Blackburn's mill-owners. The Conservatives, Hornby, Briggs, Feilden and Townley, claimed in the local press that they were the only ones who sought to keep to the spirit of the Act. Though this was partly a way of attacking the Whig/Liberal government, that tactic allowed them to acquire a powerful influence over the factory reform movement in Blackburn. The radical Richard Oastler, on a visit to the town in 1836, told his audience how to ruin textile machinery with a stocking needle if mill-owners failed to enforce the factory acts, but his advice was not needed. Such action was pre-empted by the majority of factory masters taking up the cause themselves. They even called for a ten-hour working day and supported the abolition of the Corn Laws.[12] In this latter cause the mill-owners treated 1,200 demonstrators to tea at the James Street school in 1845.[13] The mill-owners led; the workers followed. We must accept that, while they stood to gain much from these tactics, the Blackburn mill-owners were undoubtedly motivated in part by genuine humanitarian and philanthropic beliefs and principles.

As we have already seen, the middle classes also sought to ensure that the new Poor Law worked as humanely as possible, and they attempted to ameliorate its most draconian provisions and to avoid or evade some of the requirements which were dictated by central government. Before the 1834 Poor Law Amendment Act the giving of outdoor relief was standard procedure in Blackburn, as it was everywhere else, and there were only about 250 people, mainly the elderly, resident in local workhouses. When the new Act came into force in the town in 1838 the select vestry members, the magistrates and the overseers of the poor were at pains to suggest that little would change, so there was little popular discontent. Locally, the main organised opposition to the legislation had come from the Operatives Conservative Association, which was naturally patronised by many leading mill-owners including W. H. Hornby, so they could demonstrate that they had endeavoured to limit its impact. Eleven of the twelve newly appointed guardians were major employers or professionals, the remaining one being a shopkeeper, and they were heavily criticised by the Poor Law Commissioners in London for being too lenient towards the poor, and told to reduce the 'luxuries' in the workhouse and the amount of outdoor relief.[14] By ignoring these instructions and publicly coming out against other iniquities of the Poor Law, such as the splitting-up of husbands and wives in the workhouse, they obtained the support of the labouring classes and ensured that anti-poor law agitation was notably absent in Blackburn when compared with the experience of some other parts of the north-west. When it did occur, it was swiftly defused. Thus, in 1862 nearly 400 working-class men hold a meeting in Blackburn market place to demand an end to the labour test demanded by the Poor Law Guardians before they would grant poor relief. They succeeded. The Guardians knew when to bend.

In 1827 the vicar and churchwardens of Blackburn St Mary decided to levy an extra rate to pay for new heating and lighting in the parish church, which had recently been rebuilt. This rate demand caused an outcry, and placards appeared all over the town calling on the people of Blackburn to fight a tax from a pre-industrial age. Led by a spinner, Edward Hammond, a mass protest meeting was held in the parish church itself. It turned rowdy, and prayer cushions were torn, hymnbooks ripped and pews damaged. The vocal strength of the demonstrators forced the church to allow a vote on the imposition of the extra rate. Public meetings were held on Blakey Moor, and handbills, broadsheets and pamphlets printed. On polling day a mass picket was staged. Many voters found themselves 'jostled by them to the great injury to their apparel', and though the majority of ratepayers agreed that the rate should be levied this time, a lesson had been learned. Never again did the churchwardens try to raise one.[15] For them, too, it was time to bend with the wind of change, rather than resist it. The success of the employers and the leading groups in the town, in controlling, directing or influencing many and varied working-class movements, rather than trying to oppose them or simply standing aloof, can be seen in the response to the deaths and funeral processions of prominent mill-owners. It was not uncommon to see hundreds

When the New Poor Law was introduced in 1834, instructing towns such as Blackburn to build new workhouses to be run on much stricter lines than before, the main mill-owners believed the law inappropriate to cater for the poor of Blackburn and dragged their feet implementing it. This alliance with the common people of the town is explained in this Conservative election poster of 1841.
BLACKBURN LIBRARY LOCAL HISTORY COLLECTION

**IS POVERTY A CRIME?**
**THE NEW**
**Poor Law!!**
*Inhabitants of Blackburn!*

Our Conservative Candidates—FEILDEN AND HORNBY—have, in the most unqualified language, expressed their abhorrence of the horrible and barbourous enactment which bears the above name; but this pet *Measure of the* WHIGS, *of course, meets no opposition from Mr. Turner.* Who are the true friends of the Labouring classes? Men who, like *Feilden and Hornby,* exert their influence *against the treating of poverty as a crime,* —against the separation of man and wife,—against lodging and boarding the poor, distressed, and heart-broken pauper worse, than a convicted felon, or a murderer; or, men who, like *Mr. Turner,* clamours for *Cheap Bread,* in order that they may have an excuse for lowering the wages of their *already half-paid and half-famishing workpeople?* Let conscience answer this.
**CANDIDUS.**

Blackburn, 28th June, 1841.

of workers walking behind the funeral cortege while thousands of others lined the streets. Though class divisions did exist, and at times led to conflict, Blackburn's relative quiescence was remarkable.

Political agitation was, perhaps, a different matter. During the early nineteenth century growing political awareness, interest and participation came hand in hand with urban growth. Only four Blackburn men were arrested for political offences between 1789 and 1803, a much lower number than in other north-western towns of comparable size,[16] but this tiny and insignificant group of radicals began to grow as political change, franchise reform and other issues became more prominent. As a result meetings of up to 2,000 were seen in 1831, demanding parliamentary reform. Comparable popular gatherings were held in the 1860s, when franchise reform was again a burning issue, and parades and demonstrations were held. In the meantime, though, elections had emerged as increasingly violent affairs. There was violence in Blackburn during five of the nine general elections held between 1832 and 1859, and on two occasions the military had to be called in from Preston. During the 1830s and 1840s public participation usually took the form of spontaneous general rioting, when shops, public houses and committee rooms were wrecked. In 1842, after an investigation into the disputed 1841 election allowed the result to stand, the Bull Inn, used by the Conservatives, was attacked. The Riot Act was read and the 60th Rifles were called in to restore order.[17] Nationally, the main expression of working-class consciousness was the Chartist movement, which emerged in 1838–39, reached its maximum size and power in 1842, raised its head once more in 1848, and then dwindled away. The name derived from the fact that its agenda for social and political reform was set out in the

Blakey Moor was a traditional meeting place. This open space, photographed in 1887, was situated in the area now covered by the original Blackburn College building, by what was the Blakey Moor Central School and a large section of the King George's Hall and Magistrates building complex. It was here in 1827 that the local people gathered to organise resistance against the ancient ley-rate imposed by the Church of England. It was also here where 5,000 weavers met in 1878 before marching off to burn down Clayton Manor in Wilpshire. It was also the town's traditional red-light district.

form of a Great Charter (itself echoing the name Magna Carta). In 1838 and 1839 large Chartist meetings were held in Blackburn, prompting the vicar to publish a sermon against the movement that was later bound and presented to the queen. But despite his fears, the response of the people of Blackburn was 'somewhat apathetic' according to the Chartists themselves.[18] The call for a general strike in August 1839 passed off peacefully, in contrast to the violent agitation at nearby Bolton. The historian Duncan Bythell claims that this was because the employment opportunities at this time were better in Blackburn than in the surrounding districts.[19] If Chartism was a 'knife and fork' issue, then the workers of Blackburn apparently had a full enough plate.

The events of the year 1842 were very different. Mass meetings were being held in March, at which Richard Marsden, a Preston Chartist leader, called for militant action. In August a regional meeting was held in Bolton, attended by Blackburn delegates. They returned with the news that there was to be a general strike, intended to force the government to grant the terms of the charter. Stoppages started in many Blackburn mills the next day. Meanwhile, strikers from Stalybridge and Manchester, who had come out on the 8 August and then marched on neighbouring towns to turn out the workers, arrived in Blackburn. Newly sworn special constables and the 72nd Highlanders awaited them. Mill after mill was attacked, some successfully, others not, as police used their cutlasses and the soldiers their muskets. When peace was restored one woman was dead. The strike lasted a further three weeks before crumbling. Eleven of the rioters were transported to Tasmania and 58 received prison sentences.[20] The mill-owners, under severe pressure and using their power over the forces of law and order, had successfully crushed the agitation and had deterred further public expression of the radical agenda. Chartism virtually died out in Blackburn, though in 1848 there was an attempt to set up a co-operative venture based on Feargus O'Connor's plan for resettling working families on the land. The Operatives Sick and Burial Club purchased a small plot near Pleasington on which a dozen families settled, but it failed miserably after only three years.[21] Chartism in Blackburn never acquired the powerful, though temporary, influence which it did in some other places in Lancashire. In the years around 1840 the mills in the town were the largest in the northwest at the time, with an average of about 280 workers per mill.[22] As we have seen, this allowed paternalism and mill loyalty to develop, defusing the pressures of agitation. As the *Blackburn Standard* proudly claimed in 1839, after a regional Chartist meeting, 'Blackburn, to its lasting honour, be it said, contributed very little either to the strength, interest or importance of the day's proceedings ... Indeed it may with truth be said that in few towns of its size and importance in the manufacturing districts are to be found in a greater degree the elements of pacific organization or where the spirit of industry the co-operative discharge of social duties are more strongly valued.'[23]

Political violence carried on into the 1850s and 1860s but – curiously – this time it was organised by the town's elite. Some elements among the political classes decided to use and manipulate the potentially violent energies of the working classes for their own ends. Mill-owners on each side of the political party divide began to recruit 'bludgeon men' to break up rival political meetings and to defend their own. These schemes, which were no more than modern-day representatives of strategies used by politicians for generations, led to fierce street battles, vicious running fights and attacks on rival public houses that supplied free beer to supporters. In 1853 several public houses at Bank Top and Whalley Banks which supported the Liberal cause were almost gutted. In 1868 the local Conservatives hired 6,000 bludgeon men, the Liberals 'only' 3,000 men. The result was that it was claimed that Liberals could not reach the polling booths 'without extreme personal danger'. The Riot Act was read and the police and military called out. Clubs, picking-sticks, hammers, bricks and paving stones were all used, and it was said that 'the cracking of heads sounded like so much crockery being broken'.[24] If violence to further political aims was inevitable then perhaps the elite felt that it was better channel it in such a way that it furthered their own ends.

The more normal, everyday, type of crime is poorly documented before the nineteenth century, and satisfactory statistics do not appear until the

On the right of this picture of Darwen Street in 1929 is the old Queen's Head Inn on the corner of Dandy Walk. It was here that in 1842 rioting Chartists were held as prisoners by the military. Shots were fired when fellow Chartists tried to aid their escape. The shop on the left was where one of Blackburn's cotton kings, Henry Harrison, was born in 1834. He amassed great wealth and was elected mayor. All was demolished in the 1970s.

1860s. References to local crime included highwaymen in 1793; pickpockets who apparently descended in droves from Manchester on fair days; and body snatching in 1827, when two men were surprised removing the corpse of a recently drowned woman from the graveyard of the Independent chapel. The major crime in the late eighteenth and early nineteenth century, if the food riots or machine-breaking rampages are ignored, was probably 'moutre-snatching', the embezzlement by handloom weavers of the cotton thread left by the putters-out. From the mid nineteenth century, statistics are more forthcoming though still fragmentary.[25] Serious crime was relatively limited. Between 1851 and 1885 there was an annual average of one murder, two manslaughters and one rape in the town. Muggings over the period fell from just under 30 per year to under ten. Robberies from shops and houses averaged about 200 per annum. Prostitution was a problem, and the number of known prostitutes rose from 96 in 1855 to 127 in 1861. A peak was reached during the Cotton Famine years as unemployed female weavers were forced onto the streets to earn an income, but the number of prostitutes recorded fell back to 48 by 1880. During the 1870s the annual total of reported crimes averaged 4,450, which suggests that Victorian Blackburn was not a law-abiding town – there were just 500 reported crimes per annum during the 1930s – but the nineteenth-century figures were first matched, and then exceeded, in the 1960s. The total passed 4,000 in 1968, but it must be noted that the definitions of crime had altered, people were far more likely to report crimes, and recording procedures were much more rigorous, so this does not necessarily mean that we are comparing like with like.

This row of cottages at Ramsgreave, built in 1841–42 and photographed here around 1970, was soon known locally as 'Little Paris'. The reason is said to be because the wives and daughters of the handloom weavers, whose trade had fallen on hard times with the introduction of the power loom, resorted to part-time prostitution to supplement the family income.

A large percentage of the nineteenth-century crime figures involved drunkenness or drink-related offences. Back in 1835 the vicar, in a description of the town's working class, had alluded to the problem of drink. He lambasted 'their immorality in every respect, their gross, filthy habits, their ruffian-like brutality beggar all description. The Sabbath breaking and drunkenness are dreadful. The beer shops have increased the latter to a frightful extent.'[26] The view that drink increased crime was supported by the chaplain of Preston prison: 'There is a greater proportion of the uneducated classes in Blackburn than in Preston and the passion for liquor is a source of ruin and disgrace, more fruitful than any other source combined.'[27] Drink certainly was a problem. The annual number of drunkenness cases brought before the magistrates after 1862 rose steadily from approximately 400 to over 1,000 (in 1876 and 1877). The figures remained at that level until the mid-1880s and then began to decline slowly. While drink received much of the attention, many of the crimes were directly or indirectly the result of extreme poverty, where hopelessness and despair were major factors. According to the police statistics, the lower working classes committed the most recorded offences, but it is important to acknowledge that this may simply in part reflect the fact that the police gave by far the greater part of their attention to this stratum of society. In 1879 the Irish, who lived in the poorest areas of the town and did most of the menial and unskilled labouring jobs, made up 28 per cent of all men and 34 per cent of all women who were arrested. Of the 1,986 people arrested in 1881, ten years after Forster's Education Act, 837 were illiterate, 1120 could only 'read and write imperfectly', and only 29 were fully literate. This is another indication that most crime – or

'The Sabbath breaking and drunkenness are dreadful. The beer shops have increased the latter to a frightful extent.'

VICAR OF BLACKBURN, 1835

Some crimes capture the imagination of the public and one such in Blackburn was the murder of Alice Beetham. The story of this murder, in 1912, of an eighteen-year-old mill worker, who had her throat cut with a razor by her lover Arthur Birkett, is told on this delicate souvenir silk. This tragedy, which occurred at Jubilee Mill, is related in full, complete with memorial poems and photograph.

at least most arrests — took place among the most disadvantaged groups in Blackburn society. The town had a large 'floating' population of vagrants, the homeless, and the dispossessed. In 1861 there 107,675 registrations (that is, for a night's accommodation) in the 36 registered lodging houses in Blackburn. The chief constable attributed much of the crime committed in the town to these men on the tramp. Before 1914, though, robbery and theft were at surprisingly low levels, which could be interpreted as evidence that Blackburn's ruling middle-classes successfully kept control of their own interests — although the same low level of property crime holds good for many other parts of the British Isles. Looking back in 1914, the town's elite could be satisfied. They ruled over a place which had weathered the storms of sporadic violence and working-class anger, and which was a relatively peaceful, settled and law-abiding community. In some senses they had achieved this, by virtue of their control as magistrates and other figures of public authority, with greater success than their equivalents in other towns of Lancashire and Yorkshire. They were entitled, perhaps, to be proud of Blackburn, and proud of its place in the world. How proud the workforce themselves were is another matter.

# CHAPTER SIX

# 'Behind every other town in England': education, 1750–1914

BEFORE INDUSTRIALISATION AFFECTED BLACKBURN the educational opportunities for its children were limited. For the most part, only those from the wealthier or, paradoxically, the very poor families were catered for. Like many other towns in northern England, Blackburn had a grammar school. In 1514 a chantry chapel was founded in Blackburn parish church under the will of Thomas Stanley, first earl of Derby, who had died in 1509. Associated with this chantry was a small school taught by the priest, and it was from this that the grammar school traced its origins. It was refounded and given a royal charter by Queen Elizabeth I in the late sixteenth century and despite many vicissitudes, and much criticism of poor standards, and even though its buildings were often dilapidated and decaying, the school clung tenaciously to life and provided a bare modicum of learning for its few fee-paying pupils from comfortable middle-class backgrounds.

At the other end of the spectrum were establishments such as the Girls Charity School, founded in 1763 to enable ninety chosen daughters of the poor to be 'clothed and educated in knitting and sewing, reading, writing and arithmetic'.[1] There was also a scattering of dame schools and other private establishments. These were normally, as their name suggests, run by women, who took up the occupation because they were unable to do any other work, or because it provided a much-needed second income, or because of a genuine interest in education. The main attraction of these schools, as far as parents were concerned, was that they were cheap and, as industrialisation progressed, they formed a child-minding service in an area where female labour was needed either in the mills or in domestic service. The standard and breadth of teaching varied widely but for many families that was of secondary importance. Such schools saw their heyday at the beginning of the nineteenth century.[2] Even the workhouses had a small school. But for the majority of Blackburn's children, those who fell between these two extremes there was little provision. During the first half of the century this lack of provision began to change, as educational opportunities were made available by a range of private and religious bodies, with the town's manufacturers and social leaders prominent in the moves towards better facilities and wider opportunities. The motives of the elite did not only involve education in the 'pure' sense, but also embraced social order and control, and the production of a suitable workforce for cotton mills and factories.

Private schools originated in the eighteenth century but carried on expanding as dame schools fell into disrepute and declined. Whereas the latter were never more than basic and rudimentary in their facilities and the education they offered, the private schools could appeal to the aspirations or, less charitably, the pretensions of the emergent middle classes and petty bourgeoisie. In 1839 there were 39 such schools in Blackburn, the vast majority of them being small day schools with an average of only 29 pupils.[3] The expanding middle class in Blackburn, including the 'shopocracy' of traders and small merchants, saw the value and need of an education for their children and could afford to pay for it. Some of these schools catered for middle-class girls, an important development since schooling for girls had been very limited indeed until this time. They would typically, take girls from the ages of seven to seventeen, and a sample newspaper advertisement placed by Miss Clayton in 1805, and describing her school in Penny Street, gives a flavour of the type of education on offer: the school catered for 'the education of a few young ladies' in writing, arithmetic, plain, fancy and ornamental needlework, drawing, dancing, music, French and geography. The cost was 25 guineas per annum for boarders and four guineas for day scholars.[4] The number of private schools fell after 1850s, as demand from the lower middle classes declined following the development of better-organized and eventually public-funded elementary education in

Education for the children of the working classes of the town was virtually non-existent at the start of the nineteenth century. Benefactors like a certain William Leyland attempted to help. He built a Girls Charity School in 1763 in Thunder Alley (now Town Hall Street) to educate ninety girls from families of the poor. The building was demolished in 1928.

COTTON TOWN PROJECT

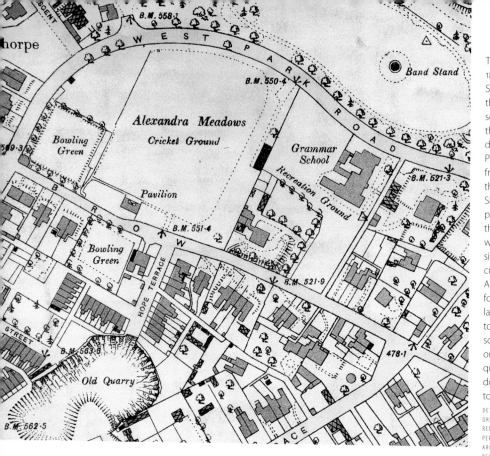

Blackburn. Those specifically catering for middle-class young ladies survived a little longer, but eventually experienced severe competition and withered as state-funded secondary education for girls expanded.

Education for the working classes was first provided on a significant scale from the penultimate decade of the eighteenth century, as religious denominations began to interest themselves in the provision of schools which offered a straightforward curriculum together with clear inculcation of the principles

of religion, albeit, a partisan view which depended on which denomination was involved. Although daytime weekday education remained unusual, the first major involvement of religious bodies with education was the provision of Sunday schools. The first in Blackburn was opened by the Church of England in 1786. It catered for 300 children and although its work was limited to teaching religious knowledge, any study of the bible required the children to learn to read. Such schooling was, therefore, a considerable step forward for the working-classes, and the provision of Sunday schools began to grow. Religious rivalry was a contributory factor. During the Napoleonic Wars the Independents, Baptists, Methodists and Roman Catholics all decided to open Sunday schools, and by 1824 the Church of England, though first in the race, had fallen behind in the provision of places: in that year 1,100 children attended Anglican Sunday schools but 1,276 were pupils at those run by the Nonconformists and a smaller number of others went to a Catholic school.

The Reverend John William Whittaker, who in 1822 became vicar of

This was St Paul's Elementary School, built between New Park Street and Alma Street and facing St Paul's Street, pictured around 1956, when St Paul's church that stood in front of it was demolished. Education was linked to religion from the early nineteenth century, first in the guise of Sunday schools and then by elementary schools. The site of the church and the graveyard is now an open space in the middle of the Blackburn College campus and the Art Building stands on the site of the school that also soon faced demolition.

Blackburn, made serious efforts to maintain the Anglican challenge. The Anglican Sunday school movement should, he considered, provide 'moral restraint' in a town where population growth had apparently outstripped civic authority, and should also compete vigorously with the other denominations rather than being supine.[5]

He co-ordinated a town-wide offensive against such encroachment on what he saw as the home ground of the Established Church. The other religious bodies reacted by meeting the new challenge and further expanding their own provision. In 1842 statistics prepared by the great Lancashire historian and social reformer Edward Baines showed that in Blackburn the provision of Sunday school places had grown rapidly, and that the Anglicans now had the largest share:

Table 6  *Sunday school provision, 1842*

|  | Sunday school places | Number of teachers |
|---|---|---|
| Church of England | 2223 | 203 |
| Independents | 1455 | 163 |
| Methodists | 1205 | 127 |
| Baptists | 400 | 42 |
| Roman Catholics | 370 | 32 |
| Other denominations | 670 | 54 |
| Total | 6323 | 621 |

Growth continued for many years, so that in 1875 Blackburn had a Sunday school attendance of 21,000 out of a total town population of 80,000, and 9,500 of these (45 per cent) went to Church of England establishments, compared with 35 per cent in 1842. Whittaker was doubtless very pleased, though less so that 8,000 attended a plethora of Nonconformist Sunday schools and 3,500 trooped off to Roman Catholic ones.

As was the case throughout the country, the religious involvement in the Sunday school movement soon encouraged the denominations to consider weekday schooling as well. In the voluntary day school sector religious rivalry was again the main motive for the expansion of provision. The Nonconformists were first off the mark. The Independents set up a Lancastrian school in Ainsworth Street in 1810 – the Lancastrian method, devised by the clergyman Joseph Lancaster, was a fashionable educational theory at the time. The Church of England took rapid action to compete, and in 1811 the existing Sunday school in Thunder Alley became a National day school.[6] By 1824 it taught up to 800 pupils, using the rival Madras system which depended heavily upon the employment of pupil monitors. These early ventures were against the context of national moves towards the involvement of the churches in education, which included the establishment of the Nonconformist British and Foreign Schools

Society in 1810 and the National Society for the Education of the poor in the Principles of the Established Church (usually known for understandable convenience as the National Society) in 1811. Whittaker not only revitalised the Anglican Sunday school movement in the town but also worked with the National Society to encourage the expansion of the day school provision. Inevitably, the Nonconformists and the Roman Catholics had to follow suit. Provision was slow, however, and in 1842 when, as we have seen, there were 6,323 Sunday scholars, the weekday provision was far less:

Table 7 *Day school provision, 1842*

|  | Number of schools | Scholars |
|---|---|---|
| Dame and unregulated infant schools | 10 | 340 |
| Private schools | 18 | 539 |
| Public (i.e. state-sponsored) schools | 17 | 1865 |
| Total | 45 | 2744 |

Even in 1870, when the government passed Forster's Education Act which introduced universal elementary education, and even allowed local School Boards to make it compulsory if they wished, Blackburn had only 19 Voluntary schools, just two more than in 1842, but some of these now included infant and junior schools and many had been extended and rebuilt, so pupil numbers had grown proportionately more rapidly. There were now 13,073 children who attended these schools, of whom 6,901 went to a Church of England school, 2,317 to a Roman Catholic school, and 2,743 to a Nonconformist one.[7]

The second element encouraging the growth of elementary education in Blackburn prior to 1870 was the town's employers. They first involved

themselves in the Sunday school movement. Thus, Joseph Feilden donated land for such a school in the Billinge and Mile End area of the town, while Joseph Eccles started a Sunday school at Stakes Hall in 1843.[8] Mill-owners financed, directly or indirectly, a large proportion of the Sunday school movement in the town, for reasons which were clearly explained by one of their number, John Baynes, in 1857: 'Does not the experience of every manufacturer testify to the truth [that] those workmen and workwomen who arc the most sober, steady, respectable and intelligent have been, or still are, connected with the Sunday schools.'[9] The same motive, together with loyalty to the church to which they belonged and the fact that schooling would instil discipline and a work ethic into pupils, was behind the involvement of the employers. It was enlightened self-interest, and this also dictated that most such schools would be in the vicinity of a benefactor's mill. That assured a steady supply of basically educated new employees, and would help to ensure the gratitude and loyalty of their parents who also worked at the mill. Eccles built a British Society school near his Nova Scotia mills in 1835, and Hornby constructed one alongside his Brookhouse mills in 1839 and had his crest proudly and conspicuously carved in stone above the main entrance. Religious rivalry was apparent here, too. Hopwood built an Anglican school near his mills at Grimshaw Park in 1850, and this later became Christ Church school. In the same year the Pilkingtons financed the building of a Congregationalist school virtually next door in Park Road.[10] Grimshaw Park, formerly without any voluntary schools, now had two new ones in the space of a few months. Religious rivalry in education was sometimes taken even further. In 1880 James Briggs, a Nonconformist, took all the half-timers who worked at his mill out of the local Anglican school and sent them to one that he had just built. Robert Hopwood Hutchinson was publicly attacked in 1874 for only employing children from Church of England schools at his mills. In 1879 a rule at Boothman's 'Punch-noggin' mill stated quite openly that all children who worked there would attend the Anglican All Saints school and no other.[11]

But notwithstanding all these schools, Blackburn before 1870 still had a seriously low rate of literacy. A survey of marriage registers, which shows how many people in the town were capable of signing their names, reveals that in the period from 1754 to 1777 33 per cent could do so, but that between 1800 and 1820 the figure fell to 31 per cent, and even in the 1860s it was only 45 per cent.[12] A contemporary commented in 1844 that, 'Blackburn with its teeming population is at the present time behind every other town in England in intelligence, for it appears that out of every one hundred men only 39 can write their name; and out of 100 women only eleven are able to do so while in London 89 men and 76 women out of every 100 are able to read and write.'[13] Even those who could sign their name may well not have been fully literate in the modern sense. The close relationship between the Anglican Church and a key group of leading

*'Does not the experience of every manufacturer testify to the truth [that] those workmen and work-women who arc the most sober, steady, respectable and intelligent have been, or still are, connected with the Sunday schools.'*

Boys and girls were taught separately in the town's elementary schools and often had their own entrances. Such schools, that taught the basic three Rs, were the sole providers of education for the overwhelming majority of Blackburn's children. Here are two class photographs from the late nineteenth century of pupils, dressed in their best, who attended St Paul's School. The adults are most likely the class teacher and the headmaster and headmistress.

employers culminated in the working of the Blackburn School Board, which was established under the Education Act of 1870. Such Boards were created by government order in places where educational provision was inadequate, since the Act stipulated the provision of a school place for every child that wanted one. Since the Borough intended to make education compulsory, a School Board was established to tackle any deficiencies. The Boards were elected by the ratepayers but regulated and supervised by the government. At Blackburn there were originally 29 candidates for the 13 seats but pre-election manoeuvring and agreements meant that eventually no contest was held and the ratepayers were denied their democratic participation in the process. It was, in short, a fix. Cotton manufacturers were in the majority, holding seven seats, and W. H. Hornby was in the chair, while churchmen held three seats. The remaining places were filled from the professions or even, towards the end of the century, by tradesmen, but the overall result, was a continuous 'cotton Anglican' majority, a dominance that was used to good effect This ratio remained throughout the life of the Board, until under the provisions of the 1902 Education Act it was superseded by Blackburn Corporation as local education authority.[14]

In its thirty-two years the School Board only used ratepayers' money to build three schools, and one existing school was taken over from the Nonconformists. The churches, especially the Church of England, had already built most of the schools in Blackburn, and those in authority saw no reason to alter that pattern. Co-operation between the School Board and the churches was so close that when it was decided that a school was needed in the Dukes Brow area, the Board informed the Church of England of the fact and then delayed action until the Church authorities raised the necessary finance to build one. By 1900 church schools dominated elementary education in the town. In that year 12,500 pupils attended the 25 Anglican schools; 6,350 the eleven Nonconformist schools; and 4,350 the eight Roman Catholic schools; a total of 23,200 against only 1,500 pupils who attended the four Board schools.[15] Such figures are in stark contrast to those elsewhere in the northwest. At Bolton the average attendance at Church schools was 14,540 compared with 10,056 at Board schools, and in Oldham only 8,236 attended Church schools against the 11,099 who went daily to Board schools.[16] In Blackburn the middle-class cotton interest and the churches, especially the Church of England, had elementary education comfortably in their grip. But elementary education in Blackburn was not notably successful in educational terms, and the middle-class elite must bear much of the blame. The motives behind school building were not

These girls in aprons and bobcaps are in the Laundry Room at Blakey Moor Central School in the interwar years. They are being taught the skills it was felt they would need to fill their role in society. For girls this was as wife and mother so here they are being taught ironing skills. This gender division within the curriculum was set in the nineteenth century elementary schools. Note how the irons are being held with cloths. This was because before the electric iron they were heated by being placed on the cooking range.
COTTON TOWN PROJECT

At the turn of the
twentieth century
worries over the
physical fitness of
the next generation
were widespread,
and as a result
physical education
in schools was
overhauled with
a major input by
the armed services.
The result was a set
table of activities
introduced by the
government. In
this picture local
schoolgirls take part
in synchronised
exercises with
military precision.
BLACKBURN LIBRARY LOCAL
HISTORY COLLECTION

primarily to do with education for its own sake, and the consequence was that not enough attention was paid to results, except those of loyalty, diligence and the work ethic. The quality of the teaching may not always have been of the best, but what was more culpable was the town's ambivalent attitude towards education in general.

Blackburn, like many other cotton towns, developed a strong tradition of half-time schooling, whereby children were released from factory work to attend school for only part of each day. Child labour had been an integral part of the cotton industry as far back as the domestic system of manufacture, and it did not depart from the mills with the passing of the numerous Factory Acts. This legislation alleviated the conditions under which the children worked and limited the age range and working hours available to employers, but acceptance of the principle that children should not work but should be educated was very slow to take hold and there were many steps to be taken before it was enshrined in statute at the time of the First World War. Until 1870 schooling was in any case not compulsory, so many children, even in the 1860s, did not attend school, even though they were prevented, at least officially, from undertaking employment. The minimum age at which children could be employed full-time was raised to ten following the passing of the Factory Act of 1874 and Sandon's Education Act of 1876; to eleven in 1893; and to twelve in 1899, but the major exemption was that with permission from the school board a child under those ages could be 'exempted' from schooling for half the day in order to work in industry or other trades. In order to claim exemption from full-time schooling, parents had to apply to the board and show that their child had reached a certain standard of education.

The Blackburn board, dominated by cotton manufacturers, not unexpectedly favoured this system since their cheap labour supplies depended on it and it refused even to set an educational standard: any parent who applied could obtain the exemption or 'half-timers' certificate. Eventually, in 1880, the Board of Education ordered the School Board to conform to standards, but these were set at the bare minimum. Education could not stand in the way of the hiring of

BOARD OF EDUCATION.
Form 146 b.

SCHEDULE III.

COUNTY BOROUGH OF BLACKBURN.

Local Education Authority

LABOUR CERTIFICATE, No. 2 (for partial exemption only).

AGE AND EMPLOYMENT.

I certify that *Freda Murphy* residing at *3 Swan Street* was on the *19th* day of *February* 191*3*, not less than twelve years of age, having been born on the *16th* day of *February 1901*, as appears by the Registrar's Certificate (     ) now produced to me, and has been shown to the satisfaction of the local education authority for this district to be beneficially employed.

(Signed)

(¹) Clerk to the Local Education Authority.

(¹) or other officer.

PREVIOUS ATTENDANCE.

I certify that *Freda Murphy* residing at *3 Swan Street* has made 300 attendances in not more than two schools during each year for five preceding years, whether consecutive or not, as shown by the (²) certificate furnished by the Principal Teacher of the (³) *St Mary's* School.

(Signed)

(¹) Clerk to the Local Education Authority.

Dated the *19th* day of *Feby* 191*3*.

When a Child under 14 years of age is out of employment, this Certificate is suspended, and the Child must attend School Full Time.

labour. Only in 1884 was the school board forced to introduce a rule that an official certificate should be issued to early school-leavers to show that exemption had been formally granted, thus making the illegal employment of children far more difficult.[17] In 1872, after education for 5–13 year olds in the borough had been made compulsory, 2,784 boys and 2,844 girls in Blackburn were half-timers, and forty years later the numbers were still very high. In 1902 there were 2,110 half-timers and in 1914 the figure was still 1,600. Blackburn had far more such children than other textile towns. In 1882 in the major industrial towns of Yorkshire and Lancashire an average of 10 per cent of children were half-timers, but in Blackburn the figure was 25 per cent, and it did not fall to below 10 per cent until 1902. Even these figures hide the true story. In 1909 at Christchurch Church of England School, 92 of the 118 twelve to fourteen year olds in the top class were half-timers; at Bank Top Council School 35 out of 46; and at St Alban's Catholic School, 79 out of 122. Whatever the type of school, half-time working and, therefore, half-time education were the usual fate of the majority of children in Blackburn.[18]

A shortage of school places was never a major problem in Blackburn, although the Newcastle Commission of 1858, which investigated the extent of working-class education, highlighted it as a pressing issue nationally. In 1871 there were, in theory, 16,908 places available in the town's voluntary school sector but only 11,961 of these were filled. Their geographical spread was also adequate, and only one school in the town was found to have genuine overcrowding.[19] Even after elementary education was made compulsory, provision was adequate. In 1875 total accommodation had risen to 18,933 places but only 13,073 pupils were recorded as receiving at least some schooling. By 1901, after the Church of England had expanded its school provision and had come to

This exemption certificate, given to a girl just three days after her twelfth birthday, would allow her to be excused full-time education and thus be able to work in the mill as a half-timer. In a town that had no tradition of education or culture, both the local elite and many of the parents encouraged the granting of such exemptions.

COTTON TOWN PROJECT

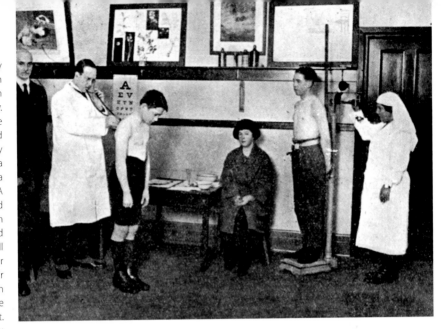

dominate elementary education in the borough, there was an excess of 7,000 places.[20] The problem was simple. Many children just did not go to school in the first place, and had they done so the provision of places would have been a much more serious question. Even those who did go to school tended to have poor attendance rates, and the prevalence of half-time schooling exacerbated that difficulty. Immediately before the school board was set up in 1871, of the 17,453 children of school age in the borough only 12,807 were on the school registers, and many of the latter only attended sporadically. Thus, of the 10,532 pupils on the registers of publicly inspected schools an average of only 7,023

Though discipline inside school was strict, once children escaped into the streets their natural exuberance took over as this picture of schoolchildren crowding down Whalley Range in 1905 shows. Sensing the excitement of having their photograph taken, they swarm towards the photographer helped by the total lack of traffic.

J. HALSALL COLLECTION

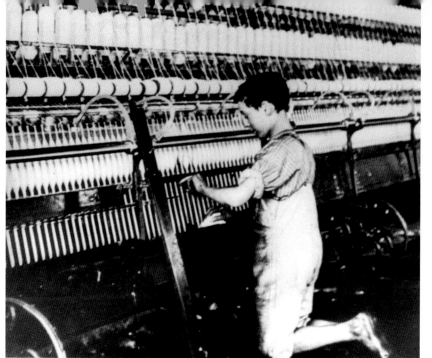

The young men of Blackburn often entered spinning or weaving mills at an early age as half-timers. In Blackburn's weaving mills many were not even paid at first but learned the trade helping to clean and look after the looms that their family worked. Such help might allow a mother or sister to work an extra loom and therefore bring home more money.
COTTON TOWN PROJECT

turned up each day. Three years after education was made compulsory the attendance rate was no better. Of the 14,846 pupils attending inspected schools at the time of the 1873 survey, only 9,609 came daily – the absence rate was 35 per cent.

Several reasons, in addition to the support for the half-time system by the employers, help explain the poor attendance record and the generally low esteem in which education was held by many of the people of Blackburn. There was no tradition of education or culture in the town and, as will be seen, no significant self-improvement movement. Parental pressure was on the side of the half-time system and at one stage there was even a School Grievance Committee which complained against the decision to use parental income as a yardstick in any decision regarding the granting of exemption from full-time education. Parents also complained that doctors were objecting to too many such applications on medical grounds. Many of Blackburn's parents wanted their children to work in the mills as soon as possible, so that they could begin earning, and the work ethic of the town was centred on employment and wage-earning, not on education and self-improvement. Neither, of course, did the prevalence of poverty help matters. Not only was a child's wage essential to the household budgeting, but many parents could not afford to pay the school fees, which were among the highest in the north-west. The 1870 Education Act allowed school boards to use rate money to replace the income from school fees, but the Blackburn Board chose not to do so and in the late 1890s it was still charging fees for elementary education, though 93 per cent of state schools in England and Wales had ended them. Until 1898 Blackburn also had a system whereby the Poor

Law Guardians, not the School Board, paid the fees on behalf of parents who could not afford them. Though the board recommended which parents should receive financial help, the Guardians insisted on a separate vetting procedure and many parents avoided what they felt was the stigma of such an interview. The Poor Law Guardians were also far from generous. Of the 504 applicants for fee aid in 1872 only 287 were accepted. The attitude among the middle-class decision-makers towards education for the working classes is revealed by the number of attendance officers employed to enforce compulsory education. In 1882 a survey of the 22 largest northern towns revealed an average of one officer for 2,739 children, but in Blackburn it was one per 4,199. Little wonder that many children were able, quite illegally, to avoid schooling.

Secondary education in Blackburn before 1914 was very limited. The Taunton Commission of 1869, which investigated the national state of secondary education, reported that the Queen Elizabeth's Grammar School had 83-day pupils and thirteen boarders, that its buildings were in a poor condition, and that it had a very poor record of university entrance. It provided a somewhat unsatisfactory and inadequate education for a relatively small minority of the town's middle-class children, and as late as 1894 it only admitted three scholars a year from the elementary schools of the borough. In 1905 there were still only 137 pupils on the roll. One reason for its continued weakness was that Blackburn did not have a large middle class to supply it with pupils, but more significant was that its extremely old-fashioned curriculum probably deterred many of the more ambitious and intellectual parents from choosing it as a place of education for their sons. The diet of classical learning served up at the grammar school was hardly geared to the skills they believed were more relevant to the modern world of commerce. For that reason, many manufacturers chose to send their sons to private commercial academies, including Hooles Academy which combined 'gentlemanly polish' with the 'distinctly commercial',[21] while the really wealthy naturally preferred to send their sons away to boarding schools and public schools. In 1871 217 of Blackburn's children were being educated outside the borough.

The grammar school only took boys, so there was a growing awareness of the inadequacy of secondary education provision for girls. In 1883 a girls' high school was opened, situated in a private house on Preston New Road and modelled on those being founded in many towns by the Girls' Public Day School Trust. The entry age was nine, and the school had 150 pupils within ten years and 210 by 1914. Its academic standing was not high, but that was not the main reason why Blackburn's middle class sent their daughters there: 'The School is scarcely of first grade character but owes its existence and such success as it attains to social considerations rather than to any superiority in the range and character of the educational advantages which it offers.'[22] For the parents the social standing which attendance conferred on their daughters was

*'The School is scarcely of first grade character but owes its existence and such success as it attains to social considerations rather than to any superiority in the range and character of the educational advantages which it offers.'*
INSPECTOR OF SCHOOLS

of greater importance than their academic achievement. Roman Catholic girls might receive a secondary education at the Convent of Notre Dame School, founded in 1908 by the amalgamation of the Convent Higher Grade School and the pupil teacher centre. By 1914 it had 160 pupils aged between 9 and 18. Academic success received a higher priority here since the school's main ambition was to turn out future Catholic schoolmistresses, who could carry on the work and help to make up a national shortage. Only a few working-class children benefited from secondary education before 1918, not least because all the schools were mainly fee-paying. The Girls' High School allocated 10 per cent of its annual intake to free scholarship places from 1903, in return for a grant from the new local education authority, and a total of 22 scholarship boys attended Queen Elizabeth's Grammar School by 1905. Some scholarships were financed by charitable trusts, others by the local education authority. A modest level of extended education, for a few other working-class children, was provided by four higher-grade schools attached to established voluntary elementary schools. Nevertheless, the little secondary education that was available in Blackburn by 1914 was almost entirely a middle-class preserve.

Adult education never had a strong tradition in the town, which once again presents a contrast with the experience of many larger industrial communities. Mechanics' institutes were founded in numerous towns during the 1820s and 1830s. They were attended mainly by skilled working men, but sponsored, as an exercise in benevolent paternalism, by middle-class employers. The institutes usually held educational classes, provided a lending library and study facilities,

This mid-nineteenth-century photograph shows Queen Elizabeth Grammar School students standing outside the school when it was in Freckleton Street. The school was founded in 1514 and renamed Queen Elizabeth's Grammar School in 1567 when given a royal charter. The boys' dress, which included top hats, and their confident and nonchalant attitude to the camera, shows that the school catered for Blackburn's elite, although the major families of the town preferred to have their sons educated outside the borough at various public schools.

BLACKBURN LIBRARY LOCAL
HISTORY COLLECTION

the 1830s and 1840s and as local newspapers flourished the role of the ballad singers declined – by 1855 six newspapers had been started in Blackburn and, though several were short-lived, the *Blackburn Standard* lasted until 1904 and the *Blackburn Times* and the *Northern Daily Telegraph* (later the *Lancashire Evening Telegraph*) flourished and became well established. Public perform-ances by bands, entertainers and others in the streets survived into the twentieth century, but gradually they were eclipsed by indoor commercial entertainments. Other activities included gardening and horticulture, which were encouraged by the formation of the Blackburn Floral and Horticultural Society in 1850 and the expansion of allotment-holding at the end of the century, the latter being fostered by the council in the context of national legislation which allowed local authorities to set aside land for the purpose. Historians have placed a strong emphasis on the way in which the middle classes encouraged 'rational recreation' for the masses and by the turn of the twentieth century in

Corporation Park had its grand opening on 22 October 1857. East and West Park Roads are yet to be built, but soon would be developed, with large houses for the town's middle classes who wanted to move out of the smoke-filled valley in which Blackburn's early cotton mills had been built. At the top of the park captured Russian Crimean war cannons sat in their specially constructed stone redoubts. Blackburn Corporation finally sacrificed these to the scrap metal campaign in the early years of the Second World War in order to set an example to the people of the town.

Drawn by A. Maclure.

London, Liverpool & Manchester.

VIEW OF BLACKBURN AND THE PARK.

*Permission to William Pilkington Esqr. The Worshipful the Mayor of Blackburn, on the occasion of*

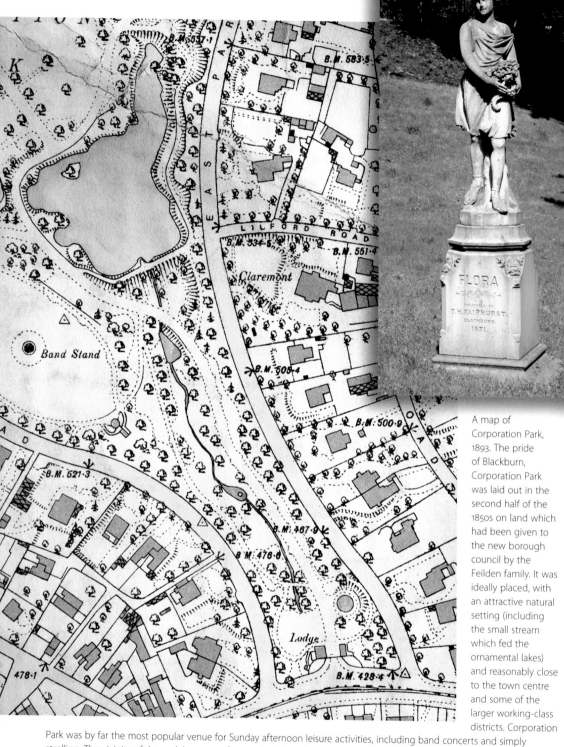

A map of Corporation Park, 1893. The pride of Blackburn, Corporation Park was laid out in the second half of the 1850s on land which had been given to the new borough council by the Feilden family. It was ideally placed, with an attractive natural setting (including the small stream which fed the ornamental lakes) and reasonably close to the town centre and some of the larger working-class districts. Corporation Park was by far the most popular venue for Sunday afternoon leisure activities, including band concerts and simply strolling. The vicinity of the park became a favoured residential area for middle-class citizens, whose detached houses and semi-detached villas, set back from broad gently curving tree-lined roads benefited from the attractive outlook across the park.

DETAIL OF THE 1893 ORDNANCE SURVEY MAP, REPRODUCED BY KIND PERMISSION OF THE COUNTY ARCHIVIST, LANCASHIRE RECORD OFFICE

Blackburn the town council included a number of the 'shopocracy' and even some 'superior working-class' men, so there was a good deal of support for improving activities such as gardening.

A clearer example of the encouragement of 'rational recreation' is the growth of municipal leisure facilities after the town was incorporated in 1851. Corporation Park, covering 50 acres between Preston New Road and the crest of Revidge Hill, was bought from Joseph Feilden in 1855. The total cost to the Corporation, including landscaping, was £14,702. The old reservoirs were made into ornamental lakes; terraces and carriageways were built; fountains installed; and a battery constructed at the top of the hill provided a place to exhibit two Crimean war cannon. The opening of the park in 1857 was one of the great events in mid-Victorian Blackburn, attended by many thousands of citizens amid much celebration and ceremony. In 1885 the 30-acre Queen's Park was opened, its boating lake added to the town's amenities, and swimming baths were provided at Belper Street (1906) and Blakey Moor (1911). The landscaping and design of the parks was clearly middle-class in character, with the carriage drives and elegant balustrades, and Corporation Park was located in a mainly middle-class area of the town, the nearby streets of detached and semi-detached houses benefiting from the views across the park itself. This was very typical of the Victorian industrial town – the main urban parks in, for example, Bolton, Preston and Manchester are similarly designed and located – but the aim was to

These cottages, next to the Corporation Park Hotel on Revidge, overlook Corporation Park. At the turn of the twentieth century they sold tea and 'red' cakes 'at any hour', according to the sign outside the door to those, including 'picnic parties', who strolled to the top of the park.

COTTON TOWN PROJECT, © LANCASHIRE EVENING TELEGRAPH

provide a 'green lung' for the increasingly smoky and congested working-class areas, and the huge numbers of people who visited the parks on Sundays and holidays are testimony to the fact that they served that purpose well.

Markets and fairs were also traditional events associated with entertainment. On market days, although the main business was buying and selling, there was plenty of drinking, socialising and amusements. The annual fairs were more significant in this respect, particularly because Blackburn had no special or traditional 'wakes' days. The town fairs were held three times a year: on Easter Monday, for two days at Whitsun and one day in October. Originally trading was the main function of these fairs, with entertainment being of secondary importance, but as the commercial role of the fairs diminished their pleasure function grew instead. Thus, among the main attractions at the 1849 Easter Fair were, topping the bill in the freak shows, a large-headed girl, rabbit-eyed children and a lady giant, while boxing, ring-tossing, shooting popguns, the wheel of fortune and sword swallowing were just some of the many sideshows. Those who showed animals joined together to form circuses and these began to visit Blackburn regularly in the second half of the nineteenth century. In 1887, for example, 'Sanger's extensive circus and Hippodrome took up quarters in the Market Square. At noon on Monday [they] passed through the principal thoroughfares with a valuable stud of horses and accompanied by a band.'[10] Other important changes in leisure habits were consequent upon the new industrial disciplines. Over the north-west as a whole, many customary holidays disappeared in the first half of the nineteenth century, as did the 'free Monday' or 'Saint Monday' traditionally taken by many self-employed hand-loom weavers. To ensure efficiency it was necessary for factory machinery to be worked to capacity, so long hours had to be enforced and holidays reduced. Soon, apart from the summer 'wakes', only Christmas Day and Good Friday were left as holidays. In Blackburn the absence of a local 'wakes day' meant that the inhabitants traditionally observed the Easter fair as the main holiday event, so Easter Monday was the main holiday rather than Good Friday. In addition, Whitsun remained important with its traditional Whit walks of pre-industrial origin. These were given added strength in the mid-nineteenth century as both church and chapel attempted to reassert the influence of religion on people's lives. The walks became a symbol of sectarian strength and parish pride and were still an essential feature of Whitsuntide celebrations in 1914. Fair days, too, were slowly lost after 1850 both as holidays and as events. Pleasure fairs were opposed by various groups, including the 'respectable' middle classes, tradespeople and employers. They became more overtly working-class events in the mid-nineteenth century, and since publicans' booths, or beer tents, were a common sight there was growing opposition on the grounds of the danger to public morality and order. Market traders complained that they were thrown off their pitches for the fair days, and shopkeepers claimed that they lost custom,

Church parades, especially at Whitsun, were a common sight in Blackburn, with young girls dressed up for the occasion and Rose Queens often the centre of attention. Mothers would spend many hours proudly making special dresses for their daughters. This parade is one held by Audley Range Congregational church along Queen's Road.

while employers were plagued by absenteeism at fair times and disliked having to concede intermittent holidays.

Various Acts of Parliament gave the opponents of fairs the powers that they needed. The 1847 Markets and Fairs Act and the 1858 Local Government Act granted councils the authority to create and regulate new fairs. The Fairs Acts of 1868, 1871, 1873 and 1878 then gave them the right to limit or even abolish existing fairs. By the 1880s Blackburn council had used these Acts to rid the town of the October cattle fair and reduce the Easter fair from eight to four days. In addition they had used the 1874 Licensing Act to make fairs 'dry'. The employers then sought to end the Easter fair entirely and to obtain

This map shows how Queen's Park was built on the very edge of the town, amid the fields and with the bare slopes of Whinny Edge rising to the south. Its great attraction was the ornamental boating lake, fed by natural springs and partly within some disused quarry workings. Work on the park began in Golden Jubilee Year, 1887, and when the map was made was only partly completed. Extensive planting soon softened the rather bleak character of the area.

DETAIL OF THE 1893 ORDNANCE SURVEY MAP, REPRODUCED BY KIND PERMISSION OF THE COUNTY ARCHIVIST, LANCASHIRE RECORD OFFICE

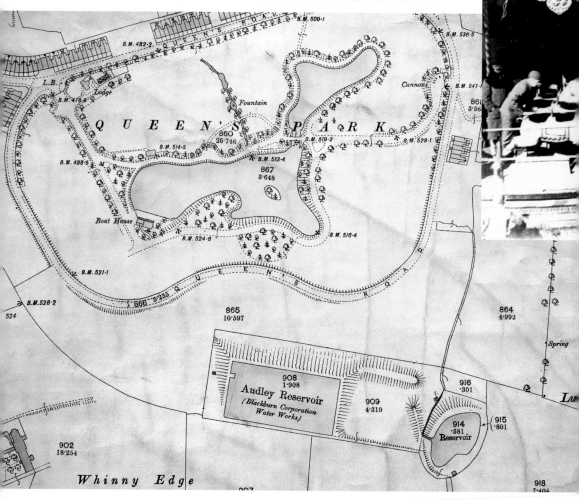

The Easter fair was a highlight of the year. By the 1930s it was still being held on the market place. Compared with work at the mill and life in the soot-blackened terraced streets, the bright lights, gaudy colours and raucous music of the fair must have seemed another world.

agreed regular holidays for the town by abolishing the Whitsuntide holiday and making Easter the main break. They hoped that such a switch would reduce absenteeism but the fair was an obstacle, for it was held to encourage people to remain in Blackburn rather than going on annual trips and so regarding Easter as the main holiday period. The holding of the fair in the town centre was banned in 1890 but it was then held on private land belonging to the Feilden family and grew even larger, attracting more people and no longer limited to an 11 p.m. finish. In 1893 the council surrendered and allowed it to return to the town centre – the small businessmen and traders, disgruntled because moving the fair had cost them trade, outvoted the mill-owners. Tradition had kept its foothold.[11]

Industrialisation at first greatly reduced the potential for leisure time, for factory workers could not come and go as they pleased or choose their own hours as handloom weavers had done and the working day was exceptionally long. Until the 1840s the only time that mill workers had free was Sundays and after 8.30 p.m. on weekdays and, since the day began at 5 a.m. or 6 a.m., the short evening was needed for eating sleeping and domestic duties, and a six-day week was standard. The 1850 Factory Act limited the working hours to a twelve-hour day, from 6 a.m. to 6 p.m. and work on Saturdays finished at 2 p.m. Most daylight hours were still taken up by work, and in the winter all the hours of daylight, but as the working day was shortened over the rest of the century the leisure activities which could be pursued in the evenings increased. For example, the theatre and the public house adapted to this opportunity. With the growth of the free Saturday afternoon in the second half of the century further changes occurred, most obviously an increase in playing or watching sport. In Blackburn, as anywhere else, national legislation was increasingly significant in determining working hours and holidays, and negotiations with local branches of trade unions were also important. In the 1830s most mills in the town only stopped for four days holiday, and it was not until the passing of the 1871 Bank Holiday Act, which added Easter Monday, Whit Monday, Boxing Day and the first Monday in August to Christmas Day and Good Friday, that the situation showed a significant improvement. At first Blackburn employers

Corporation Park was a haven of greenery in a mainly dark and dirty industrial town. Opened in what was then the main middle-class area of town, it was still within reach of many working-class terraced streets and was one place where the classes could mix during their leisure hours. Almost certainly pictured on a Sunday, these people take their chance to stroll and sit in the fresh air, dressed in their weekend best.

sought to circumvent the Act and refused to close on August Bank Holiday, and
even local banks remained open on bank holiday, but eventually the employers
were forced to acquiesce. In 1889 the mill-owners agreed with the unions that
the Whitsun holiday be abolished in favour of three days at Easter and a full
week in July at the time of the Darwen Fair, but pressure from below, in the
form of absenteeism, meant that Whit Monday and Tuesday were regained in
1891 in return for a shortening of the Easter and summer breaks. Soon Whit
Tuesday was traded in to make a full week in summer, which was transferred
to the second week in August. Most mill workers now received nine or ten
days holiday a year. Blackburn's holidays had been determined by a combination of tradition, Government legislation and bargaining between mill-owners
and trade unions.

The first theatre in Blackburn was almost certainly the Theatre Royal on
Ainsworth Street, opened sometime between 1767 and 1775. The words 'Opera
House' were added to its name in 1818, with three entrances, a gallery and a

The Council has embarked on a project to return Corporation Park to its original splendour. This pleasant green interlude is bounded by East and West Park Roads where many of the nineteenth-century middle-class villas have now been converted to offices. Near the top can be seen Alexandra Meadows, the ground of the East Lancashire Cricket and Bowls Club, founded in 1863: this club at first refused to play other local teams because of their 'questionable' social mix.

WWW.WEBBAVIATION.CO.UK

pit. As was usual in the early theatres the seating in the pit was just wooden benches. After the frontage was rebuilt in 1851 the name reverted to 'Theatre Royal'. The building was reconstructed in 1886 and refurbished in 1909, reopening as the Royal Hippodrome and Opera House with seating for 1687 people and standing room for another 700. It now had 'numerous saloons' which were 'luxuriously furnished'. The New Theatre was opened in 1787 in Market Street Lane in a building which had been used as assembly rooms. It, too, had various incarnations, as the Alhambra Palace, the Royalty Theatre, the New Royalty Theatre and finally, in the 1880s, the Lyceum Theatre of Varieties. It finally closed in 1902 when the council refused to relicence it. The building was demolished in 1953.

In 1818 the Theatre Royal and Opera House was opened in Ainsworth Street. During the first three decades of the nineteenth century the two theatres catered mainly for the middle classes, since the long hours of the working classes prevented them from attending. By 1840, as the number of workers increased and hours of work were marginally reduced, the clientele became more mixed, with a strong working-class element, and the entertainment offered changed

The Alexandra Cinema, which opened in 1909 at the junction of Eanam and Dock Street, was the first purpose-built cinema in the town and one of the earliest in the country.
COTTON TOWN PROJECT

accordingly. In earlier decades the evening was typically divided into three parts – a comedy, songs, and a farce. With the growing influx of working-class patrons the comic intervals between these sections became so popular that they were soon developed into complete performances. Both theatres were eventually dominated by music hall entertainments – the Royalty or Lyceum from as early as the 1850s, and the Theatre Royal in the Edwardian period.

From the mid-nineteenth century several 'theatres' were built specifically for the working-class clientele. The Amphitheatre, on Jubilee Street, opened in 1880 and went through a number of changes, as the Princes Theatre, the New Princes Theatre, and finally, in the 1920s, the Grand Theatre. The Palace Theatre was built as a music hall on the site of the old Wesleyan Mission in Jubilee Street in 1899. It failed within a year, but was reopened a few months later as part of the MacNaughton Vaudeville Circuit, which by 1907 had twenty halls across the country. The Blackburn one had the largest gallery in Lancashire, seating 1,000 people at a mere 2d. a ticket, and so clearly aimed at

One of a number in the town this theatre was originally built in 1880 on Jubilee Street and was renamed the Grand theatre in the 1920s. After a short-lived flirtation with the cinema the Grand was the only music or variety hall remaining in the town by 1939. For over fifty years its opulent décor had attracted thousands from the drab back streets of the town to enjoy a few hours of what must have seemed another world of bright lights, warmth and colour.
COTTON TOWN PROJECT, © LANCASHIRE EVENING TELEGRAPH

These posters range in date from 1847 to 1940 and in entertainment from music hall to variety. It is interesting to see how little the programmes changed. Singing and comedy continued to be the mainstays, interspersed with acts such as jugglers, accordion aces and whistling vocalists. In times when there was no radio or television, theatres were many and packed.

a working-class audience. Over the years many of the famous starts trod the boards there, including Vesta Tilley, Sir Harry Lauder and the world famous escapologist Houdini (though the latter only came once: as requested, a member of the audience tied him up and Houdini was still trying to free himself at midnight, much to the enjoyment of the audience). The last music hall was the Olympia Theatre, opened in 1911 in a former skating rink (roller-skating having been a short-lived craze). The entrance, lit by eight flame arc lamps, opened into a 15-foot square hall with two sets of double swing doors leading into a mahogany-panelled foyer. An internal promenade 233 feet long and 7 feet 6 inches wide circled the building, giving access to 34 private boxes and the rows of individual tip-up seats with plush armrests. The theatre was decorated with ornate plasterwork and a colour scheme of white, cream, pink and grey, and it had central heating. Its popularity is easily understood, given the drab, grey and chilly existence of so many of Blackburn's workers.

Most of those who frequented the music halls in the nineteenth century were working-class men, and they could be rowdy. One gentleman described his first

visit to the Lyceum theatre in late Victorian period. The pit where he sat was full of men, with hardly any women. They sat smoking their pipes and joined in the singing of various choruses. Then a fight erupted and within moments everyone had climbed over the seats to watch. A burly attendant hurried to the scene, broke up the brawl and evicted the culprits. In the meantime the show carried on. At the Palace Theatre, too, the manager at one time closed down the entire gallery 'as a lesson to the rowdier elements'. But by the turn of the century the theatres were actively encouraging women and families to attend. As McNaughton, the owner of the Palace Theatre explained in 1907, 'I am often asked why I call my Halls "Palaces" and "Hippodromes". This is to draw a distinction between the old "Music Halls" of the past, frequented by men only, and the new Vaudeville entertainment of the present day, to be patronised by women and children.'[12]

The theatres also adapted to another novelty. At the end of the century the moving picture came to town. Blackburn has a very special place in the history of British cinema and film, because in the mid-1990s Peter Worden made the extraordinary discovery, in a shop about to be demolished, of many reels of exceptionally early film shot by the filmmakers Mitchell and Kenyon. The films, which include many scenes in Blackburn and elsewhere in Lancashire, are of unsurpassed historical interest, and are one of the priceless archival treasures of the British Film Institute. The first ones were about two minutes in length and in the mid-1890s local and visiting entrepreneurs, such as Captain Payne,

began to show them at fairs. The first film show in a Blackburn theatre was at the Lyceum in 1896, advertised as a 'theatregraph'. It showed a man watering his garden. The water stops when a child stands on the hose. The man looks down the nozzle to check for a blockage, the boy removes his foot, and the man is soaked. The Palace Theatre began showing these short films regularly after 1900, as extra entertainment during intervals and the Theatre Royal added films to its variety bill from 1909. The first cinema in Blackburn, opened in 1907, was at the Victoria Hall at Eanam. Originally an assembly room, it became known as Charnley's Pictures. At Easter 1909 the Alexandra, the town's first purpose-built cinema and one of the first in the country, opened on a site close to the Victoria Hall at the junction of Eanam and Dock Street. The King's Hall at Bank Top followed in the same year, again a conversion of an existing hall, and then the Central Hall in Mincing Lane. This had formerly housed Ohmy's circus but in 1909, during the roller-skating craze, it opened as a rink. The craze then collapsed, the rink went out of business, and in 1910 the hall reopened as a 1,000-seat cinema with two shows daily and three on a Saturday. The rapid changes of fortune, and identity, reflect the way that popular culture in the town was now closely shaped by wider fashions and fads. Two more cinemas opened in 1910 – the Empire Electric Theatre in a hall on Aqueduct Road, Eanam, with seating for 800, and the Star Picture Palace in Plane Street, Little Harwood, purpose-built and seating 1,150. By 1914 there were six cinemas in the town. Entertainment had undergone a revolution . . .

Public houses could be seen on every street in the working-class areas of Blackburn. Here James Barlow, the landlord, and his wife stand outside the Britannia Inn on Penny Street. It is decorated for the coronation of George V in 1911. Other public houses on Penny Street at this time were the Welcome, the Pheasant, the Plough, the Ship, the Fleece and the Waterloo Hotel. There was also the Shamrock, a reminder that Penny Street was the centre of the Irish quarter of the town.
COTTON TOWN PROJECT, © LANCASHIRE EVENING TELEGRAPH

The Sportsman's Arms at the corner of Shear Brow and Pleckgate Road still stands today. Here, just after the First World War, the licensee, James Kay is pictured at the doorway with his children Alice and Richard. Even on the top of Shear Brow, overlooking the mills of the town, the smoke blackened walls are testament to the very poor air quality that the inhabitants had to breathe.

Certain public houses are among the oldest surviving buildings. The Swan Hotel on Astley Gate can still be seen with its distinctive tiled wall decoration that takes the place of the usual projecting pub sign. The other buildings facing it across the streets have all gone. Those on the right were demolished in the 1970s to facilitate the construction of the new shopping centre while the imposing building in the centre, that once housed the Poor Law Guardians, made way for new Social Security offices in the 1990s.

The public house also adapted to the changing requirements of patrons. The 1830 Beer Act encouraged the drinking of beer in an attempt to wean the workers from the pernicious evils associated with the excessive consumption of spirits. It was timely, for the rapid introduction of the power loom in Blackburn, and the consequent growth in population, generated major new demands. By 1862 there were 462 alehouses, beershops and public houses in the borough, or

Leisure does not always have to mean exercise or watching others entertain you. This marvellous picture taken in the 1890s shows two men choosing their own form of relaxation by taking their ease in the sun on Blackburn Boulevard where it adjoins the cathedral grounds. Taken most probably during the midday break, it is amusing to note that, while one reads his newspaper and the other takes a quick nap, it is still a social necessity to wear a hat.
COTTON TOWN PROJECT, BY COURTESY OF BILL OLDHAM AND BLACKBURN WEST ROTARY CLUB

one for every 23 households. Closer regulation of the trade meant that significant numbers of the smaller and more dubious establishments closed later in the century – for example, the number of beershops peaked at 309 in 1868, but the number of public houses continued to grow, from 183 in 1865, to 225 in 1870, 249 in 1879 and 255 in 1892.[13] In the latter year there were also 208 beershops, 106 off-licenses and 35 wine, spirit and sweet licenses in Blackburn, or one licensed premises for every 34 households in the borough.[14] The weakness of Nonconformism in Blackburn meant that anti-alcohol publicity was never as strong in the town as it was in, for example, Preston, the birthplace of teetotalism. Indeed, some key figures among the middle classes, and most prominently the Thwaites family, derived their wealth and status from the drink trade and were thus far from hostile to it. The 1872 Licensing Act

gave magistrates the power to close public houses at 11 p.m. Only two towns in England did not take advantage of this. One was Blackburn, where closing time remained at midnight. The temperance movement was so weak here that members from Preston were sent as 'missionaries' to preach the word of teetotalism in 1831. They were ignored and not until 1891 did Blackburn have a temperance hall, with the opening of the Lees Hall Temperance Mission in St Peter's Street. Even this failed to rouse the movement in the borough. By 1913 the average attendance at meetings there was only 78.

That drink was integral to working-class culture in nineteenth-century Blackburn was generally recognised: 'Strong drink is the secret of its own and Britain's greatness. Be sober and lead a decent and respectable life and your genuine Blackburner will wax red at the mention of your name, and dismiss you as a "–– Dissenter"'.[15] Hal Whitehead, a local folk hero, took his love of drink to extremes. He is reputed to have drunk six and a half gallons of ale at the Britannia tavern in Lord Street in just five hours. In 1891 the *Blackburn Times* noted that the new political working men's clubs were often little more than drinking dens with a billiard table inside and a bowling green outside, while in the area around King Street and Northgate public houses were said to be as common 'as blackberries on a hedge'.[16] In 1896, 26 out of the 38 trade societies in Blackburn held their meetings in public houses. Drink, and especially the public house, remained a central element in working-class popular leisure, as it had been since pre-industrial times. Blackburn's mainly Anglican, Conservative-dominated, middle-class elite made little or no move to limit it, although they made sure that they themselves kept to their own taverns and clubs or drank at home. Most public houses catered solely for working-class custom. Noting the growing success of the theatre in attracting working-class audiences, enterprising landlords began to stage various forms of variety shows

*'[Public houses in Blackburn are] as common as blackberries on a hedge.'*

Middle-class women also saw the scope for recreation grow. Lawn tennis came into vogue in the 1870s, mainly as a social game for the upper classes in which women could take part. The game was seen as one in which no special dress was needed, that required no real exertion so that ladies need not perspire and could take place in private surroundings so that those playing would not be watched by strangers. This photograph shows the courts at Beardwood Cliff on Preston New Road, now Nazareth House old people's home. Originally built by the brewer Daniel Thwaites, it became the home of the Thompson family, who had made their fortune in cotton, in 1876.

in the early 1840s. Some of the larger public houses, in areas such as Shorrock Fold and Darwen Street, had a 'music hall' or 'singing saloon' attached to the premises, offering alcohol with the entertainment which theatres were unable to do. Entertainers were hired from as far away as Manchester for Saturday night shows catering for young working-class men and women, especially those

Major events were also a cause of celebration and enjoyment. Balloons in the sky above Blackburn are not out of the ordinary today but in 1897 a balloon ascent from Market Square to celebrate Queen Victoria's Diamond Jubilee brought thousands of people out onto the streets. It took 1½ hours for it to inflate and then, with one pilot and one passenger it rose to 3,000 feet before landing near Clitheroe.

A group of canal boatmen, dressed in their best, pose outside the Navigation Inn, Mill Hill, around 1909. These men had a reputation as godless ne'er-do-wells. This was partly unjustified because due to the nature of their work it was difficult for them to attend church on a Sunday. Note that even the boy standing on the right is smoking a pipe while also at the back the man second from the left is pouring beer from a large jug in which it had been served.

earning regular wages at the factories. Competition between public houses intensified, as they sought to offer something different. Thus, in 1851 the Star and Garter installed a new self-acting organ complete with mahogany frame and see-through front. Even at the end of the century most public houses relied heavily on music licences to attract custom.[17] All this represented part of a new and independent working-class culture which emerged within the urban environment.

By the beginning of the twentieth century leisure was also available to working-class women, many of whom earned good wages at the mills. They could now attend theatres, visit music halls, go to dances at various halls and assembly rooms, or revel in the new cinemas. More of them visited public houses, though they were only allowed in the lounge areas or snugs, virtually never in the public bar. One middle-class concern which resulted from this change in women's lifestyles was the fear that they might undergo a moral decline. The Medical Officer of Health kept annual statistics concerning illegitimacy rates, as his colleagues did in towns up and down the country. In Blackburn the figures were reassuring: in 1889 4.3 per cent of births in the borough were illegitimate and in 1913 the percentage had not changed. In that year, though, the MOH produced a special report on the subject, which showed that of the 127 illegitimate births 91 were to mothers who worked in the mills (59 weavers, 18 winders, eight ring-spinners and six carders), nine to 'housekeepers', seven to servants, three to charwomen, three to laundresses and fourteen to women classed as 'others'. Of the fathers, 97 were known. Only twenty worked in the mills (17 weavers and three spinners), 11 were carters, and 50 were 'others'. This suggests that most of the relationships had been formed outside the mill ... the new leisure pursuits had a lot to answer for![18]

Middle-class mill-owners and employers frequently involved themselves, in a paternalistic way, with the leisure of their employees. For example, from the 1840s various mill-owners encouraged the formation of brass bands in their works, while others promoted healthy sporting activities. In 1841 Messrs Hornby and Kenworthy built a walled gymnasium at their Brookhouse mills near Whalley Road, providing facilities for football, tennis, skittles and quoits among other pastimes. Treats and trips became more common in the second half of the nineteenth century. One of the first was a dinner for the operatives, given by W. H. Hornby on the occasion of the opening of the gymnasium. The annual mill 'do' was expected and provided. One-off treats might be given, for instance, on the occasion of an owner's son coming of age, a family wedding or even funeral. In 1853, 1,900 operatives sat down to a feast paid for by W. H. Hornby. Mills often had their own social committee to organise trips, socials, football and cricket matches, and sports days. Railway excursion treats from Blackburn began in 1852 and workers thereafter might be taken to the seaside for the day.[19] The motive, on the part of the employers, for the holding, and usually the financing, of such trips, treats or leisure facilities is difficult to determine. The historian Patrick Joyce claimed they were part of a new industrial paternalism, fostered by the town's employers, that grew up in the 1840s based on the image of the old Tory squire: a form of urban *noblesse oblige*.[20] He argued that it was partly a deliberate attempt at social control, to keep the working classes happy with their lot, and to divert them from potentially more dangerous thoughts and paths, but also that a fit, suitably deferential and grateful workforce would be an economic asset. Happy workers worked harder.

In the early 1840s the working classes of Blackburn had to be satisfied with day excursions by rail, though this allowed trips much further afield than had been possible on the Leeds and Liverpool Canal. However, the railway reached Blackpool in 1846, and the resort quickly became the destination of many thousands of holiday-makers from all over Lancashire. Outings by rail in the early 1850s on four day or weekly tickets were mainly the prerogative of the town's middle classes or better-off working classes, but fares fell rapidly and opportunities for cheap trips grew accordingly. By the 1860s the working classes could participate more fully and in the 1870s, as living standards improved and holiday time was extended, and the working classes began to take prolonged visits to the seaside, as the custom of taking weekend and weekly holidays became firmly entrenched in local culture. Between 1880 and 1914 most mills and public houses operated 'going-off clubs', which allowed families to save for their annual holiday outings. In the summer of 1912, no fewer than 126 excursion trains left Blackburn including nine to Morecambe, eleven to Southport and 65 to Blackpool. A deserted Blackburn, not a crowded one, was the symbol of holiday weeks.

*'Be sober and lead a decent life and your genuine Blackburner will wax red at the mention of your name and dismiss you as a "— Dissenter".'*

The middle classes encouraged other aspects of self-improvement, promoting the idea that leisure time could be usefully employed in worthy pursuits. For example, Blackburn had had a subscription library since 1787 when the vicar, the Reverend Thomas Starkie, opened one with 2,000 volumes in the old grammar school in the parish yard. It served the higher echelons of town society, but in 1848 it closed. Several smaller rivals had also been and gone in the meantime. By this time, though, there was support for the idea of a free public library which would be available for the townspeople as a whole. In 1850 parliament passed an Act allowing local authorities to use rate money to finance and run such schemes, and after incorporation in 1852 one of the first projects contemplated by the new council was the provision of a public library. In 1859, as a somewhat interim solution, one was opened in a room in the newly built town hall, and in 1874 the new purpose-built library and museum on the corner of Richmond Terrace and Frances Street (soon to become Library Street and later still Museum Street) was completed. It began with 3,941 reference books and 2,861 volumes of fiction, many donated by the town's wealthy classes or purchased using monetary gifts, and there was also a reading room where 'quality' papers and magazines could be perused.[21]

Other middle-class attempts to mould working-class leisure habits focused on healthy sports. During the 1830s and 1840s the Blackburn Harriers held 'paper chases' or hare-and-hounds races which, they hoped, would set an example for the youth of the town to follow. Two young men would set off with bags full of paper slung over their shoulders, and fifteen minutes later the pack of runners would follow the trail. The 1839 race started on Revidge and went via Mellor, Woodfold Park, Alum Scar, Pleasington and the Yellow Hills, lasting about two hours.[22] From the 1870s a new generation of the middle classes, working in industry or the professions, encouraged team games among

Blackburn's working-class males. Many of the instigators were public-school educated and had returned to Blackburn imbued with the appropriate ethos: 'play up, play up, and play the game'. Team sports were held to mould the character, breed loyalty and team spirit, and encourage self-esteem. Those attributes could, in turn, be harnessed for self-advancement. Sport was also healthy and would counter the apparent physical deterioration among the lower classes which would, it was feared, lead to Britain's decline as a major industrial power and as an empire.

At the schools where the middle-class young men were educated, soccer was the main winter sport. Blackburn had to wait until 1920 before rugby union was introduced and the town has no rugby league tradition, but football was a local tradition that went back to the seventeenth century. By the 1870s the version played in Blackburn was the Harrow game, a cross between soccer and rugby, but in 1875 association football, or soccer, was introduced and Blackburn Rovers FC was born. A doctor and some ex-public and ex-grammar schoolboys formed the club at the St Leger Hotel. They had no ground of their own and played all their matches at the grounds of the opposition. Although at first it was no more than a sporting club for young gentlemen, the popularity of the game grew extremely rapidly and in 1878 Blackburn already had 28 clubs, including Blackburn Christchurch, Livesey United, Blackburn Park Road, Blackburn St George and Blackburn St Mark's. Most of the organisation was the work of former public schoolboys. Cricket was also encouraged. Blackburn already had a team in the 1840s, but in the last quarter of the nineteenth century many new teams sprang up, again with middle-class administrators at the helm. The heavy influence of church was also apparent, as many newly appointed, public school-educated vicars sought to introduce 'muscular Christianity' to their parishioners, on the premise that a healthy body meant a healthy mind and that mind, spirit and body should be developed together. Education would develop the mind, Christianity the spirit, and sport the body. Seen as a means of cultivating a civic spirit and instilling local pride in Blackburn's populace, as well as fostering a healthier working class, this movement succeeded. On its return from winning the FA cup in 1883, the Blackburn Olympic team were carried in a wagonette pulled by six horses, and escorted by brass bands, through the streets of the town cheered by thousands of supporters, before being entertained for the evening by the two members of parliament.

Olympic, though less well known than Rovers, holds a special place in the history of association football. The club, of working-class origins, was formed in 1878 by the amalgamation of two working men's clubs, Black Star and James Street Club, They played behind the Hole i' th' Wall Hotel on Shear Brow after changing inside it. They also played a pivotal role in breaking the public school grip on the sport. Its FA cup success in 1883 was the first such triumph by a team from the industrial working class. Blackburn Rovers had reached the final the year before but their team, other than the odd hired professional, was composed of ex-public or grammar schoolboys and, though representing an industrial town, was essentially a middle-class team which would not have felt out of place playing former pupils of top public schools. The arrival in London of Blackburn Olympic, a team made up of millhands and clerks and with a captain who was a plumber, raised more than a few eyebrows. The opposing team were the Old Etonians, imbued with the ethos that playing the game was jut as important as winning; the venue was the Oval cricket ground; and the bulk of the crowd were ladies and gentlemen. For Blackburn Olympic winning was the whole point of playing. They had a manager and a coach, and took a week off work to prepare for the match. They went to Blackpool to train on the sands and followed a special routine and diet – waking up early, each player drank a glass of port wine with two raw eggs, followed by a training session on the beach, a breakfast of porridge and haddock, and dinner of mutton and vegetables. Tea was porridge washed down with a pint of milk. Finally, each player consumed six oysters for supper. Two days before the match the team checked into a London hotel to acclimatise themselves, as every visiting team has done since.

*'Hot blooded Lancastrians, sharp of tongue, rough and ready, of uncouth garb and speech.'*

The social background of the spectators was also different. Blackburn Olympic took about one thousand supporters, on special excursion trains. Though far outnumbered in the crowd of twelve thousand, the noise they made exceeded that of the opposition supporters and their demeanour came as a shock to the respectable people supporting the Old Etonians. A London paper reported that 'London witnessed an invasion of Northern barbarians on Saturday – hot blooded Lancastrians, sharp of tongue, rough and ready, of uncouth garb and speech. A tribe of Sudanese Arabs let loose in the Strand would not excite more amusement and curiosity ... Strange oaths fell upon the Southern ears and curious words, curious but expressive, filled the air.'[23] By the end of ninety minutes the score was 1–1. Extra time was not obligatory and a replay could have been agreed, especially since Old Etonians were down to ten men through injury and substitutes were not allowed. Sam Warburton, the Olympic captain, requested to play extra time, a request that the Old Etonian captain, due to his code of gentlemanly manners, felt obliged to accede. The eleven fit men of Blackburn Olympic went on to win 2–1. As the cup was presented one slightly disappointed Blackburn supporter was heard to say that it was a bit small and resembled a kettle. Sam Warburton replied that whatever it looked like, it would be welcome in Blackburn and would not be returning to London. His words were prophetic, for in the twelve years between this match and the time it was stolen at Aston Villa, no club from the south won the F.A Cup. More important was that the grip of the public school sides had been forever broken, and association football from this moment became ever more closely linked to the culture of the working classes.

Just as the town's middle class encouraged soccer and cricket, they also approved of pastimes as whippet racing and crown green bowling, regarding them as respectable sports. But these sports were different from soccer and cricket, for they were generated from within existing working-class culture and were expressions of separateness and independence. Among the reasons why Blackburn's middle class encouraged such sports as these, as well as the team games and the working men's clubs, was because their committees, treasurerships, secretaryships and other posts produced a hierarchical administrative structure which could be climbed and which allowed 'betterment'. This offered men and their families social pre-eminence and respectability. Those pastimes may have been part of an independent working-class culture but the structure of that culture was acceptable to the town's middle class, because it had a civilising influence. The encouragement of 'respectable' sports, and the evangelical spirit of healthy Christianity, could potentially have lowered class barriers, but – despite paternalism – the opposite occurred. In the second half of the nineteenth century class divisions were intensified, sometimes deliberately. For example, there were musical performances which were exclusively for the middle classes. Serious music for the newly moneyed citizens was provided at the Angel Inn on King Street in 1837, and a Gentlemen's Glee Club was founded at the King's Arms in Northgate in 1849. A Handel Society flourished from 1752 to 1865. The performance of 'Joshua' in 1851 was to an audience paying the enormous sum of 7s. 6d. (37.5p) a ticket.[24] Dotted around the town were several halls and assembly rooms in which dances and banquets were held. At the beginning of the nineteenth century, for example, such facilities were offered by 'The Hotel' at 33 King Street (until 1815, Sudell Street). Here the chandeliered assembly rooms were opened with a major ball in June 1804 to celebrate the birthday of George III. Another grand banquet was held there to

When it was photographed in the 1960s, this fine Georgian building in King Street was derelict. Once known as The Hotel, and built in 1804, within a few years of its opening it had become established as one of the town's chief coaching inns. It contained seven eating rooms, twenty-five bedrooms, newspaper and billiard rooms and had stabling for twenty horses. For many years it was the social hub for the town's elite, with many balls being held in the main assembly room there.
COTTON TOWN PROJECT

celebrate the victory at Waterloo in 1815. In these rooms, during the first half of the nineteenth century, the great and good of the town would dine and dance the night away while their carriages awaited.

The elite also had exclusive clubs. The Union Club was founded in 1849 at a meeting in 'The Hotel' in King Street, as a non-political and non-sectarian institution for the upper middle classes. After using three rented rooms in Fleming Square the club moved to larger rented accommodation in Church Street, originally built for the cotton master Henry Sudell. In 1922 the Union Club purchased its own property at 45 Preston New Road. With a billiard room in the basement, two lounges and a bar on the ground floor, a dining room above and the steward's flat at the top of the house, it was still proudly catering for the elite when it celebrated its centenary in 1959.[25] Two overtly political clubs followed in 1864: the Reform Club, for gentlemen of Liberal politics, was in Victoria Street near the new market place, and the Conservative Club was in King William Street. In addition there was the County Club in New Market Street. For Conservative and Liberal supporters of a lower social class new working men's clubs were opened in the last quarter of the century. They often had crown bowling greens, but the leading families kept to their own Blackburn Subscription Bowling Club. In the early eighteenth century this was at the foot of Cicely Hole, but in 1844 the new railway company wanted the land for the station and until the 1860s the club was based close to the old grammar school next to St Peter's church, before finally moving to its present site on Shear Bank Road. Most of Blackburn's gentry belonged to it – the Feildens, Sudells, Cardwells, Hornbys, Thwaites, Osbaldestons, Liveseys, Pilkingtons, Walmsleys and Birleys – and, as late as 1875, membership was strictly limited to a maximum of 100 gentlemen.

Introducing team sport to the masses was one thing; but playing with them or against them was another matter. The superior ranks of society formed their own teams and played their own kind, as in cricket, or resorted to exclusive sports such as golf, hockey or lawn tennis. Surrounded by high subscriptions and membership quotas, middle-class sportsmen avoided working-class intrusion. The East Lancashire Cricket Club, the third in Blackburn, was founded in 1863 on the Alexandra Meadows by a group of officers from the local Volunteer Force. Solidly middle-class and based around a nucleus of the Hornby family, it maintained its exclusive membership through ballot and blackballing. The club played matches all over Lancashire but avoided playing the two other local clubs because they had a rather questionable social mix. In 1868, however, the East Lancashire CC did consent to play the touring Australian Aboriginal team.[26] Examples of the retreat to exclusivity can be seen in local golf and hockey clubs. Blackburn Golf Club was founded in 1894, soon after the clubs at Pleasington and Wilpshire. It was laid out on rented land on Revidge Heights, and limited membership to 70, each paying an annual subscription of two guineas. The lower orders were kept at bay: A. Greenwood, a prominent cotton manufacturer, first club captain and chief driving force behind the founding of the club, saw to that.[27] In 1904 Herbert Troop, a young brewer, started Blackburn Hockey Club (originally called Brownhill Hockey Club) on a field behind the Hare and Hounds at Lammack. The idea originated during a discussion with a group of young middle-class friends who also played a little soccer. They all 'felt the urge to get out of the commonplace into a more distinctive game'. The first two vice-captains exemplified the successful social level of the club: Alfred Livesey was the head of the firm of loom makers of that name, and Miss C. Bailey was daughter of the borough treasurer.[28]

This rescued chamber pot, from the Old Bull Hotel, is a reminder of how stays in even the best of hotels have changed: residents who did not wish to walk down corridors in the middle of the night to the shared lavatories could use such a pot that was kept under the bed. In the morning the chambermaid would have the disagreeable task of emptying it.
COTTON TOWN PROJECT,

Soccer was abandoned by the middle classes as the working classes took over as players and spectators. The game became imbued with working-class values and was incorporated into a separate popular culture that became ever more socially distinct from middle-class recreational habits. Some 8,000 people watched the joint sports day held by Blackburn's football and cricket clubs in 1875 and 10,000 watched Blackburn Rovers play Darwen in 1880. Crowd violence helped to keep the middle classes away from the game. The 1880 match against Darwen was abandoned when the crowd, incensed at alleged foul play,

Built in 1907 the Bull's Head Hotel, on the edge of the town near the Wilpshire boundary, catered for a slightly upmarket clientele. The landlord and his staff can be seen proudly posing at the entrance of the newly built building. With stables at the rear of the premises traps and wagonettes could be hired for the day for a leisurely ride into the Ribble valley.
COTTON TOWN PROJECT, © LANCASHIRE EVENING TELEGRAPH

J.W. PARKER
BULLS HEAD
WILPSHIRE

TRAPS.
AND

invaded the pitch. Ten years later, during the same fixture, the crowd not only invaded the pitch but also destroyed the goalposts and ransacked the grandstand. The ex-public schoolboys had apparently omitted to teach the working classes how to be good losers. The professionalisation of soccer has often been cited as one reason for the middle-class exodus from the game. Yet was there really a separation? What had started out as a way of bringing healthy sport to the masses and inculcating team spirit soon became big business, with fast-increasing gate receipts as rising standards of living allowed workers to spend more of their income on leisure activities. Prestige and a high public profile could be gained from a connection with a successful football club. What middle-class entrepreneur would turn his back on that? Is it any wonder that the north of England, the cradle of capitalism, was also the cradle of professional soccer, the greatest of spectator sports? Blackburn took its part in that development.

In 1884, after the FA refused to sanction professionalism, a meeting of Lancashire clubs in Blackburn exerted powerful pressure by founding a short-lived rival, the British Football Association. Blackburn Rovers was also the first club to lure Scottish footballers south of the border, with the offer of a team place and a well-paid supplementary job. Blackburn was at the forefront of the movement which forced the FA to accept professionalism, and prominent among the instigators were the town's industrial and professional middle classes. As one commentator wrote, 'The exalted position attained by the Rovers F.C. in sporting circles is due not only to the players who have distinguished themselves on the field but to the fine example set by the gentlemen who have guided its destinies.'[29] In 1895 these gentlemen included the two sitting MPs, W. Coddington and W. H. Hornby; John Rutherford JP, and E. S. Morley MD JP.[30] The town's middle classes were not against professionalism *per se*: the exclusive East Lancashire Cricket Club, from the start, employed two professionals, one lured from Blackburn Cricket Club and the other from Yorkshire.[31] Winning was important to Blackburn's middle classes. The commercialisation of sport would hardly have been possible without a major improvement in communications. Trams at home football and cricket matches and railways offering cheap excursion tickets for away matches not only allowed teams to travel but also made the outings possible for armies of spectators. Saturday afternoon sport gained in popularity up to 1914, and attendances at Blackburn Rovers home matches by this date were almost always in five figures. Crown green bowling also attracted large crowds, with competitions such as the Talbot from 1873 and the Waterloo from 1907 bringing growing numbers of entries and supporters.

Any discussion of Blackburn's cultural history would be incomplete if it did not mention the Blackburn poets. This was not an oral tradition but a written one – nearly fifty poets born before 1880 had their poems published, the earliest being born at the close of the eighteenth century but most in the 1840s and 1850s. It was thus an urban phenomenon, one which had its heyday in the last quarter of the nineteenth century. Most were from the working classes and many were power loom workers. Theirs was a 'popular' culture in the truest sense: there was even a poets' corner near Blakey Moor where public recitations took place.[32] The movement had largely died away by 1914, although John Baron, the son of a card grinder and himself a shop floor worker in local

As the façade of Belper Street Baths shows the Corporation built these facilities in 1905. Sexual decorum was still important in the Edwardian years as the separate entrances for ladies and gentlemen indicate. Though relatively recently built when this photograph was taken, it is noticeable how the stonework already shows discoloration through ingrained soot.

This small beerhouse on the corner of Nab Lane and Bradshaw Street, known as Poets Corner, played an important part in the cultural history of the town in the mid nineteenth century. William Billington, Blackburn's greatest lyric poet and author, who died in 1884 at the age of 57, served up the drink and among his customers were the many famous working-class dialect poets that the town produced. At his death a tombstone bearing his portrait was erected by public subscription in Blackburn Cemetery.
COTTON TOWN PROJECT

engineering firms, had one poem a week published in the local newspaper for 33 years until his death in 1922. Over 1,000 poems were published in this way and his entire output numbered over 4,000. This legacy is a reminder that cultural patterns can be local, rather than being part of regional or national trends.

Premiership football has been played at Ewood since 1992, a year after local steel entrepreneur Jack Walker (1929–2000) invested heavily in his local club. Under manager Kenny Dalglish the club won the Premiership in 1995. This photograph shows the Jack Walker stand.
PHOTOGRAPH: CARNEGIE

Leisure in early twentieth century urban Blackburn was certainly different from that experienced in earlier rural times, but it was not entirely distinct and separate. Traditional festivals, fairs, markets, games and sports all helped to mould the leisure patterns and habits of urban Blackburn. Admittedly completely fresh pursuits, such as the music hall and professional soccer, grew up in this new environment, and encouragement and ideas also came from the new middle classes. Their motives were mixed and changed over time – the need for a disciplined workforce merged with the sense of paternalism and the desire for grateful loyal employees. These motives in turn intermingled with attempts to produce a healthier working class imbued with team spirit. By 1914, though, leisure was more class-based than it had been in pre-industrial society. A distinctive urban working-class culture had emerged, much of it originating among the workers themselves.

# CHAPTER EIGHT

# 'Reforming manners and morals': religion, 1750–1914

S INCE SAXON TIMES St Mary's church has stood at the heart of Blackburn, and for centuries it was sufficient to cater for the religious needs of the great majority of the surrounding community. After the Reformation it was of course no longer controlled by the Catholics but by the Church of England, and from the middle of the seventeenth century the small but growing number of Nonconformists were also excluded. But Catholicism was relatively weak here, compared with other parts of Lancashire, and – unlike the south-east of the county – the same could also be said for Nonconformism. The circumstances changed radically, however, with the rapid population growth of

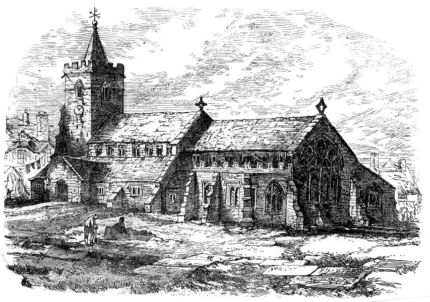

This engraving is of the parish church of St Mary in one of its many reincarnations over the centuries before it was rebuilt in 1819. The grave-diggers are preparing for a burial, but by the mid nineteenth century the churchyard was full and becoming a health hazard. In 1857 Blackburn opened a purpose-built cemetery off Whalley New Road. Compare the structure shown here with that depicted on Lang's map of 1759 (page 96).

the later eighteenth century. Urbanisation and industrialisation not only meant that there was a pressing need for new places of worship, but also changed the religious composition of the population. There were growing numbers of Catholics, especially from the mid-1840s onwards, and Nonconformity also grew quickly from the 1780s. The virtual monopoly of the Church of England was threatened, and during the nineteenth century there was a hard fought struggle between the denominations for the souls of the population. That struggle could be seen in attempts to increase the size of their respective congregations, in the effect that it had on the working and leisure hours of the community, and in the educational and political arenas.

Throughout the diocese of Chester the revival of the Church of England was late in starting, and Blackburn's experience was very typical of that of most major industrial towns in the North West. Not until the 1820s did the Church really wake up to the problems of competition for men's souls, and of the grave lack of space for worship in places which were now major centres but only recently had been small towns with a single church. In Blackburn the Reverend John William Whittaker, who became vicar in 1822, began the revival, although it is fair to point out that two churches, St John's in 1789 and St Peter's in 1820, had already helped to supplement the provision offered by St Mary's. In 1821 the population of the town was 21,940, so even with the two recent additions each church ministered to an average of over 7,000 inhabitants. By 1831 St Paul's had been added but the ratio had hardly altered, since the population had risen to over 27,000. In the late 1830s Whittaker planned

Opposite the old grammar school in Freckleton Street can be seen St Peter's churchyard. It was the practice here to set the memorial stones flat over the graves, just as had been done for centuries inside churches for parishioners of importance. The graveyard can still be seen, though the church was partially demolished in 1976, leaving just the tower.

COTTON TOWN PROJECT

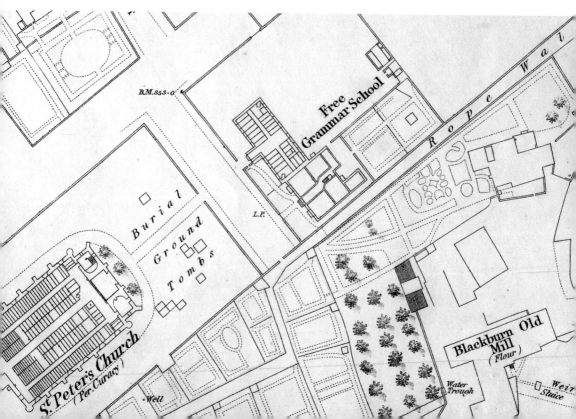

However, they certainly saw religion as an important and influential element in holding together the fabric of society. We have seen how religion and elementary education, including Sunday schools, were greatly intertwined in Blackburn and how deeply employers involved themselves in this aspect of the community. When all teachers and helpers are taken into account, an estimated 21,000 out of a population of 80,000 in 1875 had Sunday school connections. Employers encouraged this, and there is some truth in the claim that mill salesmen, managers and overlookers owed their jobs as much to their diligence in attending church and chapel and being involved in Sunday schools, as to their application to their work.[4] An important section of the working classes saw church attendance and participating in church or chapel activities as a vehicle for attaining respectability. Employers saw religion as having a civilising influence on their workforces, and that they naturally encouraged. Religion was seen as a tool of social control, or a means of 'reforming the manners and morals of the lower orders'.[5] Christian doctrine, particularly in the Church of England, upheld the pattern of society and the belief that everyone had their place. It inculcated respect for rank and property and encouraged everyone to be content with their lot. The employers regarded church attendance by their workers as being so important that in 1834 Tuesday was made the pay day, on the premise that if pay day was Saturday the combination of drunkenness and hangovers resulted, among the workers, in low attendance at Sunday worship. This change merely led to absenteeism and low productivity on Wednesdays so it was soon ended. Production came before church attendance in order of priority.

The churches did their best to improve the social habits of the working classes. At St Philip's there was a bowling green and tennis courts. Church institutes offered a wide variety of leisure pursuits. St Luke's, in Dickinson Street had a billiard hall and reading and refreshment rooms. Rambles, field days and picnics were organised. At St Matthew's the clubs and societies included a burial society, temperance society, book club, savings and holiday clubs, cricket and football teams, cookery and dressmaking classes and a scripture union. Not all attempts were successful and it was claimed in the 1860s that attempts to make church institutes into social and educational centres for the working classes had failed. From that point on some targeted middle-class youths.[6] Organised religion reflected the divisions of social class, especially in the Church of England. Those employers who helped to build churches near their mills did not feel that they had constantly to attend them, and many worshipped only occasionally at 'their' church, more frequently at the church near their home. Leading Tory employers in the early part of the nineteenth century used St John's in the centre of the town, where the major families had family vaults. As the middle-class suburbs to the north-west grew, the most important Tory employers moved to new houses and new churches, notably St James's at the top of Shear Brow and St Silas' on Preston New Road. For the middling Tory employers St Peter's and St Paul's were popular. Even Congregationalist employers had their preferences. The most prosperous tended to use the Old Chapel Street and James Street chapels. Inside the churches more dividing lines were seen. Many pews were rented, some purchased. At All Saints only half the 860 seats were free. The very poor were even discouraged from attending at all: 'For those who are too poorly clad to come to church', a cottage in Bolton Road at first sufficed, and after 1888 a mission room at the local ragged school.[7] Holy Trinity church had most of its free sittings in the gallery, perhaps in the belief that smells tend to

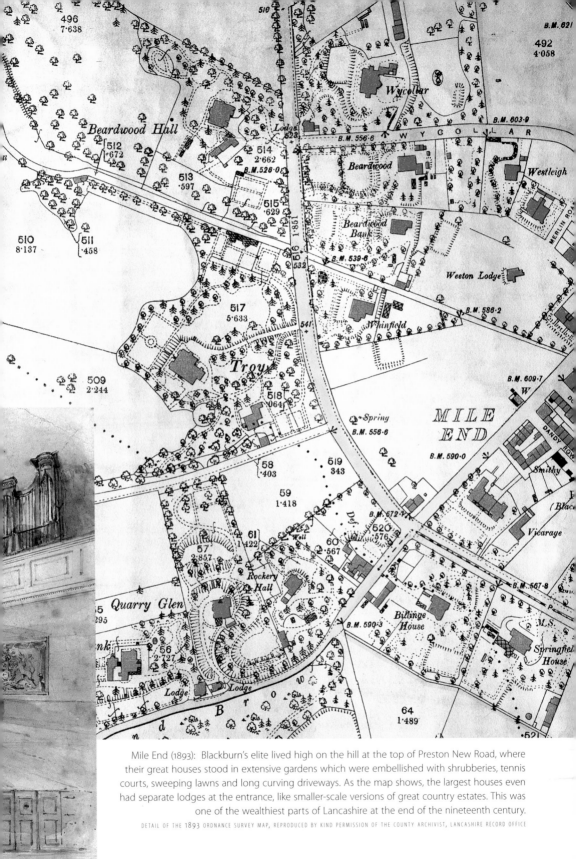

Mile End (1893): Blackburn's elite lived high on the hill at the top of Preston New Road, where their great houses stood in extensive gardens which were embellished with shrubberies, tennis courts, sweeping lawns and long curving driveways. As the map shows, the largest houses even had separate lodges at the entrance, like smaller-scale versions of great country estates. This was one of the wealthiest parts of Lancashire at the end of the nineteenth century.

DETAIL OF THE 1893 ORDNANCE SURVEY MAP, REPRODUCED BY KIND PERMISSION OF THE COUNTY ARCHIVIST, LANCASHIRE RECORD OFFICE

rise rather than descend. St Peter's had 700 rented pews while at Christchurch fewer than half of the seats were free. The vicar defended this by claiming that 'our operatives are prepared to pay rather than be penned up in "free seats" as if paupers.'[8]

The best example of the careful segregation of congregations was at James Street Congregationalist church, as late as the Edwardian period. To rent the front pews cost £10 a year, and here could be found the mill-owning families such as the Birtwistles and the Dugdales. Behind them, paying slightly less, came the mill managers, travellers and salesmen. Further back still, at £3 per annum per seat, sat the overlookers, clothlookers and local shopkeepers. In the rented pews at the rear, which cost only 8s. (40p) a year, came the middle-class widows. The working classes, mainly skilled men and their families, sat at the back of the church in the free seats.[9] Such divisions were long-lasting and were the cause of resentment among many of the lower orders. There was trouble over pew payments in 1839, during the early Chartist period, when a large number of people marched to a service at the parish church, sat in the reserved pews and refused to move. They asked the vicar to give a sermon based on the text 'Go to now ye rich, weep and howl for the miseries that are coming to you'. It had no effect. The meek failed to inherit, and rented pews

The church of St Mary, being the parish church of the town, was the focal point of the Church of England in Blackburn. The success of its vicars in holding at bay the encroachment of Nonconformism and Catholicism ensured that Blackburn remained a predominantly Anglican town.

Around 1900 there had, for a number of years, been a worry that church attendance among the working classes had been falling. Here we see the Luther Protestant Van taking the message direct to the people in the Salford area of town in the form of preaching the word and the distribution of literature.

COTTON TOWN PROJECT

persisted into the twentieth century. Even in 1939 only a handful of churches had totally free seating, and in most between 30 per cent and 50 per cent of the pews were still rented.[10] At St Silas's church the pew rental system ended as recently as 1982.[11]

Perhaps this was one reason why so many of the working classes were not churchgoers, even though most had attended church schools or Sunday schools or both. When the Reverend Whittaker came to Blackburn in 1822, church attendance was at a very low ebb. St Mary's was being rebuilt, St John's was usually barely one-third full, and the newly built St Peter's saw only an average of fifty worshippers on a Sunday. Church attendance had picked up by the time of the religious census in 1851. Because of the way the census was carried out it is difficult to extract accurate figures, but it reveals that in Blackburn some 18,240 attendances at church or chapel services were recorded that day out of a total population of 46,536 that is, approximately 30 per cent of those available to attend. How many were the same people attending more than one service is not known. The percentage varied between the denominations: among Anglicans, attendance was about 13 per cent of the potential (though it is claimed that Anglican figures were seriously underestimated here); among Methodists 5 per cent; and among Catholics a derisory 3.1 per cent. The figures can also be compared with other Lancashire towns: Blackburn, in its total attendance, was eleventh among the top fifteen towns in Lancashire and Cheshire (well below Warrington, with 46 per cent attendance, and Wigan, with 40 per cent, but well above Preston, with only 20 per cent). Although the census does not reveal this, it is fair to suppose that attendance rates were much better among the middle classes than the lower classes, and the very low figure for Roman

in the context of the general state of health in the town, that 18 per cent of Blackburn men were deemed to be unfit to serve.[3] Of those that did go, four won the Victoria Cross.

The war affected the local economy. As the men patriotically went off to serve King and Country, the women left behind found themselves more involved in industry and running essential services. Here, as in all the cotton towns, women had always worked in industry, but the wartime economy required them to take heavy labouring jobs, or other work that had hitherto been a male preserve. Thus, they were employed on the town's trams for the first time, while 300 women served with the borough police in the Women's Police Aid Detachment.[4] The greater involvement of women in arduous work, and the dearth of young men in the town, is perhaps reflected in the rate of illegitimate births, which in 1915 was 3.7 per cent, compared to the pre-war average of 4.4 per cent. The rate did creep up later, and in 1919, when the surviving young men returned home, it reached 6 per cent, though it almost immediately fell back to the pre-war level. Life on the Home Front during the Great War became progressively harder. The town centre grew dark as restrictions were placed on lighting. Gas-lamps were masked and illuminated shop windows and advertisements were banned, partly because of fear of air attack but also to save fuel. What were locally known as 'Curfew Orders' meant that public entertainment ended at 10.30 p.m. and no food could be served after 9.30 p.m. in hotels, restaurants or shops. Public clocks were not allowed to chime after dark.[5] Drinking was discouraged. Licensing hours were cut, the alcoholic strength of beer reduced, taxes increased, and even buying a round or 'treating' was banned. Of course,

The Athletes Volunteer Force was slowly equipped with both uniforms and arms by self-finance and public subscription. This explains why some have uniforms and others do not. This means that one gentleman has to continue to wear his flat cap with his newly purchased tunic. Another can be seen wearing a black armband to signify that a family member, probably his son, had already given his life for his country.

these measures were universal, not limited to Blackburn, because citizens were expected to get a good night's sleep in order to put their full energies into producing goods for the war effort.

There was full employment, because of the war effort and the loss of manpower as volunteers and from 1916 conscripts were taken out of industry. Wages rose rapidly in real terms, food became dearer as imports declined – a combination of the loss of merchant vessels because of enemy action and the use of cargo space for military materials meant that supplies were ever more constricted and in 1917 rationing was introduced. The local Food Control Committee set up headquarters in Richmond Terrace in September 1917 and oversaw the organisation of the system, issuing 112,000 ration cards.[6] The first article to be rationed was sugar, but many other foodstuffs followed, and schemes were set up to ensure that special groups such as children and invalids could obtain extra milk. The committee also pressed, though unsuccessfully, for extra meat rations to be given to women weavers on the grounds that this would benefit the nation by encouraging greater output. With official permission, however, they helped to organize local jam making using wild fruit. The first annual report of the committee commented that local people had greeted rationing with stoicism, realizing that it was for the greater good and happily accepting it since it applied

When the men went off to war in 1914 women had to take over many of their jobs. Here two women tram-workers are pictured in their new uniforms on the Cherry Tree route. Though many enjoyed such new experiences once the men returned most had to return to the home or to jobs deemed more suitable for women. Not one woman retained her job on Blackburn's trams when the war ended.
J. HALSALL COLLECTION

Calderstones Hospital, just outside Blackburn in the Ribble Valley, was built as an asylum for the mentally ill. Before it could be opened the First World War broke out and it was pressed into service as Queen Mary's Military Hospital, with 2,110 beds. In all more than 57,000 wounded troops were treated here. In this photograph patients are about to watch the weekly cinema show held on Saturdays.
COTTON TOWN PROJECT

A short branch line was built from the Blackburn–Clitheroe railway just north of Whalley to take trains carrying the wounded back from the trenches direct to Calderstones Hospital. It could take just twenty-four hours to transport from them from France. Many would arrive with Flanders mud still on their uniforms.

to all equally.[7] Whether this was true or just an attempt to keep up wartime morale is open to question.

Across Britain, the end of the war brought not only a wave of immense relief and euphoria, heavily tinged with regret and grieving for the unparalleled loss of life, but also a heady sense that the world could now be a better place and that changes to benefit society as a whole might be set in motion. News of the imminent signing of the armistice was first received at the offices of the *Blackburn Times* at 10.35 a.m. on Monday 11 November 1918. The Union Jack was immediately hoisted and a notice placed in the front window of the building. The word quickly spread round the town. Flags and bunting, stored away since the visit of the king and queen in 1913, made their appearance. Mill buzzers began to blow and church bells were rung. By common consent all work ended at lunchtime. Thousands thronged the streets centring on King William Street. The cheering of the crowds was punctuated by the sound of fireworks and in a few places bonfires were lit and effigies of the kaiser were burnt. The rejoicing lasted several days: the Employers Federation decided to close down all mills until breakfast on Wednesday 13 November and the mayor, himself a mill-owner, not only allowed his 2,000 workers to remain on holiday until Thursday but also promised them a bonus of £1 each. In addition, all schools in the borough were closed for the week.[8] Amid the rejoicing the townspeople also looked forward to the return of loved ones and to a better life than the one they had led before the war. Aspirations had grown and the prime minister had promised to build 'a land fit for heroes'. But before British people, and those of other war-ravaged European countries, could move into that optimistically imagined golden age, fate had a tragic trick to play. From the mid-autumn of

1918, through to the end of 1919, the influenza pandemic, or 'Spanish flu' as it was known in Britain, raged, killing more people worldwide than had died in the fighting during four years of war. A key reason for the high death toll was the weakened physical condition of people after years of conflict and privation. The epidemic reached Blackburn in October 1918 and lasted throughout the winter. So many fell ill in the town that the Medical Officer of Health took out a front-page advertisement in the local paper advising the people what to do. They were told to keep away from crowds if at all possible, and not to visit places of entertainment or use trams. Sufferers were to be isolated at home, the handkerchiefs used for coughs or sneezes were to be boiled, and spittoons and other receptacles disinfected. The advice ended with the stark warning that this illness killed.[9] The average annual death rate in Blackburn from influenza in the first years of the twentieth century was around 22. In 1918 it rose to 338, virtually all in the last three months. Another 187 died in the first three months of 1919.[10] These are almost certainly not the true figures, for many victims weakened by catching influenza succumbed to other illnesses such as

COUNTY BOROUGH OF BLACKBURN — HEALTH DEPT —

pneumonia. Death rates from those diseases and conditions also rose dramatically during that winter. The tragedy was not confined to those in Blackburn, for soldiers and nurses serving in France and elsewhere overseas also fell victim. The weekly roll of honour published in the *Blackburn Times* began to list those who had died not only on active service but from influenza. Men and women who had survived the horrors of the war now died of illness while dreaming of their return.

The epidemic, and the trauma which it represented, were followed by what seemed at first to be not just a recovery in the town's economy, but a spectacular demonstration of its resilience and strength. Here, as in other Lancashire cotton towns, the wartime shortfalls and lack of investment were followed by reconstruction. Cotton firms borrowed heavily to rebuild, modernise and re-equip, and output rose dramatically during 1919 and 1920. In Lancashire as a whole the average dividends paid by cotton firms rose from 7.50 per cent in 1917 to 21.25 per cent in 1919 and an astonishing 40.21 per cent in 1920. In 1921 Blackburn had 36,700 employees working in its textile industries, more than any other Lancashire town, and they accounted for 51.6 per cent of the entire labour force (for comparison, the figure in Burnley was 52.2 per cent and in Nelson 69.2 per cent, but for places such as Oldham, Bolton and Preston the percentages were substantially lower). But in retrospect it is clear that the postwar boom was an artificial one, made up largely of short-term measures to return cotton to a viable footing but not based on evidence of demand or market expansion. In fact, the industry had quite the opposite problem, for the war had enforced a dramatic change in global textile markets and trading patterns. Cut off from supplies of cotton cloth from Lancashire, places such as Japan, India and the United States, all of which had fast-growing cotton industries even before the war, had taken the opportunity further to develop domestic output, and no longer needed Lancashire cloth. Lancashire was totally unprepared for what happened during the next fifteen years. For example, exports of cotton textiles to the USA fell from 163 million yards in 1924 to 11 million in 1931. Exports to Brazil over the same period fell from 63.5 million yards to three million. But it was the dramatic fall in the export of the plain grey cloth to India, a fabric in which Blackburn mills specialised, that hurt this town the most. In 1913 India had imported 3,000 million yards of cotton cloth, but throughout the interwar period purchases declined rapidly and by 1936 had fallen below 500 million yards. The Indian cotton industry produced 1,105 million yards of cloth in 1913: in 1931 the output was 2,561 million yards and growing fast. Ironically, Indian cotton mills were helped by the purchase of second-hand looms from Lancashire mills as they closed down, dozens each year. In addition, the Blackburn Technical College, with its world-wide reputation for high-quality textile courses, trained overseas students from competitor countries, an irony noted by J.B. Priestley when he visited the town in 1933:

*'There began to appear, at places like Blackburn's Technical College ... certain quiet, industrious, smiling young men from the East, most anxious to learn all that Lancashire could teach them about the processes of calico manufacture.'*

J.B. PRIESTLEY, 1934

Blackburn College was famed for its training programmes for the weaving industry. Students came from far and wide, including Asia and South America, to be trained on the latest machinery and to learn the latest techniques. Sadly for the Blackburn textile industry, many of the foreign students returned home to help develop local industries and help accelerate the demise of the cotton industry in the town. The weaving sheds have now been converted into the main entrance and student service area of the College.

COTTON TOWN PROJECT

'There began to appear, at places like Blackburn's Technical college ... certain quiet, industrious, smiling young men from the East, most anxious to learn all that Lancashire could teach them about the processes of calico manufacture. They sat through their courses, missing nothing, smiled at their instructors for the last time and disappeared into the blue. A little later, as a result of this ... there also disappeared into the blue a good deal of Lancashire's trade with the East.'[11] Blackburn helped to accelerate her own decline.

Imported cotton cloth became a factor in Indian nationalist politics when, in 1921, Mahatma Gandhi called for it to be boycotted in favour of Indian hand-woven cloth. Nine years later, in 1930, the Congress Party espoused the same policy. Other factors also helped to increase Blackburn's woes. The worldwide fall in the price of primary products hit India's earnings and reduced the local market, while an unstable rate of exchange was also damaging. In April 1919 one rupee equalled 1*s*. 6*d*. (7.5p); by February 1920 it was 2*s*. 10*d*. (14p); by

*'Compared to the poverty and pauperism of the starving millions of India, the poverty of Lancashire dwindles into insignificance.'*
M.K. GANDHI, 1931

March 1921 it was back to 1*s*. 3*d*. (6p). The raising of tariff barriers on imports into India also hurt: in March 1921 they were increased 3.5 per cent to 11 per cent; in 1930 to 15 per cent; in March 1931 to 20 per cent; and in October of the same year to 25 per cent. This further protected and encouraged the growth of the domestic Indian cotton industry. When Gandhi was in Britain for political talks in 1931 he visited the Blackburn area. After being invited to see, first-hand, the effect on the local mills of the loss of the Indian market, he explained that, 'the poverty I have seen distresses me but compared to the poverty and pauperism of the starving millions of India, the poverty of Lancashire dwindles into insignificance.'[12] He had a valid point, but it was certainly lost on Blackburn's unemployed.

But what ensured the terminal collapse of Lancashire's, and Blackburn's, cotton industry, was the rise of the industry in Japan. In 1913 virtually all

Many ordinary Blackburn people rather took the Indian nationalist politician Mohandas Karamchand (Mahatma) Gandhi to heart when he visited the area and met them in 1931. The authorities had hoped that a first-hand look at the poverty caused by the local decline of cotton production, to a great extent brought about by the loss of the Indian market, would move him. It did, but not enough to help Blackburn.

India's cotton cloth imports came from Lancashire and most from Blackburn. By 1930 only 50 per cent were from Lancashire, the other 50 per cent being almost all from Japan. With a modern industry using the latest automatic looms, benefiting from an abundant supply of cheap labour, and a workforce prepared to work longer hours than their Lancashire counterparts, the Japanese could undercut the prices of cloth by between 12.5 per cent and 60 per cent. This not only allowed her manufacturers to take over the Indian trade, but by 1930 even meant that Japan was beginning to infiltrate Britain's domestic market.[13] Producers in Lancashire and Blackburn were saddled with equipment which was increasingly outdated but too expensive to replace and, some have argued, they were also slow to recognise the growing importance, and potential, of artificial fibres.

In 1918 there were about 150 mills in Blackburn, with 90,000 working looms. As the postwar boom came to an abrupt halt in the winter of 1920–1921, contraction began. Some 25,000 looms had already been stopped by October 1921, by Christmas 1921 40,000, and by February 1922 48,000. Though a slight recovery then took place, one-third of all looms in the town still lay idle in April 1923.[14] The industry never recovered. Between 1919 and May 1936, 79 mills had closed down and 44 of those were rendered forever inoperative as the machinery had been sold off or dismantled. In Blackburn alone, some 26,116 looms had been scrapped, but that was still not enough. Many of the rest were idle or working

Blackburn was a town of chimneys belching out smoke from the mills and the hearths of hundreds of terraced houses. With Blackburn in the bottom of a valley, much of the pollution failed to escape and the result was an almost constant smoke haze or smog. Many in the town suffered chest problems and life expectancy was made even shorter. The clean air acts of the 1950s finally brought an improvement to the town's atmosphere.

COTTON TOWN PROJECT, © LANCASHIRE EVENING TELEGRAPH

'Knocker Ups' such as this man were a common early morning sight throughout the terraced streets of Blackburn up until the mid twentieth century. They rattled the upstairs windows with their poles to awaken the occupants. They were the forerunners of alarm clocks and alarm radios and ensured that workers were woken to dress, have breakfast and get to work on time.

ART·HAVIN·NOAN·THIS MORNIN,'SLEEPY·YED

short-time and no capital was available to invest in modern machinery.[15] By 1939 the town's once-mighty weaving industry had been severely reduced and its small spinning base was almost totally eliminated.

If Blackburn and other towns in mid-Lancashire were to survive then their economic structure had to change, but the reshaping of the local economy and the potential for attracting new employment were limited by the fact that the district was not initially designated a development area under the Special Areas Act of 1934. This meant that it was not eligible for financial help in attracting new industry, something that was inexplicable to local people since its levels of unemployment were comparable to those in the four areas designated: South Wales, West Cumberland, Durham and Tyneside and South West Scotland. The average unemployment rates for those regions in 1931 were 39, 36.8, 34.4 and 33.6 per cent respectively. These figures may be compared with the 40.1 per cent unemployment in the Lancashire weaving district as a whole. By the middle of first six months of 1936 the comparable rates were 44.4 per cent, 36.4 per cent, 27.6 per cent and 22.9 per cent, but in Blackburn borough the figure was 27.2 per cent The reason why special area status was not at first given to the weaving district of Lancashire was that the county was judged as a whole, and as some parts were not so hard hit (especially around the Manchester area) the overall level of unemployment did not compare with the four selected areas.[16] The unfairness of this was recognized when under the Special Areas (Amendment) Act of 1937, Blackburn and the immediately surrounding area were included, and the Special Area Commissioner was empowered to grant loans to new companies prepared to settle in the town.

Blackburn Council had already been encouraging this, having set up an Industrial Development Sub-Committee in 1935. This offered companies sites or buildings in the town at low rents or low purchase price,[17] and from 1937, with the aid of the Special Area Commissioner, more inducements could be offered. Some success was forthcoming. A Czechoslovak firm producing man-made fibres came to Blackburn in 1937; Griffin Mills were taken over by a German firm making slippers; and a French firm making fine fabrics was also enticed to the town. In January 1937, with the threat of further European conflict beginning to loom, the government opened a gas mask factory – the first in the world – in Garden Street to produce half a million masks a week for the civilian population. Housed in a converted cotton mill, it soon employed 450 women. At the same time a Royal Ordnance Factory was promised by the government on a site at Lower Darwen, which would eventually provide bring work for over 2,000 people.[18] Blackburn's first industrial estate, at Whitebirk, was also opened in 1938. Mullards, owned by Philips of Mitcham, was the first firm on the site, manufacturing radio valves and related products. Meanwhile, some of the town's other industries began to prosper. In 1902 William Livesey of Greenbank Ironworks, with some partners, had formed British Northrop

William Livesey, who owned the Greenbank Iron Works, originally founded the British Northrop Loom Company in 1902 to import the newly invented automatic loom from the USA. At its peak the firm employed 2,700 workers at its site in the Little Harwood area but by the late 1950s decline had set in and by 1968 the workforce dropped below 500. A fire in 1982 destroyed most of the original works and only one building remains today.

COTTON TOWN PROJECT, © LANCASHIRE EVENING TELEGRAPH

Loom Co. Limited. The firm purchased the rights to the new automatic loom recently invented by the American J. H. Northrop, and within three years it was manufacturing the loom in Blackburn at Greenbank. Two years later, in 1907, the first purpose-built plant was erected and by 1914 this was employing 220 men. During the interwar years, as the cotton industry declined in Blackburn and the rest of Lancashire, this firm supplied the fast-growing industries of South America and the Far East. During 1929–1931 their success resulted in major extensions to the factory along Philips Road, next to the future Whitebirk industrial estate.[19] The breweries also survived: at Eanam, Daniel Thwaites & Co.'s Star brewery; at Salford, that of Dutton and Co.; and the Lion brewery at Little Harwood. The last-named, owned by Nuttall & Co. until 1924, was taken over by Matthew Brown & Co. of Preston who then transferred their entire brewing operation to Blackburn, extending and modernising their premises in the 1930s.[20]

Nevertheless, cotton remained Blackburn's greatest industry and much the largest employer throughout the interwar years.[21] Thus, the severe decline within the industry immediately and directly affected levels of unemployment in the town. By the 1930s these were consistently high.

Table 8 *Unemployment in the 1930s*

| Year | Percentage of insured unemployed[22] |
|------|-------------------------------------|
| 1929 | 14.5 |
| 1930 | 41.8 |
| 1931 | 47.0 |
| 1932 | 35.1 |
| 1936 | 28.8 |
| 1937 | 21.5 |
| 1938 | 31.4 |

The worst monthly figure was in June 1930, when unemployment reached 51.8 per cent. But these figures, bad though they are, do not tell the entire story, for they hide short-time working and underemployment. This was most serious when weavers were given fewer looms to work, because they were paid by the piece and so, as they produced much less, they were paid much less. But because they were still in work these people were not eligible for unemployment benefit or any other form of state financial support. In 1936, when rather more than a quarter of the workforce were officially unemployed, it was estimated that about the same percentage were underemployed. There was also an acute problem of long-term unemployment. In the weaving trade, employability depended on having the ability to operate four looms or more at maximum efficiency. Those unemployed for more than twelve months

Just as a needle needs threading so did the shuttles in the weaving mills. The way this was done was by sucking the cotton thread through, an action that became known as 'kissing the shuttle'.

COTTON TOWN PROJECT, BY COURTESY OF WALLY AND HOWARD TALBOT

were often deemed by the mill managers to be unemployable, because they had lost their fine skills.[23] All this meant that wage levels in the town fell sharply. As earnings were based on piece rates, and employers were constantly and successfully flouting local agreements, accurate figures are difficult to come by. However, in Burnley, four-loom weavers in 1922 averaged £2 6s. (£2.30) per week.[24] This was somewhat lower than wages during the boom period of 1919–20. Levels would have been little different in Blackburn. But by 1936 a four-loom weaver in Blackburn only earned £1 11s. 6d. (£1.58),[25] while those on fewer than four looms would earn even less.

The plight of the unemployed was alleviated by unemployment insurance. The original Act of 1911 was extended in the 1920s to cover most manual

workers. In addition the period of benefit was increased and additional benefits were added for dependants, which took some of the pressure off the resources of the poor law and the Board of Guardians. After the Poor Law was abolished in 1929 financial help was the responsibility of the Public Assistance Committees. Benefits were not notably generous: in 1936 an unemployed single man would receive 17s. (85p), but if he had exhausted his period of insurance benefit he would receive a maximum of 15s. (75p) unemployment assistance.[26] High unemployment in the town placed great pressure on the borough's libraries, for with nothing else to do hundreds of out-of-work citizens descended on the reading rooms each day. The council opened further reading rooms at All Saints School, Bent Street School, the Queen's Hall Mission and the assembly rooms in Bottomgate.[27] Another effect of high unemployment was a slow but accelerating decline in population, exacerbated by a falling birth rate. A comparatively low birth rate had always been a feature of the town, because of the high incidence of working women, but now a low birth rate was not compensated by migration into Blackburn. Instead there was an outward flow of migrants. During the decade 1921–31 the population fell by 6,529, to 122,971 and the decline accelerated during the 1930s. The migration rate of 3.7 per cent for 1921–1931 rose to 6.9 per cent and this, together with the excess of deaths over births, led to a decline in Blackburn's population during 1931–39 of 9 per cent. Those who left were predominantly younger people, who went elsewhere in search of employment and had fewer ties to restrain them. Thus, Blackburn also had an increasingly aged population profile.[28]

High unemployment also affected the unions. The decline of the cotton industry was accompanied by industrial unrest, as employers sought to cut costs in order to compete and survive. The workers and their unions attempted to keep jobs and maintain wage levels. Two of the biggest disputes became known as the 'more looms lockout' and the 'Great Strike'. The seeds of these bitter disputes were sown in Burnley. In 1928 the employers and the unions agreed on a one-year pilot scheme whereby a weaver would operate six or eight looms set at a slower speed, rather than the usual four at normal speed. In return the weaver would receive an increased set wage of 50s. It was found that the scheme brought savings on the wage bill of 20 per cent, together with a fall of 7 per cent in total production costs, without the need for capital expenditure and with better wages for those weavers who remained in work. As a result 41 of the Burnley mills agreed to adopt the system, though the unions opposed it on the grounds that it needed fewer weavers and therefore increased unemployment. A strike was immediately called in the mills which implemented the scheme, and the mill-owners association in Burnley retaliated by ordering a lock-out of workers. They then urged similar action in all the mill towns. A number of Blackburn mills which held, in total, 55 per cent of all the looms in the town obeyed the instruction, leaving workers with no job to go to. The lock-out was not popular with the Blackburn mill-owners since 'more loom' working was

After a post-war boom following the First World War, demand for cotton fell quite dramatically and pressure was put on for wage reductions and the laying off of workers. The result was a number of strikes. This group of strikers in Cowell Street in the Nab Lane area in 1920 were most probably ensuring that no strike-breakers entered the mill. In the centre their leaders appear to be in negotiation with the police sent to ensure that order was kept.
COTTON TOWN PROJECT

only worthwhile when plain cloth was woven. With support falling the lockout was called off after two weeks. However, the consequences of this failed move were severe for, as they now had no confidence in their association, employers now attempted individual ways of cutting costs. Those that did not follow the 'more loom' system still had to compete for customers with those that did, so they cut wages and some attempted to move away from the 48-hour week agreement signed in 1919. Amid this chaos all collective agreements made with the unions were ended in January 1932. By far the most important casualty was the 'list', which had stipulated agreed rates of pay across the town's mills.

Industrial mayhem broke out again across Lancashire. Between 1929 and 1932 a total of 20 million working days were lost in the cotton industry and the mills in Blackburn saw more than their share. The situation in the town in July 1932, six months after the and of collective agreements, shows how mill-owners tried different ways to cut costs and survive, all of which were to the detriment of their workers. Twenty-one firms had closed. Sixteen reduced the agreed uniform list of wages by 12 per cent and another 21 had reduced wages by 22 per cent. Seven mills altered the wage structure and previous working conditions so much that it was impossible to put a precise figure on the fall in wages. At three mills the 'more loom' system had been introduced. Only a few owners kept to the uniform wage list agreed previously with the unions.[29] The dispute was finally settled through direct government intervention. Overseen by representatives of the Ministry of Labour, the Midland Hotel Agreement was signed in September 1932. The 48-hour week was re-instituted, as were all previous collective agreements, but though the 'list' was restored it was with a 15½ per cent wage cut. Industrial peace did not immediately result, since a few employers failed to adhere to the agreement and only when it was given full legal force through an Act of Parliament did widespread industrial action cease. This, too, was at a cost to the workers, for it involved a further 5.7 per cent wage cut. Between 1933 and 1939, though, only 716,000 work-days were lost in the cotton industry, just 3.25 per cent of the figure for 1929–1932.

But mills were still closing and the cotton industry in the town was in headlong decline. Industrial action failed to protect wage levels or jobs in Blackburn, not least because of mass blacklegging, or 'knobsticking' as it was called locally. This brought successive defeats. Many of the blackleggers were women,[30] though why they failed to support their union is unclear. They were perhaps less politically motivated than men, and they also needed the stamps to qualify for unemployment benefit – the Unemployment Insurance (Anomalies) Regulations of 1931 had made it much more difficult for married women to claim benefit. Perhaps, too, many women put their families, and especially their children, before their union or their fellow workers. Whatever their motive, such people were expelled from their union, while others left as they became unemployed and found it difficult to keep up the payment of weekly dues. As a result the membership of the Blackburn Weavers Association fell by 48.3 per cent between 1929 and 1938. This had a devastating effect upon union income and, together with the intermittent drain caused by the payment of strike pay, meant that the unions were in serious financial difficulties. In the 4½ years to the summer of 1933 the textile unions in Blackburn paid out £150,000 but received an income of only £107,000. As a result, they were forced to stop benefits to members who had not been given back their jobs after the 'Great Strike' of 1932.[31] Declining membership, dwindling finances and mass 'knobsticking' steadily weakened Blackburn's trade union movement throughout this period. What militancy there had been, either at leadership or rank and file level, soon evaporated. For the remainder of the 1930s calm prevailed in the field of industrial relations.

Apathy in the industrial sphere was matched in the wider political arena. The National Unemployed Workers Movement (NUWM), formed in London in 1921 and a Communist front organization, was very active nationally but never strong in Blackburn. It often crossed swords with the Blackburn Weavers Association and found little support for its attempts to highlight the plight of the unemployed. The NUWM, like other organizations at this time, arranged and coordinated hunger marches, but Blackburn was relatively uninterested

The twentieth century saw the Liberal position in local politics strengthened slightly but only when they ran in harness with the Conservatives. However, this short-lived resurgence did mean that David Lloyd George came to speak in the town. Here he is supporting John Duckworth who was MP for Blackburn between 1923 and 1929.

registered as unemployed, having given up the hope of paid employment and being ineligible to claim unemployment benefit.[39]

Older women suffered disproportionately. In 1931, 38.3 per cent of unemployed women were between the ages of 18 and 34, and 50.4 per cent were aged 35 or over. The difference was even more pronounced with long-term unemployment. Women over 45 were eleven times more likely to be unemployed for more than twelve months than those under 25. Women applicants under 30 to the Unemployment Assistance Board made up only 6.8 per cent of the total, but 35.7 per cent were between 30 and 45 and 64.3 per cent were over 45.[40] Married women, too, were clearly the subject of discrimination when workers were laid off or when they tried to obtain new jobs. In 1931, 56 per cent of married women were unemployed compared with 44 per cent of single women. Married women were also more likely to be the long-term unemployed. There was no serious unemployment among young women in Blackburn in 1938 but there was a steady increase in long-term unemployment for those over 24, who were more likely to be married.[41] One reason for the high incidence of unemployment among women was a refusal by many to entertain the thought of any other job than in a factory or mill. Attempts to coerce unemployed mill girls to enter domestic service failed because such work was, not unreasonably, seen as an inferior occupation. This antipathy to domestic service even meant a reluctance to taking seasonal work as domestics in Blackpool and Southport, or as canteen workers in army camps in the south.[42] But the main reason, surely, was male chauvinism and the belief that a woman's rightful place was within the home. This was partly the resurfacing of views that had lain dormant when there was an acknowledged need for a second wage. Since in the 1930s it was often the case that only one wage was possible, the general view was that it should be the man's. In other industries this had always been the case. Women were never employed on the trams prior to 1914, and though in 1917 there were twelve women drivers, 42 conductresses and two female ticket inspectors, all lost their jobs when peace came. The trams returned to having male-only employment for the entire inter-war period.[43]

That society as a whole preferred to see women in the home, or at least in jobs deemed more suitable to their sex, can be seen in other ways. The *Blackburn Times* publicly supported the idea that unemployed female weavers should become domestic servants and gave highly favourable reports of domestic service training centres in the town. It also voiced the opinion that unemployment benefit for married women was a 'marriage subsidy or state dowry'.[44] The Pilgrim Trust held out the hope that the high unemployment rate among Blackburn women would improve their skill in household management, which they considered to be 'bad' or 'indifferent' when compared with the mining areas of South Wales, where women traditionally did not work. The clubs opened up for unemployed women also revealed such an attitude by the types of activities that they encouraged. At the YWCA, for example, dress-making, millinery, cooking, first aid, shorthand and typing were the order of the day, while at the New Sunshine Club the main activities were remodelling and making clothes.[45] Women's unemployment may have had a beneficial impact upon the infant mortality rate in the town, although, as in the nineteenth century, this remained far higher than the national average. The rate per 1,000 fell from 109 in 1921 to 80 in 1929 and 67 in 1938, but this must be compared with the national average of 83, 74 and 53 respectively. Of towns with a population of over 100,000, only Stoke and Burnley matched Blackburn's figures, and they too had a tradition of large numbers of married women in work. The high incidence of mothers dying in childbirth was also a characteristic inherited from the previous century. Between 1924 and 1929 this averaged 6.7 per thousand births.[46] These statistics reveal a regrettable and unsatisfactory situation which was mainly the consequence of so many women working virtually to the end of their pregnancies in order not to lose too much in wages. The resulting damage to the health of the women of the town was plain. Mary Hamilton, the borough's Labour member of parliament from 1929 to 1931, noted that in 1924, 'At the first women's meeting I addressed, I was disappointed to see so few young faces, only realizing later that many of these worn, haggard women were young, but looked, almost invariably, older than their age.'[47]

The town had a low birth rate. It had started to fall during the last quarter of the nineteenth century, and by 1914 it was 20.8 births per 1000, compared with 41.2 per 1000 in 1871. In 1920 the figure had fallen to 20.1 per 1000, when the national average was 25.4. It remained low throughout the interwar period, although fewer women worked, falling to 12.0 by 1933 (when the national figure was 14.7).[48] One reason for the national downward trend was the growing use of contraceptives by the working classes, but this does not directly explain why Blackburn's birth rate continued to be lower than the national average. The answer was almost certainly that it was an economic decision. High unemployment and low wages meant that single men put off marriage and married men and their wives tried to limit the size of the family. The health of the children of the borough also came under scrutiny during these years. Most children were still born at home and only a few expectant mothers attended Springfield Municipal Maternity Home, even though the charges were flexible according to a family's income. Of greater benefit to the majority of mothers were the six maternity and child welfare centres around the town in various locations such as Harwood Street and Prince's Street schools and the parochial halls and institutes at Cornelian Street and Griffin Street. At each a female doctor was present and the town had five health visitors who advised on childcare.[49]

Blackburn Corporation also operated a school medical service, which in 1927 had a full-time school medical officer assisted by two doctors (one full-time and one part-time), a school dentist and six nurses. In 1931 the dental service

'At the first women's meeting … I was disappointed to see so few young faces, only realizing later that many of these worn, haggard women were young, but looked, almost invariably, older than their age.'
MARY HAMILTON, 1924

found that 90 per cent of schoolchildren inspected had dental problems and 70 per cent required dental treatment.[50] At least children now had access to dental treatment, but this ended when they left school. On the creation of the National Health Service in 1948 many people in the town immediately requested to have all their teeth extracted and false ones fitted, knowing that the inconvenience of dentures was more than recompensed by the knowledge that they would never have to suffer from toothache again. Each child was inspected by the school medical service four times during their time at school, at the ages of five, eight, and twelve and just before they left. Those considered in need of fresh air were sent to special open-air classes held in, for example, Corporation Park. Others, in need of the benefits of sunlight, might be taken to ultra-violet light clinics to sit under lamps – by 1931 there were two such clinics, at the hospital and at the council's health centre on Victoria Street.

Blackburn's housing was a legacy of the nineteenth century and had altered little. The environmental and public health problems associated with Victorian working-class residential areas were perhaps less here than in some other towns in industrial Lancashire, but nonetheless Blackburn was, according to a

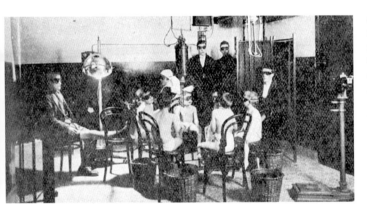

Corporation Hospital had an artificial light clinic which contained two carbon arc lamps and a mercury vapour lamp. Those who it was deemed would benefit from this artificial sunlight ranged from young boys stripped to their underpants to men with rolled up trouser legs (interestingly, he was allowed to keep his boots on).
BLACKBURN LIBRARY LOCAL HISTORY COLLECTION

In a time when many children were brought up in poverty in homes that were often cold and damp and whose nutritional intake was inadequate, physical defects occurred in many. 80,000 to 100,000 children were estimated to be, what was termed then, crippled. Such children in Blackburn attended a Remedial Exercises Clinic in the town hall staffed by a Remedial Gymnast.
BLACKBURN LIBRARY LOCAL HISTORY COLLECTION

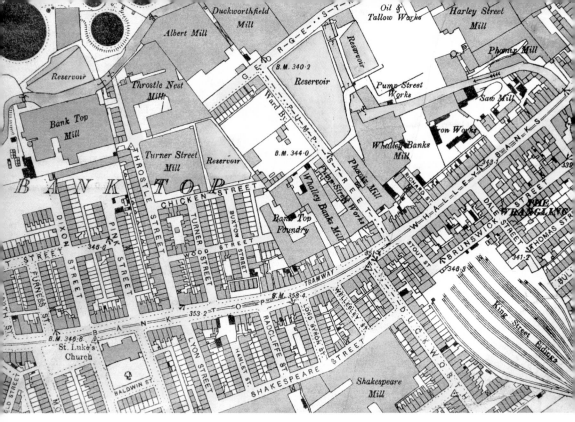

The Wrangling and King Street sidings (1893): a classic landscape of uncontrolled and unplanned early nineteenth-century development is shown on this map. Densely packed slum housing is crammed into every available space – note how on Harrison Street (*right centre*) the houses not only front straight onto the street, but are also directly above the polluted waters of the Blakewater at the back. The area along Whalley Banks had some of the town's worst housing deprivation and was an early target for slum clearance policies.

DETAIL OF THE 1893 ORDNANCE SURVEY MAP, REPRODUCED BY KIND PERMISSION OF THE COUNTY ARCHIVIST, LANCASHIRE RECORD OFFICE

contemporary observer, 'One of those typical Lancashire industrial centres ... Smoke darkens their skies; the little two-storey houses are set – no gardens – up and down the cobbled streets; from the tiny "lobby" you step straight to the roadway ... no trees, no grass, no playgrounds for the children.'[51] The Pilgrim Trust saw the town in the same grey light: 'The predominant impression which Blackburn leaves is that of grimness, unmitigated by any natural pleasantness, for the city is too large for much sense of the surrounding country to penetrate it. Everywhere is a forest of tall black chimneys, against a sky that seems always drab, everywhere cobbled streets, with the unrelieved black of the mill girls' overalls and the clatter of wooden clogs.'[52] But though the housing was perceived as being unattractive, that was not in itself a reason for action. Neither were the environmental problems of pollution and blackness deemed to be reasons for housing renewal. In the case of Blackburn, as with some other towns, such as Nelson and Bury, much of the housing was in reality in quite good condition, because the overwhelming bulk of it dated from the last quarter of the nineteenth century and so many properties were less than fifty years old. In the housing survey which was obligatory under the 1930 Housing Act, the

*'Smoke darkens their skies; the little two-storey houses are set — no gardens — up and down the cobbled streets; from the tiny "lobby" you step straight to the roadway ... no trees, no grass, no playgrounds for the children.'*

borough council found that only 38 houses in Blackburn should be designated for slum clearance, which accords with the view of Neville Chamberlain, who as minister of health in visited Blackburn in 1927 and was shown the worst of the town's housing. He is reported as exclaiming, 'Is this all you have got to show me? It is not very bad. It is nothing like Manchester or Birmingham.'[53]

Neither was overcrowding a problem. Though little new house-building had taken place in the first two decades of the twentieth century, the declining population meant that in 1921 the official statistic for overcrowding in Blackburn was only 3.9 per cent, compared with an average of 9.6 per cent for the whole of England and Wales.[54] The sanitary condition of the housing stock had also been improved. In 1920 22,755 houses had a fresh-water flush system for their lavatories, a major advance on the position twenty years earlier. Even so, over 12,000 properties still had simple pail or tub closets that had to be emptied by the night soil men each week. Between 1920 and 1922, as part of a programme of public works schemes to relieve unemployment, the corporation compelled landlords to install fresh water lavatories in their properties. The council helped by paying half the cost from the rates, money that would be quickly recouped since privy waste would no longer have to be collected. The result of this massive and highly effective strategy was that by 1922 only 109 tub closets remained in the entire borough. A visit to a lavatory still entailed going down the backyard but at least the stench and the excrement had been eliminated. Refuse disposal was based on wooden ashtubs, to be found in most backyards, which were filled with the household refuse and, like the pail or tub closets, were emptied weekly. The tubs were so heavy that they could not be lifted and

emptied directly into the dustcarts, so had to be first emptied onto the street so that the refuse could be shovelled into the carts. This was an unhygienic, messy and time-consuming procedure, so in 1924–25 the town's 27,000 ashtubs were replaced by galvanized iron dustbins. Life, in some ways at least, was becoming a great deal more civilised.[55]

Storing food was a continuing problem, although many houses had a pantry. This usually was against an outside wall so that it could be well-ventilated with wire mesh rather than glass in the window, and it might have stone-flagged floors and a stone shelf at waist and window height to keep food fresh and cool. However, because of the difficulties in storing food, and because budgets did not allow for anything but small purchases at any one time, most people bought what they needed daily. To cater for this, corner grocery shops abounded. In 1939 Blackburn had nearly five hundred of them, and in addition there were nearly 200 butchers, while for cheap meals that needed no preparation over 150 fish and chip shops sold ready cooked food for those who lived in the terraced streets. Small local businesses of other sorts abounded. Thus, since many in the town lived in or on the edge of poverty, goods were repaired rather than being thrown away and replaced. On the eve of the Second World War, for example, the town had more than 150 boot and shoe dealers and repairers, and 21 of these still advertised as cloggers.[56]

The decline in the population and the absence of slum clearance schemes meant that the level of new house-building in the interwar years was notably low. There was very little private building, although the construction of council

houses, required under successive legislation, was not insignificant. Between
1919 and 1939 the Corporation constructed a total of 1,993 council houses at
a cost of just over £1 million, financed mainly through government subsidies
under the Housing Acts. In contrast only £40,000 in subsidies was paid to
private house-builders by 1934. The lack of a sizeable middle class in the town,
allied with the lack of industrial growth – and indeed, the dramatic decline of
the key industry – meant that the middle-class suburbs of the interwar years,
so typical and so common elsewhere, are largely absent from Blackburn. One
potentially important change in housing circumstances that did get under way
had no immediate effect on the townscape. This was the first movement away
from rented accommodation towards owner occupation in the terraced streets.
The council advanced £135,000 to tenants, under the various Small Dwellings
Acquisition Acts, to enable them to buy the homes in which they lived.[57] New
council estates were the only major change in the built environment and, just

as mill colonies had helped to reshape the town in the early nineteenth century, the municipal schemes did so in the 1920s and 1930s. The Addison Housing Act of 1919 imposed a duty on all local authorities to survey the housing needs of their area and submit plans to the Ministry of Health for new building to make up any shortfall. Impressed by the pre-war Garden City movement that had stressed the benefits of planned, low density housing incorporating public and private open space, the new ministry insisted that houses, each with a garden, had to be of a certain size and standard and were to be built at a density of no more than twelve per acre. This meant that virtually all such building would inevitably be on the outskirts of towns, where undeveloped land was more readily available and the sites were more suitable for landscaping.

Blackburn Corporation chose three rural sites on the northern, eastern and south-western boundaries of the town, at Brownhill, Intack and Green Lane respectively. Green Lane and Intack were the first to be built, but problems soon became apparent. Building on the outskirts certainly allowed tenants to breathe fresh air and meant that housing layouts were less cramped, but what of the journey to work? When the Brownhill estate was being planned this difficulty was addressed. The estate was built on both sides of a new dual carriageway, which would eventually form part of the Blackburn ring road, and it was decided that the central reservation should be sufficiently wide for the construction of a tramway or light railway. The road was built, but the tramway never was. Other problems also came to light. Extra land was purchased at Green Lane for a playing field, and the Brownhill plans included a sixteen-acre public park complete with bandstand and ornamental pool, but none of the new estates had a shop or public house. The Church of England was allowed to purchase land at Brownhill for a new parish church but that was all. The error, made

A scene from the mid-1920s showing the construction of the 4¼-mile ring road linking Yew Tree to Whitebirk. Seen here is the Brownhill Arms, and the line of cottages by its side, all of which can still be seen today virtually unchanged. What has altered is the appearance of the large Brownhill roundabout. The dual carriageway being built was originally meant to have a tram system in the central section to transport the workers from the Brownhill council estate which was also just being erected on land in the foreground of the picture.

COTTON TOWN PROJECT, © LANCASHIRE EVENING TELEGRAPH

by almost all local authorities and repeated throughout the interwar period, of erecting isolated estates made up solely of housing units and lacking any sense of community, was made in Blackburn.[58] Even the standard of municipal housing declined as the subsequent Chamberlain, Wheatley and Greenwood Housing Acts of 1923, 1924 and 1930 reduced the size and quality of the houses so that more homes could be built more cheaply.

The relative dearth of new building experienced in Blackburn in the interwar period was reflected in the provision – or non-provision – of new schools. By 1936 the Blackburn Education Committee, which was set up in 1903, had built only five new elementary schools, most of them before 1914. As a result Victorian schools still dominated education in the town. They were 'in the main, old fashioned and badly planned: dark and draughty, with desks of the most uncomfortable type, and classrooms that were much too large.'[59] The position regarding secondary schools was even less satisfactory. The council did not build a single one before the Second World War, so that the only secondary education in the town was at Queen Elizabeth's Grammar School, the Girls' High School (which remained a private limited company until 1932), and the two Roman Catholic schools, Notre Dame and St Mary's College, while the Church of England opened St Hilda's and St Peter's in 1939.[60] Just as in Victorian times, it was felt that for the bulk of the children of Blackburn, a sound elementary education based on the three Rs was quite adequate to fit them for a working life. It is not surprising that just before the national abolition of half-time education in 1920, 30 per cent of all boys and girls in the borough aged between 10–13 had employment and nearly 50 per cent of those aged over twelve.[61] Neither is it surprising that the only new educational venture

embarked upon in these years was the setting up of juvenile instruction centres. Margaret Bondfield, the minister of labour, opened the first in October 1930. They gave practical training to some of the unemployed youth of the town. The only other aspect of education which showed growth and promise was the technical college, which had 4,000 full- and part-time students by 1935. All followed mainly practical courses of instruction. The belief, held by the cotton masters of the nineteenth century, that education should be geared to the world of work and the needs of the local economy apparently still held good. The lack of any pressure to alter the situation seems to suggest that parents likewise held to the views of their own parents and grandparents, that schooling should end as early as possible so that a wage could be earned.

During the first half of the twentieth century there were also major changes to the transport systems of Blackburn and the surrounding area. The peak year for passenger journeys on the borough's trams was 1921, when 18.25 million journeys were made, an average of 50,000 per day. The rapid growth in unemployment, and the simultaneous rise of motor transport, ensured that this figure would never be surpassed. The increase in motor transport brought traffic congestion in the busy town centre streets, and although a range of improvements was introduced such as traffic lights from 1932, the situation

In October 1929 the Corporation took delivery of its first twelve motor buses: six 30-seat single-decked Leyland Tigers and six 48-seat double-decked Leyland Titans. Some of them are being proudly inspected in front of the town hall. The last of them were taken out of service in 1948. Note also the copper ball atop the Market Hall tower, nearing the top of the pole at 12.40 p.m. (see page 140).

COTTON TOWN PROJECT, © LANCASHIRE EVENING TELEGRAPH

grew steadily worse and the trams received much of the blame. Blackburn was unusually late among the free-standing towns of Lancashire and Yorkshire in getting rid of its trams. Although the Audley route closed in 1935, and in 1938 the council took the decision to replace trams completely with motor-buses within five years, the war intervened and the last services survived until 1949.[62] Needless to say, this did not end the problem of congestion – rather, the inexorable increase in road traffic soon cancelled out any limited benefits in that respect. The Corporation did almost nothing to change the street pattern of the town centre until much more recent times, partly because of lack of money and partly because Blackburn, unlike some other industrial towns, was a relatively late convert to the idea of full-scale central area redevelopment.

Nonetheless, road-building was not entirely absent from its plans, for during the late 1920s and into the 1930s the Corporation planned, designed and built a generously laid out dual carriageway ring road from the Preston New Road at the bottom of Billinge Hill, via Brownhill and Whitebirk, to the major junction of the Accrington, Oswaldtwistle and Haslingden roads at Intack. The road was intended to take most of the through traffic from Preston to East Lancashire and over to Yorkshire out of the town centre, and also to give access to new residential and industrial areas, all of which objectives it achieved. One notable success was that whereas the contemporary ring roads at, for example,

Bolton and Preston were almost immediately edged by new housing and so lost much of the advantage of a fast route around the edge of the town, at Blackburn service roads and infrequent junctions helped to maintain the free movement of traffic and gave plenty of space for future improvements. The railway network remained intact during the interwar period, and it was not until the dramatic rise in private motoring during the 1950s and 1960s that the contraction of local services had its impact. The passenger trains between Blackburn and Burnley via Great Harwood and Padiham were withdrawn in 1957; those on the line to Chorley in 1960; and to Clitheroe and Hellifield in 1962. The routes to Burnley and East Lancashire; to Manchester via Darwen and Bolton; and to Preston and Blackpool survived, although local services were substantially reduced, stations became unstaffed, and most of the through trains to London, Liverpool and more distant towns and cities were withdrawn.

Between the wars leisure patterns altered, partly because of changing tastes and fashions and partly because increasingly harsh economic conditions meant that people had less money – or no money – in their pockets. During the summer holiday weeks of 1921, which were shortly after the great industrial recession had set in, train bookings at Blackburn station were down 66 per cent from their pre-war levels, and they never recovered. That many Blackburners

Photographed in 1935, decorated for the silver jubilee of King George V, the Savoy cinema on Bolton Road, purpose-built in 1922 to seat just over 1,000, was just one of the fifteen cinemas that Blackburn had at that time. A weekly visit to the 'flicks' had become a part of life for many in the town, especially the young.

COTTON TOWN PROJECT

could not afford a full week of holiday meant that instead they sought cheap day excursions, as their grandparents and great-grandparents might have done back in the 1840s and 1850s. Quite a few of those who still took a week's holiday in Blackpool or another resort returned twice during the holiday: once to sign on and once to draw benefit.[63] But in the town itself, the new forms of entertainment, already appearing in the Edwardian period, continued to grow and evolve, while older-established pastimes dwindled. The four theatres or music halls in the town (the Princes, the Palace, the Theatre Royal and the Olympia) had their swan song. The first to go was the Olympia, the most recently opened – after only ten years as a music hall it became a cinema. The Palace closed in 1934, its size making it uneconomic as a theatre. Its owner, McNaughton, reopened it as a cinema in 1936 with seating for 1,250. The third to disappear was the Theatre Royal, which was shut down in 1937 and in the following year was reborn as the Cinema Royal with seating for 1,600 and a café. The Princes Theatre, renamed the Grand Theatre in the 1920s, was also turned into a cinema in the early 1930s but then had a new lease of life as a music or variety hall, so that in 1939 Blackburn still had one live theatre, booking the stars of the day such as Gracie Fields and George Formby.

From this it is clear that the great growth area was the cinema, for this was the golden age of the Dream Palace. In 1918 there were six cinemas in Blackburn, but in 1939 there were fourteen. The first postwar example was the Exchange Hall Cinema (1919), housed in part of the 1865 Cotton Exchange. By 1900 this had become a multi-purpose hall used occasionally by travelling

FAIENCE BY SHAWS.

THE RIALTO CINEMA, BLACKBURN
DRESSINGS IN SHAWS VITREOUS GREY FAIENCE
NIGHT VIEW SHOWING FLOODLIGHTING

film shows and by 1914 was showing films and variety acts. Having been transformed into a cinema, showing films every night together with daily matinees, it became the Majestic in 1924, and in 1932, modernised so that it could show the 'talkies', it could seat 1,400 people. In 1920 two more purpose-built cinemas opened: the Palladium on New Chapel Street, Mill Hill seating around 700 and the Regent on King Street, seating 1,350 and reincarnated as the Roxy in 1939. Finally, in 1922, the Savoy was built on Bolton Road, seating 1,031. In the 1930s there was a new wave of openings. As well as the Theatre Royal which became the Cinema Royal, and the Palace, there was the purpose-built Rialto on Penny Street (1931, with 1,878 seats), equipped with a stage for live shows, an organ

The building of
the King George's
complex was
begun in 1913 and
completed after the
war. It had three
dance halls, one of
which could hold
1,200 dancers. In
addition the larger
King George's
Hall shown below
had a stage that
could hold a
sixty-strong dance
band. Dancing was
so popular that
lunchtime dances
were held here
in addition to the
usual evening and
weekend ones.
PHOTOGRAPHS: CARNEGIE

that rose from the depths, and the now obligatory café. At the end of the 1930s,
Blackburn's cinemas had a total capacity of 16,000, or more than one-eighth of
the entire population of the borough. Though Sunday showings were not yet
allowed most cinemas offered two shows daily and some three from Monday to
Saturday. Programmes were changed on Mondays and Thursdays. The choice
as to what to watch, when to watch or where to watch was wide.

Blackburn town centre was bombed only twice. The second occasion occurred just before midnight on 31 August 1940. Ainsworth Street was hit and two people were killed and eight injured. The next day, as a police sergeant keeps guard against looters, local residents and businessmen come out to view the damage.
COTTON TOWN PROJECT, © LANCASHIRE EVENING TELEGRAPH

families were shocked at the state of the children who had come from the depths of the Manchester slums, but the operation went relatively smoothly. A second wave of evacuees arrived in Blackburn from London in July 1944, escaping the attacks from the V1 and V2 rockets. They were dispersed to Haslingden and Darwen.[4] During the salvage campaign of the early war years the ornamental iron gates of Corporation Park and Queen's Park were removed, as were most of their boundary railings. The same fate awaited the two Russian cannons, mementoes of the Crimean War, which had stood proudly above Corporation Park.[5]

More profound, perhaps, was the effect of the war on Blackburn's wartime economy and the peacetime economic conditions which followed. At the start of the war the gas mask factory in Garden Street more than doubled its labour force to 1,000, mainly women, while by 1944 the Royal Ordnance Factory, which specialised in fuses for anti-aircraft shells, employed 5,000 workers of whom 85 per cent were female. Special day nurseries were opened so that young mothers could work there. British Northrop switched from making automatic looms to the production of aircraft components and machine tools, while Mullards mass-produced valves for military electronic systems.[6] When

In the first few days of the Second World War over one thousand evacuee children from the Manchester area arrived at Blackburn station as part of Operation Pied Piper. The policeman holding the baby was P.C. Alec Lamb while on the right can be seen P.C. John Bolton. The boy being held up in the foreground is clutching his gas mask holder.
BY COURTESY OF MRS E. BOLTON AND PETER WORDEN

During the Second World War the Government opened a number of restaurants in the major towns and cities to ensure nutritious yet cheap food for the people. They were based on the cafeteria system whereby the customer queued at a hatch, ordered from a limited menu displayed on a blackboard, and was handed his food on a plate. This one was in Mayson Street and shows the uniformed serving ladies handing out the already prepared dishes to office workers wearing their trilbies.
COTTON TOWN PROJECT

the war ended in 1945 not all the jobs in the military supply industries disappeared. For example, production of munitions at the Royal Ordnance Factory was cut back, but the factory took on other work to keep employment levels up – the workforce were even producing alarm clock mechanisms – but the outbreak of the Korean War in 1950 brought more work and the War Office,

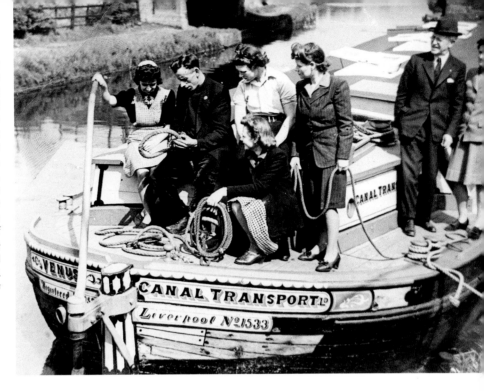

Due to men being called up to serve in the armed forces in the Second World War, women were trained to take their place in the workforce. Here, at Whitebirk, a group of trainee barge crews are being given a demonstration of knot tying under the watchful eye of local dignitaries.

Blackburn had its own 'Dad's Army' ready to help repel any invasion and to guard strategic sites against a 'fifth column'. Here, in 1943, No. 1 Mobile Company proudly marches past the General Post Office on Darwen Street during the 'Wings for Victory' Parade.

and later the Ministry of Defence, retained the factory as an integral part of Britain's military supply strategy. Some 3,000 workers, mostly women, were still employed there in 1980.[7] Mullards diversified into a new and fast-expanding industry, manufacturing television set components such as transistors, valves and capacitors at its 46-acre Blackburn site.[8] British Northrop returned to the production of automatic looms and in 1953 was employing 2,000 workers at its Daisyfield factory. As demand for looms declined in the late 1950s the company diversified into commodities as varied as earth-moving machinery and furniture.[9] Some other Blackburn firms also expanded or developed in the 1950s and 1960s. The Scapa Group, which started business in the 1920s in a disused skating rink, employed 1,000 workers by 1967 producing felt for the paper-making industry.[10] C. Walker & Sons Ltd at Guide became Great Britain's largest steel stockholder, with an annual turnover of 180,000 tons in 1975 compared with just 1,000 tons in 1956.[11]

But though the war accelerated the town's move from textiles to engineering and other forms of manufacturing, Blackburn was still shackled to its past. Not only was the borough's rapidly ageing nineteenth-century housing stock in increasing need of renewal but, for all the industrial restructuring since the mid-1930s, the town was still heavily reliant on the ever-dwindling cotton industry. Structural unemployment remained a major concern. Although there was a brief boom in the textile industries in 1948–50, the relentless decline of the industry was otherwise uninterrupted. In 1931 there had been 33,326 jobs in the cotton mills of Blackburn, but in 1957 employment in this sector had shrunk to only 12,491, and showed no sign of stabilising: in 1965 the figure was 7,495; in 1977, 6,572; and in 1981 only 3,404 workers. There were still 50 working mills in 1955, but twenty of these closed between then and 1960 and by 1983 only five were left; the rump of a once proud and dominant industry.[12] The switch to engineering soaked up quite a few of the jobs that cotton had shed. By 1951 engineering employed 8,178 workers, almost exactly twice the number twenty years earlier, and the Corporation was actively pursuing the potential of engineering and allied trades as it tackled the restructuring of Blackburn's industrial base. Further industrial sites were provided at Whitebirk, and major new trading estates were laid out at Roman Road in the 1960s and Shadsworth in the 1970s. Since then, more land has been developed for this purpose at Whitebirk (Glenfield Park), and the council has provided new sites for small industrial units near the town centre.

Nevertheless, this continuous attempt to attract new industry to Blackburn, though very effective by its own criteria, did not keep pace with the loss of jobs, partly because new industries were vastly less labour-intensive than those

At Mullards, wire of very fine dimensions, often one tenth of the thickness of a human hair, was made as part of the production process of valves and cathode ray tubes for televisions. The wire factory in Blackburn produced enough each year to encircle the equator ten times over.

The railways, too, saw considerable change in the post-war years. This photograph marks the end of an era. In 1954 Bobby was the last horse left at Blackburn's railway station, where it had been used for shunting and delivery runs. Forty years earlier the station had 180 working horses.

which were closing, and partly because some of the relatively new arrivals have themselves shrunk or closed. By the 1980s cotton had largely gone, but the contraction of other large-scale employers was being experienced. The employees at the Royal Ordnance Factory could now be counted in their hundreds rather than thousands, Mullards had slimmed down dramatically, and British Northrop had closed. In terms of employment and the size of its working-class base, Blackburn had remained disproportionately committed to manufacturing, even by the standards of a region with a heavy bias towards manufacturing. The service, professional and electronic-age industries were seriously under-represented, as the figures in Tables 10 and 11 suggest.[13] All this means that for much of the second half of the twentieth century, high local unemployment levels were normal and long-term unemployment remained a major social and economic problem. The unemployment rate in 1977 was 6.5 per cent, and by July 1980 it had risen to 9 per cent, and to 15.3 per cent in August 1982. It did not fall below 15 per cent until 1986. Although Lancashire as a whole experienced a rate above the national average throughout this period, the county figures were still consistently around 4 per cent lower than those in Blackburn.[14] This pattern persisted. In 1993 the unemployment rate in the new borough of Blackburn with Darwen was 11.2 per cent, compared with the national figure of 9.8 per cent, and a council report admitted that 'in comparison to the other districts of Lancashire, Blackburn can be seen to have the highest rate of unemployment in Lancashire.'[15]

Table 10  *Socio-economic groups (percentage of total employment), 1981*

|  | Blackburn | Lancashire |
|---|---|---|
| Employers, professional and managerial | 11.4 | 15.5 |
| Other non-manual | 27.2 | 30.7 |
| Skilled manual | 30.9 | 27.4 |
| Semi-skilled manual | 22.4 | 19.7 |
| Unskilled manual | 7.1 | 5.5 |
| Others | 1.1 | 1.1 |

Table 11  *Employment by industry (percentage of total), 1981*

|  | Blackburn | Lancashire |
|---|---|---|
| Agricultural | 0.5 | 2.2 |
| Energy and water | 1.4 | 2.3 |
| Manufacturing | 40.6 | 32.8 |
| Construction | 5.4 | 6.2 |
| Distribution and catering | 18.9 | 20.7 |
| Transport | 5.6 | 5.2 |
| Other services | 27.5 | 30.6 |

With most of the town's firms taking the same traditional holidays in the summer for two weeks, Blackburn became a ghost town as the inhabitants departed for the seaside. Holiday time for this couple in 1964 starts or ends in the pouring rain as they rush to the bus stands on the Boulevard.

COTTON TOWN PROJECT, © LANCASHIRE EVENING TELEGRAPH

Blackburn's population decline, well under way by the early 1930s, continued after the Second World War. The total population in 1951 was 111,218, a drop of 11,574 since the previous census of 1931, but by 1961 it had declined even further, to 106,242 and in 1971 had fallen to 101,825, a figure last recorded in the mid-1870s. The average birth rate in the 1930s was 12.00 per 1,000, but, as the troops arrived home, the rate rose to 19.1 in 1947. It fell slightly thereafter, to 13.91 in 1957, but ten years later (in 1967) had risen again, to 18.44, and was, most unusually for Blackburn, higher than the national average (which was then 17.2). Therefore, the population decline took place despite a higher birth rate that the town had experienced between the wars. The cause is, of course, the prolonged exodus of families and young people looking for better paid work and improved prospects elsewhere. Blackburn joined with Darwen to form a new enlarged borough in 1974, so comparative population statistics for the more recent past are more difficult to establish, but the population of Blackburn town did rise temporarily, reaching 106,501 in 1981, because of immigration from Asia. By the late 1980s, though, such migration was itself slowing down and the population began to fall once more. The population of the new borough fell by a further 4,000 to 1991, when the birth rate well above the national average, and the detailed breakdown of the statistics reveals that between 1981 and 1987 there were 2,600 more births than deaths, but an overall loss of 8,300 because of high levels of out-migration. This contrasted with the experience of Lancashire as a whole, where there was an excess of deaths over births but a net increase of 900 because of in-migration. The illegitimacy rate showed dramatic changes: for the first half of the twentieth century the average

Just as cholera and typhoid were feared in the nineteenth century, polio was seen in the same way in the twentieth century. In 1965 Blackburn suffered an outbreak. Mass vaccination was ordered, and vaccination points were opened all over Blackburn, this one being at the clinic on Cedar Street. People of all ages and all classes queued together.

rate was 4.4 per cent, and even in the late 1950s the rate was still less than 5 per cent. During the 1960s, however, a major change took place, with an increase from 4.9 per cent in 1960 to 10.4 per cent in 1967, a rate maintained through to 1971 when Blackburn, Hyndburn and Ribble Valley Health Authority was formed and local statistics were no longer available.[16]

Apart from its industrial structure Blackburn's major inheritance from its past was the housing stock, which was displaying major physical and environmental problems by the early 1950s. As already noted, most houses had been built in the second half of the nineteenth century. During the post-war period, when there was not only renewed optimism about the overhauling and modernising of the national infrastructure, but also a new enthusiasm for industrial

For many years Blackburn appeared to be in a time warp. This was New Garden Street in 1957. Other than the main roads most streets in Blackburn were still setted and since working class men could only afford a bicycle at best the streets were clear of parked cars. This allowed the milk cart to travel unhindered while delivering the early morning pint for the breakfast cup of tea.

After the Second
World War entire
streets of houses in
the town still had
no bathroom or
indoor lavatories.
In the 1960s the
council embarked
on a slum clearance
programme leaving
scenes reminiscent
of the aftermath of
the bombing which
other towns and
cities faced twenty
years earlier. This is
Birley Street in the
Larkhill area of the
town, photographed
in the midst of
demolition.
COTTON TOWN PROJECT

building methods, large-scale strategies, and social engineering on a grand scale, the fact that many of these properties lacked one or more of the basic amenities was seen as an acute problem which needed to be dealt with urgently by concerted action. In 1955 some 2,000 properties in the town were categorised as slums and earmarked for demolition in the near future.[17] Two years previously an investigation had been made into the living conditions of the families who dwelt in such properties. The findings were extremely disturbing, revealing a shocking image of filth, degradation and squalor, in housing which was manifestly unfit for human habitation and shamed a civilised community. There were homes where the only light was from candles, and other researchers discovered that 'Walls black streaked with dampness enclose dank kitchens with collapsed fireplaces. Bedroom walls bulge and ceilings droop alarmingly. A family of five people sleep, eat and live in one room, four of them sleeping in the one double bed.' At another house it was found that the weather dictated where and how the family slept: 'Slight rain necessitates manoeuvring of the beds. Heavy rain showers made it necessary to move downstairs to sleep, while in a real downpour one just got wet, for rain dripped through the roof on to the floor and then through the downstairs ceiling.'[18] For many families, there were daily battles against mice and cockroaches inside the houses and rats in the yards. It is little wonder that Blackburn had a council house waiting list of 3,500 families in the mid-1950s.

There was little systematic renewal before 1960, when the government began to apply heavy pressure on local authorities to undertake large-scale renewal programmes. In 1961, some 40 per cent of Blackburn's entire housing stock was still without a fixed bath or bathroom and as many were without an indoor w.c. The council decided on a twenty-year programme to clear 11,285 houses in designated clearance areas by 1982 and to build 13,400 new homes. These were to rehouse those whose houses had been demolished and to cater for an over-crowding figure of 4.6 per cent.[19] Plans for large-scale council house building had been laid as early as 1946 when land at Shadsworth, on the outskirts of the town, was purchased. Building began there in 1953, and by 1958 the estate of

1,200 houses was completed. Further estates were begun in the 1960s as council house building accelerated in order to rehouse those families displaced through the clearance programme. There was building at Queen's Park, Roman Road, Larkhill, Audley and Millhill, and the estate at Green Lane was enlarged. All were finished by the end of the 1970s. As the table below shows, there was a move to put tenants who only required one or two bedrooms into flats, mainly in tower blocks:

Table 12  *Council housing in Blackburn, 1945–1981* [20]

|  |  | pre-1945 | 1945–1964 | 1964–1981 |
|---|---|---|---|---|
| 1 bedroom | house | 0 | 0 | 0 |
|  | flat | 124 | 800 | 2041 |
|  | bungalow | 64 | 67 | 302 |
| 2 bedrooms | house | 914 | 627 | 840 |
|  | flat | 35 | 713 | 1133 |
|  | bungalow | 0 | 0 | 20 |
| 3 bedrooms | house | 1148 | 2223 | 2253 |
|  | flat | 0 | 93 | 350 |
|  | bungalow | 0 | 0 | 5 |
| 4 bedrooms | all | 13 | 117 | 205 |
| Total |  | 2298 | 4640 | 7149 |

This emphasis on council building meant that such property made up an ever-increasing proportion of Blackburn's housing stock. In 1961 it accounted for 18.3 per cent but twenty years later this had grown to 31 per cent, compared with 19.3 per cent in Lancashire as a whole. Thanks to the right to buy system, introduced in the 1980s to allow tenants to purchase their home at a reduced price, the proportion fell to 25 per cent by 1990.[21] However, the results of this ambitious urban renewal programme were very mixed. Demolition ran ahead of schedule, so by 1970 a total of 6,281 houses had been cleared, but 58 per

cent of the housing stock was still two-up two-down Victorian terraced housing and 23.2 per cent of this remained part of the council's slum clearance plan. Some 25.8 per cent of all private households still had no fixed bath and 42.2 per cent no indoor w. c (compared with 13 per cent and 18.7 per cent for Lancashire and 12 per cent and 15 per cent for England and Wales). More seriously, though, only 4,605 new homes had been built, so there was a substantial shortfall in replacement housing, and this meant that an accelerated rate of completion was required over the next ten years to provide an estimated 8,795 further new dwellings. This would involve a rate of completion greater than even the new towns were achieving. To compound the problem, the housing committee now proposed to bring forward, to 1978, the target date for clearing the remaining 5,004 houses designated for demolition, and to add a further 750 properties to the programme.[22] Thus, even by the basic criteria of demolition versus completion figures, and the meeting of targets that the council itself had set and the government had authorised, the housing programme was far from successful.

From ginnels such as these that stretched down the rear of the terraced streets of Blackburn, coal was delivered, ash pits emptied and lavatory pails collected by the night soil men. By the 1960s, when this photograph was taken, many of the openings in the walls had been bricked up as dustbins replaced the ash pits and water flushed lavatories constructed.

But of course the bald statistics of clearance and construction tell only part of the story, for the assumption had been that the people of Blackburn would be pleased with what was being done; would recognise that it was 'for their own good' that they were being rehoused; and would be satisfied with the strategy in general. Therefore the rapid escalation of protest and opposition to the policy that engulfed the town from the end of the 1960s, and particularly from the summer of 1970, was totally unexpected and a very great shock to those charged with the task of implementing the schemes. It emerged, as protest became more vocal, more concerted and more public,

that those living in clearance areas did not want their communities destroyed, and most definitely did not want to be rehoused on peripheral various council estates or in high-rise blocks of flats. In addition, people already on the council house waiting list did not relish the idea of remaining there for many years to come, as those being rehoused took precedence over them. Faced with the wave of opposition, the full council – dramatically reversing the existing policies – turned down the housing committee's plan and instructed the committee to plan an urban housing strategy which centred not on large-scale demolition but on general improvement schemes, encouraging householders to apply for grants to renovate and modernise their homes while the council dealt with the surrounding environment.[23] These strategies should be seen in the context of a major switch in national policy – the government, by now acutely aware of the extreme unpopularity of large-scale urban renewal, and beginning to suspect that a whole series of social, environmental, financial and political problems were emerging as a result of the strategy, had already begun to publicise the new philosophy of rehabilitation, improvement and upgrading.

Having changed tack, and decided against further large-scale clearance and redevelopment, Blackburn was following the new trend and its efforts met with some success. Households lacking at least one basic amenity, such as a ready supply of hot water, a bath or indoor w.c., were reduced by 1990 to 14 per cent of the privately owned housing sector. But the difficulty was that as the years passed more of the housing stock deteriorated and required action, not least because the official standards, by which housing stock was deemed satisfactory, were continually being raised. In 1990, of the 40,000 privately

Pictured in October 1957 Alfred Woods and his wife were retired weavers who lived at 70 Eccles Street. Both had begun work in the mid 1880s as half-timers at the age of ten. Mrs Woods finally retired at the age of 64, while Alfred worked until he was 72. Flat caps, waistcoats and shawls were still common forms of dress in post Second World War years in northern cotton towns such as Blackburn.
COTTON TOWN PROJECT

While rock and roll, soon to be followed by Beatlemania, swept Britain, this back street scene from around 1960 was quite typical of areas of Blackburn. Washing can be seen hanging across the street to dry and the growth of weeds between the setts in the road indicates the almost total lack of use by any form of motorised transport. Notice also the unevenly stone flagged pavement and the dustbins waiting to be emptied.

BLACKBURN LIBRARY LOCAL HISTORY COLLECTION

owned houses in the borough of Blackburn with Darwen, 22,500 had been built before 1919 – their age was not in itself the problem, but the lower standards and limited amenities of much of the pre-1919 housing stock was clearly a continuing burden. Improvement schemes were still being carried forward, but some demolition was unavoidable – in 1989–90, for example, 452 houses were demolished in the enlarged borough. In that year, it was estimated that 8,000 homes, or 20 per cent of the private housing stock, were in need of substantial repair, while 5,000, another 12 per cent, were at least technically unfit and in principle should be cleared.[24] At the end of the 1980s, too, council house building more or less ended, because of the very restrictive policies of the Conservative government. Even before then, most new municipal housing was being built in small mixed schemes in conjunction with private enterprise developments, with a switch from large council estates on the outskirts of the town to small inner area developments, as in Daisyfield area. Furthermore, the last few years of council-house building saw an emphasis upon housing for special groups and particular needs, rather than simply for families on the general waiting list. All these trends were, of course, national in their impact, and were driven in large measure by fundamental changes in the policies of central government, but their effect upon a town such as Blackburn, which still had serious housing problems, was immediately apparent. The shortfall of decent housing grew, and the controversial question of substantial clearance and redevelopment was once again being raised, as it was elsewhere in east Lancashire.

Much of the private house building in the Blackburn area since 1950 has taken place outside the old borough boundaries, although planning constraints and issues of land ownership have imposed some limitations upon the scale and direction of development. Large estates of private housing were built at Lammack and Pleckgate in the 1950s, and there were other main areas of development at Cherry Tree, Feniscowles, Mellor and Wilpshire. The movement of population from the old core of the borough to this peripheral and suburban housing partly explains the population decline – in many ways the population figures have more meaning if 'Greater Blackburn' is considered, because the overall figure for the built-up area as a whole shows continued growth. The short-distance outward movement of the postwar period reversed the migration pattern of the nineteenth century, when many of the people coming to the town had previously lived in the ring of townships immediately outside.[25] The development of suburban housing continued apace, with numerous infill schemes and small estates being constructed in the more attractive areas (usually, those on the north and west sides of the town) and with a wide variety

Car ownership in the 1960s was still very limited, especially among the working classes of industrial towns such as Blackburn. At the end of the working day crowds flocked to the many bus stops patiently to stand four deep in queues to await the arrival of the Corporation buses to take them home for tea. Women could at least be guaranteed a seat since it was ingrained etiquette that a man never sat while a woman stood. This photograph was probably taken in the late 1940s.

of housing association, starter home and affordable housing schemes in the older industrial areas. Blackburn had, however, notably failed to attract very much of the fashionable new housing in the inner city – the designer flats and apartments, and conversions of older buildings – which have been so significant in larger places such as Manchester and which are significant elements in the evolving townscape of places such as Bolton and Preston. Its relatively poor

This square, with Victoria Street in the background, was the site where twice a week, on Wednesdays and Saturdays, Blackburn market traded. Here more than 350 stalls would be set up in what was one of the largest open-air markets in the country. It was also the home of the town's Easter fair and on Sundays preachers, political orators and buskers could all be heard. It was now felt that change was needed. The market moved to its present indoor site in 1964 when the square and all the buildings shown made way for the town's new shopping precinct.

COTTON TOWN PROJECT, © LANCASHIRE EVENING TELEGRAPH

economic performance, and marked deficiency in the service, financial and hi-tech sectors, as well as its somewhat unfashionable image and location away from the main arteries, mean that as yet this form of urban revival has, for better or worse, had little impact.

As well as tackling housing problems by undertaking large-scale clearance and renewal, the council also embarked on a major redevelopment of the town centre. Although cotton became the town's economic lifeblood in the mid-nineteenth century, Blackburn remained one of the main market towns of Lancashire, and its role as a retailing and commercial centre should not be underestimated. With the rapid decline of cotton, this role regained a higher profile, and the council decided that Blackburn should establish and reassert its former position. As with the two largest nearby centres, Preston and Burnley, the assumption was that in order to attract more shoppers and to enhance its retailing importance, much of the central area should be comprehensively redeveloped with modern architecture, much-improved traffic circulation, and a wide range of up-to-date facilities. There was also a need to address the many issues raised by traffic growth and the arrival of mass motoring. The town's

One result of the redevelopment of the town centre was that well-known streets saw great changes, as this 1962 view of Northgate facing towards King George's Hall shows. The street now ends at the junction with Lord Street West that can be seen on the centre left. All the property on both sides up to that point has been demolished.

COTTON TOWN PROJECT, © LANCASHIRE EVENING TELEGRAPH

tramways had already closed and although the use of buses remained above the national average the central area streets were increasingly congested. In 1961 the council approved plans for modern shopping complex, with pedestrian areas segregated from traffic, covered walks contrasting with new open spaces, and ample car parking. The council entered into a partnership with the private sector to undertake the project, its chosen partners being the Laing Construction Group. The plan involved building on the site of the Victorian market, so this was moved as a prelude to construction. Between 1961 and 1964 a new market building was constructed on a site between Penny Street, Salford and Ainsworth Street, and when it was completed the first phase of the shopping centre development could begin. The old market buildings, with their distinctive clock tower, were demolished and the first

stage of the shopping precinct and a new tower block extension to the town hall were built. The second phase, covering the area between Ainsworth Street and Victoria Street, was undertaken between December 1969 and November 1971, with 37 small shops and three large stores (the Co-op, Boots and Tesco) as well as a large addition to Woolworths. The centre was in three tiers: the lowest was for servicing, the middle for shopping, and the upper for car parking. The third and final phase, carried out between 1977 and 1980, covered the area between Church Street, Lord Street and Astley Gate and included two more large stores, Debenhams and W. H. Smith.[26]

Much of Blackburn's nineteenth-century town centre, including the architecturally outstanding and much-loved Thwaites Arcade and the impressive landmark of the market clock tower, disappeared with this major redevelopment. There is no doubt that in the short term the new town centre venture was a success, attracting many shoppers from further afield since it was one of the first such developments in the northwest, but the long-term benefits are more questionable. Most seriously, within a few years it began to look dated and tired. The characteristic architecture of the 1960s has rarely worked well in the climate of northern England, and many of the planning principles on which designs such as this were based have themselves been superseded or challenged. Some of the later shopping centres in other textile towns involved more sensitive approaches, trying to blend the old with the new and to link the buildings of the past with the needs of the present. The street pattern was notably ill-managed, with awkward dead ends and old streets truncated, and the access to car parks and the upper deck were insensitive and intrusive. Blackburn, in its rush to be

PREVIOUS PAGES
An aerial photograph of Blackburn town centre, showing, among other things, how relatively clean the air and buildings are.
WWW.WEBBAVIATION.COM

This was the new shopping precinct, built in the 1960s, standing on the site of the old market hall, viewed from King William Street. It shows the new town hall tower block, the entrance to Cobden Court and the replacement clock tower. For a while it reinvigorated Blackburn's retail trade attracting many customers from other East Lancashire towns.
COTTON TOWN PROJECT

One of the first churches to be demolished after the Second World War was St Paul's. The town's Victorian churches faced a twin attack from poor maintenance due to lack of finance and from declining attendances. The site of St Paul's is now part of Blackburn College's campus.

first while trying to be rid of its past, severed many of the links with a past which, for all its faults, was familiar and on a human scale. The disappearance of landmarks and buildings which people liked was a mistake – few have affection for the late twentieth-century concrete and steel, but many remember fondly the Victorian stone, brick and terracotta. The result was that one of the next major shopping developments, the Morrisons complex, sought to recall a past so recently obliterated, by incorporating a modern version of the demolished clock tower in its design. At the beginning of the twenty-first century the 1960s shopping centre underwent a large-scale remodelling and facelift in an attempt to make it more attractive as a shopping environment and more agreeable in visual and aesthetic terms.

The demolition of old Blackburn did not end with the construction of the shopping precinct. Subsequently, the Telegraph Building disappeared to make way for Morrisons and the Palace Theatre, a larger version of the successfully restored Bradford Alhambra, was demolished in 1989. When the library was moved to the former Co-operative Emporium in Northgate in 1973 the

This picture gives some idea of the sheer scale of the redevelopment of the town centre in the 1970s and this was just one of three phases. In the background is the Georgian tower of St John's that, after a protracted council chamber battle, only just managed to avoid the attentions of the demolition men.

Richmond Terrace has been the home of Blackburn's professional class for over a century. Solicitors, architects and accountants have always made their home here. This attractive Georgian terrace has now been tastefully restored complete with Victorian style lampposts.

PHOTOGRAPH: CARNEGIE

The old Technical College, a fine example of high Victorian architecture, thankfully survived the ravages of redevelopment in the 1970s and now takes pride of place on the campus of Blackburn College.

PHOTOGRAPH: CARNEGIE

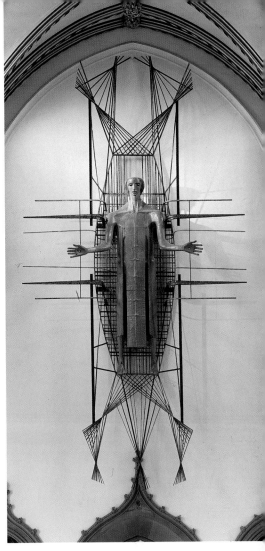

Reflecting its history as, first, the parish church for a large rural parish and, later, as cathedral church serving a new diocese, Blackburn Cathedral is very much a mixture of the old and the new in both terms of architecture and decoration. Like most towns, Blackburn also has its statue of Queen Victoria.

PHOTOGRAPHS: CARNEGIE

and building community centres on new housing estates. Implementation of both plans was slow and uncertain. During the 1950s only two new primary schools built at Lammack and Longshaw and not until 1958 were the first new secondary schools constructed, at Witton Park and Shadsworth. In 1964 the plans were in any case superseded when education provision underwent the first of a series of shake-ups. It was decided that all pupils between the ages of 11–14 would attend a junior high school, and would then either remain for one more year and leave at fifteen or transfer to one of the two senior high schools for two further years of education. This plan was implemented in 1966 and ended in 1968 when, following central government directives, the education system in the borough became comprehensive. There were to be five comprehensive schools, three of which would be for ages 11–16 and two for 11–18 year olds. This scheme was put into effect but within a short time it, too, was altered and all the schools took pupils from the ages of 11 to 18.

All five comprehensive schools were in modern buildings and all five were on the periphery of the town: Shadsworth (1958), Witton Park (1958: an amalgamation of Witton Park Secondary School and the Girls' High School), Everton (1966), Billinge (1966) and Pleckgate (1968). Queen Elizabeth's Grammar School opted out of this reorganisation and became independent. In 1984 there was yet another change, when all five comprehensive schools lost their sixth forms, and the pupils were transferred to the technical college, which was now transformed into a tertiary college. At this point that Blackburn's past again caught up with it. The influence of the churches on education in the nineteenth century meant that the Church of England and the Roman Catholic Church also had secondary schools in the borough. These voluntary-aided schools refused to join in the sixth form reorganisation, so St Mary's Roman Catholic Sixth Form College remained and St Wilfred's C of E secondary school retained its 11–18 status. Together with the now independent Queen Elizabeth's Grammar School and the independent Westholme Girls School, the separate policy pursued by these two schools meant that sixth form provision in the borough became fragmented. The existence of church and independent schools, with their own admissions policies, also resulted in the mainly Muslim ethnic minority children being unequally distributed among Blackburn's secondary schools. At the technical college the new Feilden Street building was completed

Schoolchildren have also changed. Here 1950s schoolchildren, waving their union jacks, line Victoria Street to cheer the young Queen Elizabeth as her motorcade passes. The boys are in their regulation short trousers, long socks and school caps while the girls, also smartly attired in their school uniform, are kept separate.
COTTON TOWN PROJECT

in 1964, but further building was halted when the Harris College in Preston was chosen for polytechnic status in preference to Blackburn, another sign of Blackburn's declining local importance. The next phase of building was in the 1980s when it became a tertiary college. A campus site was formed between Feilden Street, Nab Lane and Blakey Moor and a series of new buildings erected, including a new Art and Design School and a New Technology Centre. In addition the older buildings were refurbished. The institution was renamed, and Blackburn College came into existence. The plans of the late 1940s, for adult education in community centres on the new housing estates, have never come to fruition.

Leisure patterns underwent further change in the second half of the twentieth century. The closure of the Grand Theatre in 1956 and its demolition in

The Regency Club, situated in Regent Street, was a gambling club in the early 1960s. Customers climbed the stairs to play roulette, dice or cards. Officially it did not have a drinks licence but unofficially was another matter. Today it still caters for the town's nightlife, as Jazzy Kex can be found here (for southern readers this name could be translated along the lines of 'Rather nice trousers').

COTTON TOWN PROJECT, © LANCASHIRE EVENING TELEGRAPH

1958 saw the end of live theatre in the town, though the recent reopening as a theatre of the old cinema at Ewood marks not only a rebirth but also an ironic turn of fate, since it was cinemas which were responsible for the falling popularity of live performance between the wars. Indeed, the fate of cinemas echoed the experience of the theatres and music halls, for their rise had been dramatic and their decline was to be no less headlong. As television grew in popularity after 1952, the fourteen cinemas represented a major over-provision. In 1957 the Savoy, the Olympia and the New Central Hall all closed and in 1958 the newly renamed Ritz at Bank Top followed. During the 1960s six more cinemas shut their doors and when the Rialto closed in 1974 Blackburn was left with just three cinemas. These were Unit I Plus 4 in Little Harwood on the site of the Star Picture Palace; the Palace which shared the original building with a bingo hall; and the newly renamed Classic Cinema at the old Cotton Exchange. The first two only lasted until 1992 and 1984 respectively, and then the old Classic cinema, in the guise of Unit 4, 5 and 6 from 1981 and the Apollo from 1993, was the sole survivor. The cinema was almost gone from Blackburn.

Dance halls changed with the arrival of rock and roll and pop music. During the 1950s ballroom dancing still ruled, as couples waltzed around Tony's ballroom in Town Hall Street, but by the end of the decade Harold NcNulty's School of Dancing on Preston New Road, newly rechristened the Mirabelle, saw young people dancing the night away to new records. In the mid-1960s the plans for the redevelopment of the town centre included the construction of the Cavendish Club, which as was usual with such institutions underwent a bewildering series of name-changes and makeovers: it was opened by the erstwhile celebrity Simon Dee in 1968 and was later known as Romeo and Juliet's (1979) and then Peppermint Place and Utopia. In 1969 the Locarno ballroom, which could accommodate 1,000 dancers, was refurbished and reopened as the

When the Rialto cinema was built in 1931 on Penny Street it had a stage for live shows, a café and an organ which rose from the depths to entertain the 1,878 customers that could be seated. In 1959, when this photograph was probably taken, the cinema was refurbished and renamed the Odeon. At this time the organ was removed. The building was finally demolished in 1974 to make way for an office block and car park.

In the 1970s the Cavendish Club was built as part of the new shopping precinct complex which transformed, for good or ill, the centre of Blackburn. Though later renamed Romeo and Juliet's then Peppermint Place and Utopia it helped for a while to make the town become the entertainment centre for East Lancashire, with the most famous singing and comedy stars of the day performing there week in and week out.

COTTON TOWN PROJECT

Young people jived the weekend nights away at the Locarno Ballroom in the 1960s. Young men, who during weekdays tended mainly to wear overalls, dressed up for the occasion in their suits made at the local Burtons or Hepworths, often with coloured linings. Ties were obligatory and often even matching handkerchiefs were worn in the top pocket, though many were just card with material stitched on top. Girls dominated the dance floor, dancing together until a young man felt brave enough to intervene.

BY COURTESY OF LANCASHIRE EVENING TELEGRAPH

Golden Palms. Blackburn was becoming known as the entertainment centre of east Lancashire, drawing young people from long distances to see such attractions as stars of comedy (Terry Cooper, Bob Monkhouse and Norman Wisdom at the Cavendish, where the chart-topping Frank Ifield also performed) or to dance at the Locarno to groups such as Herman's Hermits. In Lower Harwood, at the Starlight Club, Susan Maugham and Alan Price entertained downstairs while gambling took place upstairs. For the young Blackburn was the place to be, and the place to be seen.

While young girls in mini-skirts and boys with lengthening hair danced in

the new nightspots, even more fundamental changes were altering Blackburn society. The town, like other places in Lancashire and Yorkshire with a strong textile tradition, became a magnet for migrants coming to Britain from South Asia, or those of Asian ancestry expelled from Uganda. The motives for this immigration are much the same as those that compelled the Irish immigrants to come to England in the nineteenth century. They were attracted by the prospect of a comparatively better life with better-paid employment. At home in India and Pakistan, rapid population increase was bringing fragmentation of agricultural holdings and acute, and seemingly insoluble, problems of poverty, while in Uganda, and other East African countries, outright persecution and expulsion, or the continuing threat of the same, was primarily responsible. A higher percentage of the migrants from Africa were from non-agricultural backgrounds, even though they had often lived in small towns and villages, and they included a higher percentage of people who had been in retailing or were qualified professionals.[32] The very rapid growth in Asian migration to the town during the late 1960s and through the 1970s is demonstrated by the census figures:

Table 13 *Total Asian migration to Blackburn*
*(those of Asian or East African Asian birth)*

| 1951 | 287 |
|------|------|
| 1961 | 652 |
| 1971 | 5,355 |
| 1981 | 15,237 |
| 1991 | 19,700 |

The immigrants to Blackburn came from three main areas: Gujarat in India, the Punjab in Pakistan, and from Uganda, Kenya, Malawi and Tanzania in East Africa. The overwhelming majority (89 per cent) were Muslim, with a further 8 per cent Hindu and 1 per cent Sikh.[33] The table below highlights the differing backgrounds, and cultural and geographical experiences, of this important new element in the town's population:

Table 14 *Background of main Asian immigrant groups in Blackburn*[34]

| Rural Indian Gujarati Muslims | 29.7 per cent |
|-------------------------------|---------------|
| Rural Pakistani Punjabi Muslims | 21.2 per cent |
| Urban Indian Gujarati Muslims | 8.7 per cent |
| Rural East African Gujarati Muslims | 8.2 per cent |
| Urban East African Gujarati Muslims | 5.6 per cent |
| Urban Pakistani Punjabi Muslims | 5.5 per cent |

As with the Irish in the nineteenth century, most immigrants found themselves in low paid employment and consequently settled in the older areas of Blackburn where they could purchase property more cheaply. It is particularly striking that very few members of the immigrant communities chose to rent housing, and this dramatically altered the overall balance between renting and owner-occupation in the town. In 1977 some 64.6 per cent of dwellings in Blackburn were owner-occupied, but among ethnic minority households the percentage was 93 per cent.[35] The newcomers tended to form their own self-contained communities, divided on first arrival along national and religious lines, but partly perpetuated by the way in which each community helps relatives, friends and past neighbours to settle and set up house on arrival in this country or on marriage. Because of this process, Gujarati Hindus tended to live in streets around Preston New Road, as did the Punjabi Sikh families. Most Gujarati Sunni Muslims, the largest ethnic group, lived in the Brookhouse area, especially in the south-west corner. The Gujarati Surtis group tended to live in the Daisyfield and Audley Range area, and the Pakistani Sunnis in the streets of the north-east corner of the Brookhouse area and in the Audley Range, Queen's Park and Green Bank areas.[36] In 1991 those with an Asian heritage (that is, including those born in England of Asian parents or who categorised themselves as being Asian) formed 19.5 per cent of the population of the former borough of Blackburn.[37] This is largely the consequence of the young age of the immigrants, which led to a higher birth rate compared with the indigenous population. In turn, that meant that the proportion of children of school age with an Asian heritage is higher than the overall figure and that implies that the percentage will continue to grow for some time to come. As noted, most immigrants were attracted to Blackburn's textile industry. In 1977, when only 10.3 per cent of the town's workforce was employed in textiles, this sector accounted for 54.1 per cent of all adults from the immigrant communities.[38] The industry's continuous decline has therefore contributed materially to the unemployment problems among Blackburn's ethnic minorities. In 1977 unemployment was 6.5 per cent in the town but among the Asian population it was 21 per cent. The same pattern still persisted in 1990, when Blackburn's unemployment rate was just under 8 per cent, but in Cathedral ward, which has a large ethnic minority community, it was over 17 per cent and it also exceeded 15 per cent in the Brookhouse, Bank Top and Queen's Park wards, other areas with a concentration of ethnic minorities.[39]

Since the overwhelming bulk of the Asian community is Muslim the skyline of Blackburn has been changed by the addition, between 1965 and 2004, of 29 mosques with their distinctive domes. In addition seven new Islamic independent schools have opened, four mixed primary schools and three girls secondary schools. Efforts are now being made to have one of the secondary schools expanded and brought within the State sector. The arrival of the large Asian community has had many other effects and consequences. One is on eating habits. As in most other towns and cities in Britain, the first ethnic restaurants only appeared in the early or mid-1960s. Normally, the first to arrive were

With the coming of thousands of immigrants from the Asia from the 1960s the skyline of Blackburn has begun to change yet again. The overwhelming majority of immigrants were Muslim and as a result, minarets and domes have started to appear over many of the terraced streets of the town.
PHOTOGRAPH: CARNEGIE

Chinese, offering a low-cost three-course luncheon or an exotic evening dining experience. In Blackburn the first were the Silver Lantern on Penny Street and the Ying Kin on Salford. But Blackburn was one of the first places in the country with Indian restaurants: in the early 1960s the Anglo-Asia restaurant opened in Town Hall Street and the Taj Mahal at Higher Eanam. Today Blackburn has one of the widest choices of Indian cuisine of any British town.

The relatively low pay earned by many of the immigrant community, together with the high rates of unemployment among this sector of the town's population, means that the areas in which they live became the most deprived

Another consequence of the changing religious mix in Blackburn is the rise of new schools. Fuelled partly by the desire for girls to be educated separately, a number of Islamic schools have been opened to take their place alongside older-established faith schools in the town.
PHOTOGRAPH: CARNEGIE

The Brookhouse area was one of the most deprived, not only in Blackburn but in the whole country. Today new housing in the foreground and background of this view intermixes with modernised terraced homes. Being an area with predominantly an Asian heritage population, the distinctive architecture of mosques and Islamic schools brings added variety to the townscape.

in Blackburn and among the most disadvantaged in the entire nation. A survey undertaken in 1984 by the General Practitioners' Committee identified the Brookhouse and Cathedral wards as the two most deprived of 9,200 wards in England and Wales. This conclusion accorded with that of Department of the Environment survey, based on 1981 census information, which indicated that the Blackburn was one of the ten most deprived local authority areas in England and Wales.[40] The position had improved only slightly by 1991, when the Blackburn was still ranked as the thirty-first most deprived local authority out of the 410 in the country. Deprivation was measured using thirteen criteria, and Blackburn was classed as 'deprived' in twelve of these: households without a car, mortality rate, unemployment rate, numbers of long-term unemployed, adults on income support, amount of derelict land, house insurance premiums, numbers passing five GCSEs, overcrowding, seventeen-year-olds not in full-time education, numbers of children in non-earning households and houses lacking the basic amenities. Compared with the rest of county Blackburn was 'far and away the most depressed part of Lancashire' and its deprivation was increasing. The infant mortality rate (33.3 per thousand births) was twice the national average.[41] Blackburn was still suffering from its legacy of nineteenth-century housing and from the collapse of the cotton industry, but these factors

*Blackburn was 'far and away the most deprived part of Lancashire.'*

also afflicted places such as Burnley, Nelson and Accrington. For a variety of reasons, the town's circumstances were apparently even more problematic and difficult to tackle. The borough also experienced rising crime, to which high unemployment and deprivation were a major contributor. In the early 1990s 14 per cent of all reported crime in Lancashire was committed in Blackburn and Darwen, even though it had only 10 per cent of the population. The town was seen as the 'crime blackspot of Lancashire': 87 per cent of offenders were resident in the borough and 75 per cent of offences were carried out by those aged 14–25.[42]

In its political complexion, the town changed significantly in the postwar period. Blackburn was a two-member constituency to 1945, and in the Labour landslide of that year the borough returned two Labour MPs including Barbara Castle, the first of the town's MPs who was a nationally renowned and influential figure. After 1945 the town was divided into two single-member seats, Blackburn East and Blackburn West. In the 1950 election Barbara Castle was returned in Blackburn East with a majority of 4,818, but Blackburn West fell to the Conservatives. The position remained the same in 1951 except that Barbara Castle's majority was reduced to 2,632. However, because of Blackburn's declining population it then became a single constituency, electing one member of parliament. Barbara Castle hung on to it in 1955, with the tiny majority of 489, and since then it has been continuously a Labour seat. In 1979 Barbara Castle retired and was succeeded by Jack Straw, Foreign Secretary in the Labour government, and in 2005 Leader of the Commons. Blackburn is a manufacturing town with a large working-class base, and has experienced

A young Barbara Castle campaigning in the 1945 general election. After winning her seat in the Labour landslide victory of that year she held it until her retirement from Westminster in 1979. Though Blackburn was an industrial town with more than its fair share of employment and housing problems the Labour party's grip was far from secure. In 1955 they only won by 459 votes, reflecting Blackburn's traditionally strong working-class Conservative support. In the 1980s the town was still a marginal seat.

COTTON TOWN PROJECT

an above average unemployment rate – and since 1945 has had only two MPs both of whom have been important political figures. Nevertheless, the Labour Party has had relatively small majorities. In 1970 Barbara Castle retained her seat with a majority of only 2,736, and in 1983 Jack Straw's was only 3,055. This increased to 6,027 in 1992 and to 9,429 in 2001. A significant proportion of this increase is the result of a personal vote and a sizeable Labour-supporting element among the ethnic community, a vote which held firm in 2005 despite the negative impact of the war in Iraq.

Nevertheless, Blackburn retains a large and traditional working-class Conservative element and in the 1970s the National Front and the National Party in Blackburn had a brief prominence. Their eventual failure was probably a testimony to the town's traditional antipathy to political extremism. The rise of the two right-wing parties began in 1971 with the 'Battle of Azalea Road'. It was alleged that residents of that street were angered by the possibility of one of their neighbours selling their property to an Asian family. The National Front sent an organiser from the Manchester area to Blackburn and a local branch of the party was formed. Although it was claimed that 'the rapid development of the Blackburn branch is the greatest success story in the Lancashire area to date',[43] the National Front remained just an undercurrent in local politics for some years. A local man, John Kingsley-Read, first became a national leader of the Front and then, in a much-publicised split, formed a breakaway group, the National Party of Great Britain. Extreme right-wing politics acquired a higher profile in Blackburn.[44] In the 1975 council elections, Kingsley-Read won a seat in St Thomas's ward and John Franklin, a fellow-member of the National Party, was elected for St Jude's ward. The media descended on Blackburn and a series of marches and counter-marches in the town were organised by the National Front, the National Party and Action Against Racism.[45] The largest, in September 1976, was organised by Action Against Racism and 3,500 people took to the streets. The provost of Blackburn, the Very Reverend Lawrence Jackson, claimed that the bulk of the marchers were not Blackburn people but outsiders bussed in from all over Britain. 'Blackburn people', he claimed, 'were conspicuous by their absence and I think this was Blackburn's own demonstration of how they want to be left to be allowed to get on peacefully.' The mayor agreed and, in true nineteenth-century entrepreneurial spirit, bemoaned 'the effect on trade in the town', claiming that many shoppers had gone to Accrington for the day.[46] The marches and demonstrations continued, though they grew fewer and attracted smaller crowds. In May 1978, despite wide advance publicity, a National Front march and a counter-demonstration went off 'like a damp squib', with fewer than 1,000 people present in total and only one demonstrator sufficiently excited to be arrested.[47] Kingsley-Read was not re-elected to the council, and Franklin had resigned without attending a single council meeting. Public apathy killed off political extremism in Blackburn, just

This image of the demolition surrounding the old Victoria Brewery, Adelaide Street, perhaps best sums up Blackburn in the post-war era. During these years an extensive urban renewal programme was embarked upon, with mixed results.

BY COURTESY OF JOHN BROWN

as it had seen off the Communists as well as Oswald Mosley and his Blackshirts in the interwar years.

During the second half of the twentieth century Blackburn did much to try to escape from the inheritance of its past, but at the start of the last decade of the century much of that legacy was still apparent. It coloured, shaped and influenced many crucial areas of life and was still a key factor in explaining the character, appearance and outlook of Blackburn. Much had been done, and very large sums of money had been spent, on housing improvements, but housing was still deteriorating and even some more recent building was becoming sub-standard. A sizeable part of the nineteenth-century town centre had been swept away, but the new structures were already looking outdated and had not met with any popular enthusiasm or affection. New industry had been attracted to replace cotton in the town's economy, yet higher than average unemployment persisted. One-fifth of the entire population was of Asian birth or heritage, compared with a minute fraction fifty years before. By all measures used to produce official statistics, parts of Blackburn experienced appalling and unacceptable levels of deprivation and disadvantage. Half a century of public investment, though it had made a huge difference to the appearance of the town, its economic structure and its physical fabric, had been unable to remedy problems and remove the evidence of deprivation. The future of Blackburn, as the new millennium approached, was still uncertain.

# CHAPTER ELEVEN

# *Renaissance*

A CROSS GREAT BRITAIN the 1980s and 1990s saw a wide variety of new and innovative strategies aimed at regenerating declining and troubled urban areas. These approaches, many of which challenged existing orthodoxies and sought to parallel, or replace, the role of the state with private enterprise initiatives, were received with varying degrees of enthusiasm by the communities concerned, and met with varying degrees of success. Blackburn became the subject of two of these new initiatives, not primarily because it courted such involvement but because of factors largely outside its control. The 1981 Toxteth riots in Liverpool forced the Conservative government to take direct and positive action to address, or at least to consider, issues of urban deprivation, decline and social malaise. Michael Heseltine was appointed to oversee the revival and regeneration of Liverpool, and under his auspices the government came to accept the principle that the business world, the local authority and the local community could work together for the benefit of all those concerned. It was accepted, albeit with qualification and hesitation, that it was not possible to rely solely on public or private initiative, but that in any successful and meaningful strategy it had to be both. Another factor, unexpectedly, was a fact-finding visit by Prince Charles to Lovell, Massachusetts, a town which had revitalised itself by a strategy which involved everyone in the community working in partnership for the common good. The prince, already actively involved in community work through the Prince's Trust, wanted to encourage a pilot scheme along similar lines in this country. Lovell was a textile town which had encountered hard times, so Halifax was chosen as a British equivalent. To prevent the Wars of the Roses breaking out again it was decided to implement a second scheme based in Lancashire. The first choice was Burnley, but that town chose not to take up the offer, and therefore Blackburn was selected instead.

The partnership was established in 1988 and in the following year Prince Charles himself came to Blackburn to launch the project officially. The scheme came within the umbrella of the Business in the Community initiative, which at that time was headed by the chairman of Barclays Bank. As a result Peter Robinson, then the manager of Barclays Bank in Clitheroe, was seconded for two years to oversee this attempt to set up a working partnership between the council and the business community in the borough. Eventually it was made a permanent post. It is said that the early meetings of the Blackburn Partnership were far from successful, for the two partners had a deep mistrust of each other. The councillors, the majority of them being Labour members, seemed to view the employers as representatives of an exploitative class, either paying lip service to the proposed partnership or only in it for what they could get out of it. In return, many employers saw the councillors as political dinosaurs, ignorant of the real world and financially inept. Nevertheless, despite this inauspicious beginning a few people, such as Councillor Bill Taylor, later knighted for his services to local government, began to see that the preconceptions of both sides were not necessarily accurate. They increasingly acknowledged that cooperation could bring real and tangible benefits. Another key visionary was Phil Watson, Blackburn born and bred, who joined the council in 1968 and finally retired as Chief Executive in 2006 when he was justly awarded the CBE in the Honours List for his services to the town's regeneration.

A further major turning point for Blackburn was the City Challenge Competition of 1992. This was a government initiative, involving more than sixty councils which bid for £32 million. On the day that the winners were to be announced, television cameras were positioned at Bolton and Preston, so nobody from the media was at the town hall when a messenger arrived with the news that Blackburn was the smallest borough in the country to win. The primary reason for the victory in the competition was that the bid from Blackburn was not made by the council alone, but rather was a joint one from the borough and its business community. The idea of 'partnership' had its first major success. The initial money from the government was only the icing on the regeneration cake. Over the next five years the City Challenge schemes brought in a total of £223 million. This included a further £5.2 million from the government but the main benefits derived from the fact that the partnership could now bid for funds from the European Community. This earned no less than £134 million of private investment, most of which was spent on three key areas: the Brookhouse/Bastwell housing renewal area, the economic infrastructure in Blackburn town centre and the redevelopment of Greenbank Business Park. These programmes achieved, and indeed exceeded, their targets. For example, 5,446 jobs were created or safeguarded as opposed to the initial target of 3,645; some 3,202 houses were built or improved (the target was 1,430); and 193,346 square metres of new or improved commercial floorspace was created, compared with a target figure of 144,870. Success bred success as further bids for more monies were entered.

A further seven-year regeneration programme was agreed in 1995. Based on an initial £19.5 million grant, very large new funding, totalling £160 million, was attracted including £118 million from the private sector. This programme focussed on a policy of attracting investment, in the form of new housing and

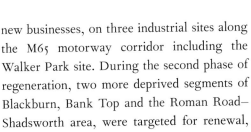

Throughout the town works of art have been commissioned and erected not only in the town centre but also on the new industrial estates. This one, entitled the Beehive can be found at Shadsworth

BLACKBURN AND DARWEN COUNCIL

Much has been done recently to try to shake off the harsh, concrete appearance of the shopping precinct. Colourful block paving has been laid, and the town hall extension has been re-clad, but giving the past a facelift has proved difficult.

PHOTOGRAPH: CARNEGIE

new businesses, on three industrial sites along the M65 motorway corridor including the Walker Park site. During the second phase of regeneration, two more deprived segments of Blackburn, Bank Top and the Roman Road– Shadsworth area, were targeted for renewal, upgrading and enhancement.[1] The motorway itself, linking Blackburn and East Lancashire with the M6, had been planned for many years, and the section from Whitebirk eastwards to Burnley and Colne had been open for some time, but the missing link, the Blackburn southern bypass and its extension to Walton Summit, was finally completed in 1997. The full impact of the M65 has yet to be assessed, but it is at once apparent that it will forge a major new reorientation of the patterns of economic activity in the borough, with new light industrial and warehousing projects focusing on motorway junctions and their feeder routes.

These were very large scale and ambitious programmes, but they were paralleled with a wide variety of smaller and more detailed community-based schemes which contributed to urban renewal and social and economic revival.

Many of these were the result of the continuing partnership between the council and the local business community. In 1994, for example, the Crime Concern Project was started in the town centre, involving the provision of a CCTV system and linking local shops by radio so that early warning of shoplifters could be given. A local Groundwork Trust was set up to improve the environment and by 1996 160,000 trees had been planted and £3.75

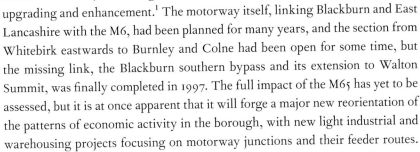

As part of bringing art to the streets of the town this eye-catching sculpture can be seen on the Boulevard. It is a far cry from the more formal and traditional ones of Gladstone, Hornby and Victoria which stand on their plinths.

PHOTOGRAPH: CARNEGIE

million raised for 444 separate practical projects to improve the environment and local landscapes of the borough.[2] The Guardian Angel Scheme, begun in 1993, was another new initiative. Experienced local businessmen volunteered to form a pool of experts willing to help and advise new entrepreneurs who were setting up or expanding businesses in Blackburn. So successful has this been that it has now been expanded to encompass the rest of East Lancashire.[3] Another scheme connecting local businesses with the wider community has been the School Friends Project, launched in 1996. This aimed to link every school in the borough with at least one local private sector company, and by 2004 all but a couple of schools had acquired partners under this initiative. The idea was that the partner company would help the school where possible, or provide an introduction to another local company which could help the school.[4] A further turning point came with the return to unitary status in 1998. Until 1974 Blackburn had been an autonomous county borough but under the local government reorganisation of that year it, like other county boroughs including Preston, Blackpool and Burnley, had become a second-tier district within the administrative county of Lancashire, based in Preston. This meant that services such as education were now the responsibility of the county council. In 1998 a further reform made Blackburn with Darwen a unitary authority, returning all the services which had been surrendered 14 years earlier. This meant that the borough could now plan for the future in an integrated and comprehensive way, taking all aspects of the town's services into consideration. Representatives of education, health and social services now joined the employers and councillors on the partnership committees.

One major area of concern was housing. During the 1990s the housing problem in Blackburn, already serious, was becoming more acute. Since 1988 the council had been prevented from cross-subsidising the council housing sector using money raised from other sources, and the availability of funding from central government was drastically reduced. The council had to formulate policies for dealing with an ageing private housing stock – it could either use limited resources available to revitalise that sector or it could repair and modernise council homes. Both policies were attempted, but council house rents had to rise at an average of 10 per cent a year in order to balance the books. This was unsustainable except for a very short period, so hard decisions had to be made regarding the council's property portfolio. Three options were put before the councillors: the status quo, attracting private sector finance, or transferring the housing stock to a new private non-profit making company. The second option was dismissed and permission was successfully sought from the government to allow the tenants to choose from the remaining two options. Though the government's rules allowed a simple majority of those voting to decide the issue the council embarked upon a campaign to encourage as many tenants as possible to vote. Under the slogan 'Key to the Future – Use your vote' a series of meetings was arranged to publicise and highlight the council's case. The result was a turnout in the ballot of 65 per cent, nearly triple the normal percentage for local elections, and an 85 per cent vote in favour of transferring the housing stock from the council to a new company registered with the Housing Corporation.

On 28 March 2001, responsibility for a total of 9,624 council properties was handed over to a new company called Twin Valley Homes. This had an elected board of eighteen non-executive directors, six of whom were nominated by the council and six elected from the tenants. Nominations were sought and then all tenants were invited to a public meeting where they received the curriculum vitae of each nominee and heard a five-minute presentation from the applicants themselves, before a vote was taken. This was grassroots local democracy in action. A further six members were then elected by these twelve on the grounds of their expertise in crucial areas such as law, accountancy or information technology. All were unpaid volunteers, and each was to serve for three years. Two from each of the three categories would then stand for reselection each year. Most of the company staff had previously worked in the housing department and the first managing director, Phil Richards, was the former Director of Housing. Change was immediate. Since the company was not subject to the borrowing restrictions that had hamstrung the council, £130 million of investment was planned in the first five years. Each tenant was promised that within that time their property would have uVPC windows and doors, double-glazing, central heating and modern kitchens and bathrooms, and everyone was told when the work would be done as a specific promise, rather than just being 'on a list'. In addition, as the work was carried out, tenants were told when the next modernisation would take place. For example, if a new kitchen was installed the tenant was told that a replacement would be provided in a certain number of years' time. For those who wanted to exercise their right to buy that scheme was kept and honoured.

Because many young couples wanted to buy their own home it was estimated that only just over 8,000 properties were needed to meet rental demand within the borough. It was therefore proposed that 1,100 properties should be demolished – those that were difficult to rent out or where repair costs were prohibitive. This plan was not fully implemented, as the views of tenants were sought and plans amended accordingly. Some properties were modernised or, where demolition did take place, new properties were built to address perceived shortages in particular areas or of particular types of dwelling. The company has been very successful and has regularly accumulated an annual surplus. As it is non-profit making this surplus has been reinvested, mainly in environmental schemes to improve the estates. Such schemes are often planned and undertaken at the request of the 22 tenants' associations that have been set up. Litter is collected, hedges are cut for those tenants who are physically incapable of doing

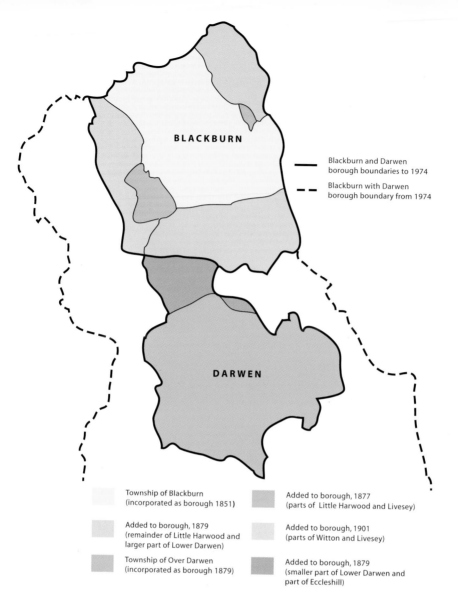

The changing boundary of the borough since 1851.

BLACKBURN

DARWEN

——— Blackburn and Darwen
borough boundaries to 1974

– – – Blackburn with Darwen
borough boundary from 1974

Township of Blackburn
(incorporated as borough 1851)

Added to borough, 1879
(remainder of Little Harwood and
larger part of Lower Darwen)

Township of Over Darwen
(incorporated as borough 1879)

Added to borough, 1877
(parts of Little Harwood and Livesey)

Added to borough, 1901
(parts of Witton and Livesey)

Added to borough, 1879
(smaller part of Lower Darwen and
part of Eccleshill)

As part of the regeneration programme the canalside, derelict for many years, is now undergoing redevelopment. On the left can be seen Eanam Wharf while on the other side of the canal the new offices of Twin Valley Homes, built by local labour with local materials, can be discerned.

it for themselves, and playgrounds modernised. The company built new offices at a cost of £3.5 million on Wharf Street opposite Eanam Wharf, on the site of Prospect Mill. As well as providing a pleasant working environment this has saved the company the annual rent of £200,000 which it paid for its previous

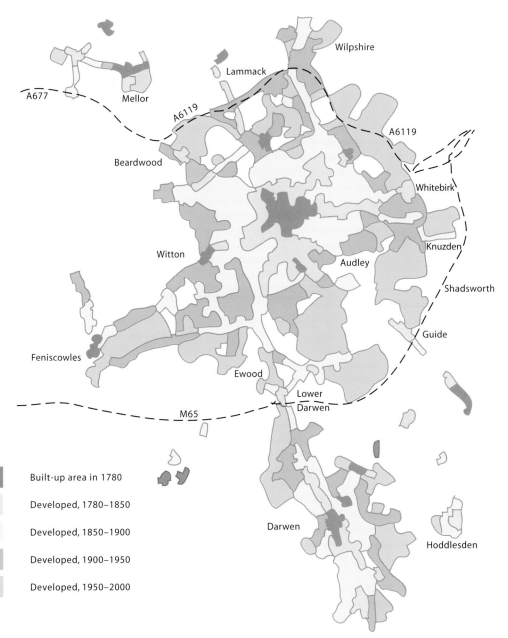

**Built-up area in 1780**

Developed, 1780–1850

Developed, 1850–1900

Developed, 1900–1950

Developed, 1950–2000

The physical growth of Blackburn, 1780–2000. This map highlights how Blackburn has not just simply grown from the centre outwards, though such a pattern can just be discerned, but how isolated colonies of development have slowly been incorporated over the years as in-filling has taken place. With the coming of the M65, however, it could well be that a major development shift to the south and south-east is a major pattern for the future.

MAP BY DR ALAN CROSBY

premises. It is justifiably proud of the fact that 80 per cent of the workforce that built the headquarters were local; 11 per cent were trainees or apprentices; and 90 per cent of the materials used were purchased within a twenty-mile radius. The latest expansion has been seen in the Pathfinder Scheme. In the Audley area a successful bid has been made to set up a 'neighbourhood management scheme', involving the devolution of all service provision to the local level but with Twin Valley Homes as the lead agent. The government is watching this scheme carefully, and if it is successful it could provide a blueprint for a new national strategy. The most recent housing scheme began in 2003/4 and was named Elevate. A Housing Market Renewal Company was set up to cover East Lancashire and allocate Government monies to improve targeted areas of housing. In Blackburn the two main areas were around the Infirmary and at Bank Top. The scheme had three main strands: house clearance where necessary, house facelift and renewal and environmental improvement. In tandem with the parent company, Twin Valley Homes provided social housing, while the private sector built new homes. The scheme has been so successful in revitalising areas of Blackburn that they have seen a 65% increase in average house values over three years, a rate of increase well above the national average.[5]

Other investment focused on upgrading the environment and landscape of the town centre, and a key element in that strategy has been the construction of a relief road, Barbara Castle Way, an orbital route designed to relieve traffic congestion in central streets and encourage new investment along its alignment. The construction of the road was part of a wider programme of investment. A town centre action plan was drawn up, giving attention to neglected areas and to modernising the increasingly outdated image of the centre. There were transport and streetscape improvements, retail developments and conservation projects, including a £5 million refurbishment of the railway station which provided modern facilities within the conserved Victorian buildings, and the pedestrianisation of Church Street complete with a series of urban sculptures. The very belated realisation that the best of the past should be kept alongside the new has been reflected in a £1.1 million programme to create a 'heritage corridor' in the centre of the town, based on Church Street and King Street and involving the restoration of key historic buildings such as the Waterloo pavilions on Church Street, one of the few surviving remnants of Regency Blackburn. These have been tastefully modernised and the early Victorian Fleming Square is now attractively refurbished. Public art commissions now grace many areas of the town, including a number of the new industrial estates, as part of the landscaping. But though Blackburn has undoubtedly changed dramatically since the mid-1990s, and further regeneration schemes and initiatives will continue to improve the town centre and other key areas, problems still exist. One aim of the town centre strategy is to upgrade Blackburn as a sub-regional shopping centre, for the town not only lacks high-quality retail names but also faces very strong competition from Preston and, to a lesser extent, from Burnley, both of which have major central area development projects in hand or approaching implementation. Environmental improvements and town centre strategies are not just window-dressing or cosmetic: they are part of a wider economic and commercial policy of attracting business and shoppers from other areas of east Lancashire, and encouraging private investment. As a result of such improvements, especially in Church Street, it is hoped that the owners of the shopping mall will invest £40 million in redeveloping parts of the central complex, especially those sections facing Church Street and Ainsworth Street and the Lord Square area. This should not just see cosmetic improvements but partial demolition and rebuilding. Also planned is the repositioning of the indoor market within the shopping mall which will leave the present indoor market site for yet further town centre redevelopment.

The need to enhance and upgrade the wider environment of the town has also been addressed. Foremost among such projects have been the very extensive and impressive projects to restore and revitalise Queen's Park and, especially, Corporation Park, which is not only central to the town in geographical terms but also occupies a place at the heart of its Victorian historical development. The clearance of woodland and scrub, and restoration of terraces, walks and landscaping features, have helped to transform the rundown appearance and have also reduced fears of crime and insecurity among users of the parks. The very attractive landscapes of parkland and woodland at Witton, with the fine viewpoint at Billinge Hill, are a popular and well-used country park, and in the south of the enlarged borough the rural landscapes of Tockholes and Roddlesworth are similarly accessible and, with new visitor facilities, trails and interpretive literature, provide a valuable resource for the people of Blackburn with Darwen and adjacent areas. Other environmental problems have also been resolved. A combination of smoke-control legislation and the dramatic decline in traditional industries means that Blackburn is now a cleaner place than it has been for two hundred years, with clear air and fresher water in its rivers and brooks. This has made a tremendous difference to the marketing potential of the town, for it is possible to portray in leaflets and promotional literature a place surrounded by rolling hills and set in a green valley with attractive countryside, something that would have been impossible fifty years ago.

Blackburn, however, still has significant demographic problems. The population of the borough has stabilised at about 137,000, but although the birth rate is higher than the national average outward migration matches it. Most unusually, the migration now tends to involve middle-aged people who have found promotion or identify better job prospects elsewhere, or who prefer to live in the rural areas outside the borough boundaries. The result is that the population of the borough has an age profile which is sharply different from that of most other places in Britain. Thus, 25.2 per cent of the population is under 16

These two images reflect the changing face of Blackburn. Above, in 1963, two local teddy boys stride out along a dismal Fleming Square. Today, though the buildings on the right have now gone the shops on the left have been totally renovated and, as well as still housing the barber's, is now also home to a range of quality shops including the unique Coffee Exchange where a pavement culture is now developing.

years old. Only nine local authority areas in the country have a higher figure, and the national average is 21 per cent. Conversely only 17.6 per cent of the population of the borough is over sixty years of age, compared with a national figure of 21 per cent.[6] The large number of young people means that the need to expand employment is imperative, but the borough also has an above-average percentage of people who have few or no qualifications, so that the unskilled element of the labour force is uncomfortably large.

The question of race and ethnicity must also be addressed by all those many institutions, public bodies and private organisations with a stake in the present state and future prospects of Blackburn. At the 2001 census people with an Asian background (that is, either born in Asia or born in Britain of Asian heritage) made up 27 per cent of the population of the borough, compared with 19.5 per cent in 1991, and that figure is certain to increase further. That it will do so is essentially because the Asian-descended population has a higher birth rate, not because of continued immigration. The rate of marriage with partners from the Indian subcontinent has declined dramatically. It now accounts for only about 10 per cent of all marriages and the figure is falling fast. In terms of community relations, Blackburn has a good record, of which it can be proud, and the issue is always near the top of the local agendas. Since almost one-third of the population is from the Asian community, their own role in the decision-making process is growing apace, and the voice of this section of the community will continue to be more audible and more decisive in future years. The importance of consulting all sections of the community is matched by the continuing need for all groups to work together for common goals. This is especially so because the beginning of the twenty-first century saw a resurgence of the far right in the old textile towns of the north-west, drawing their support not only from those who are overtly racist but also from sections of the community who feel that councils have offered too much to the ethnic minority communities while ignoring the problems of the indigenous population. So far, Blackburn has been fortunate to have escaped the full impact of this revival of the xenophobic right. Only one British National Party (BNP) councillor has been elected, in Mill Hill ward in 2003, whereas in nearby Burnley there were six councillors.

During the past 250 years Blackburn has changed continuously. It was a small country market town which emerged as a centre for the new patterns of industrialisation, then became a boom town which was one of the world's greatest textile manufacturing communities. After a period of industrial might and vigour which in retrospect seems relatively short – only four or five decades – Blackburn was dramatically transformed into a place of acute and prolonged economic and social malaise, a phase which lasted for seventy years. Finally, since 1990, the town has undergone a major revival, with courageous attempts to address its severe difficulties and large-scale investment in the future. Blackburn has come a long way and further change is planned. A start has been made to unshackle the town from the restrictions imposed by the poor quality of the built environment that was inherited from the industrial revolution and from the economic uncertainty which was brought about by the demise of cotton. Credit should be given to those who have the vision to attempt such change and, though difficulties still exist and the future of the town is still uncertain, hope is visible and the horizon is clearer than it has been for many decades.

# Notes and references

*Notes to Chapter 1: Blackburn before 1750*

1. My thanks to Dave Pack a former member of the Geography Department at Blackburn College for the geographical details.
2. P. A. Whittle, *Blackburn As It Is* (Preston, 1852).
3. R. D. S. Wilson. *The Feildens of Witton Park* (Blackburn, 1979)
4. Whittle, *Blackburn As It Is.*
5. W. A. Abram, *A History of Blackburn Town and Parish* (Blackburn, 1877).
6. Abram, *A History of Blackburn Town.*

*Notes to Chapter 2: The economy, 1750–1914*

1. *The Times*, September 1862, quoted in N. Longmate, *The Hungry Mills* (Temple Smith, London, 1978), pp. 36–7.
2. P. A. Whittle, *Blackburn As It Is*, privately published (Preston, 1852), p. 245.
3. G. Trodd, 'Political change and the working class in Blackburn and Burnley, 1880–1914,' unpublished PhD thesis, University of Lancaster, 1974.
4. D. Walsh, 'Working-class development, control and new Conservatism: Blackburn 1820–1850,' unpublished MSc dissertation, University of Salford, 1986.
5. *Manchester Guardian*, 4 December 1841.
6. For much that follows see J. G. Timmins, 'The decline of the handloom weavers in nineteenth-century Lancashire,' unpublished PhD thesis, University of Lancaster, 1990 and J. G. Timmins, *The Last Shift* (Manchester University Press, Manchester, 1993).
7. Walsh, 'Working-class development'.
8. *Blackburn Standard*, 22 December 1841.
9. D. Bythell, *The Handloom Weavers* (Cambridge University Press, Cambridge, 1969).
10. G. Trodd, 'The local elite of Blackburn and the response of the working class to its social control 1880–1890,' unpublished MA dissertation, University of Lancaster, 1974.
11. R. A. Light, 'The Lancashire power-loom breaking riots of 1826,' unpublished MA dissertation, University of Lancaster, 1982.
12. Trodd, 'Political Change'.
13. See printed census tables for 1881 and 1911.
14. Trodd, 'Political Change'.
15. *Blackburn Mail*, 12 April 1826.
16. G. C. Miller, *Blackburn: Evolution of a Cotton Town* (Blackburn Town Council, Blackburn, 1951).
17. For much that follows see M. Ellison, *Support For Secession: Lancashire and the American Civil War* (University of Chicago Press, Chicago and London), 1972.

7. For the events in the English Civil War and the Jacobite Rebellions see Abram, *A History of Blackburn Town* and George C. Miller, *Blackburn: The Evolution of a Cotton Town*, (Blackburn, 1951).
8. Quoted in L. W. Thomason 'The Growth and Decline of the Blackburn Coal Industry', unpublished study in Blackburn Library Community History Section.
9. See Thomason and Jack Nadin, *Coal Mines Around Accrington and Blackburn* (Keighley, 1999).
10. W. A. Abram, *A History of the Blackburn Parish.*

18. *Blackburn Standard*, 4 December 1861.
19. *Blackburn Standard*, 17 June 1863, 14 October 1863.
20. *Blackburn Patriot*, 5 October 1864.
21. *Blackburn Times*, 26 August 1893.
22. See for example Michael Winstanley (ed.), *Working Children in Nineteenth-Century Lancashire* (Lancashire County Books, Preston, 1995).
23. *Report of an Enquiry by the Board of Trade into working class rents, housing and retail prices together with the standard rates of wages prevailing in certain occupations in the principal industrial towns of the UK* Cd. 3864. (1908), cvii, p. 319.
24. *Inter Departmental Committee on Partial Exemption from School Attendance* PP 1909 xvii pp. 1018–22.
25. *Census of Great Britain 1911.*
26. *Board of Trade Enquiry.*
27. Trodd, 'Political Change'.
28. S. Boston, *Women Workers and the Trade Union Movement*, London, 1980, quoted in E. M. Jones, 'Deference and the Blackburn Working Class: Operatives' Struggles 1852–1878', unpublished MA dissertation, University of Warwick, 1984.
29. Trodd, 'Political Change'.
30. *Board of Trade Enquiry*, p. 91.
31. *Board of Trade Enquiry*, p. 91.
32. Trodd, 'Political Change'.
33. J. Corin, *Mating, Marriage and the Status of Women*, London, 1910, p. 128, quoted in Trodd, 'Political Change'.
34. Trodd, 'The local elite of Blackburn'.
35. Trodd, 'Political Change'.
36. Trodd, 'Political Change'.
37. *Report of the Factory Inspectors*, PP (1842), xxii.
38. Trodd, 'Political Change'.
39. *List of Mines 1873*, *The Collieries of Lancashire in 1879* and *List of Mines 1896* quoted in Jack Nadin, *Coal Mines Around Accrington and Blackburn* (Keighley, 1999).

40. *Blackburn Weekly Express*, 30 June 1888.
41. *Report on Child Labour in Coal-Mines 1841*, quoted in Nadin, *Coal Mines* p. 85.

42. *Blackburn Mail*, 22 December 1819
43. *Blackburn Times*, 1 June 1836
44. *Blackburn Standard*, 14 February 1885.

*Notes to Chapter 3: Elites and political power before 1914*

1. R. D. S. Wilson, *The Feildens of Witton Park* (Blackburn, 1979).
2. P. A. Whittle, *Blackburn As It Is* (privately published, Preston, 1852).
3. *Blackburn Times*, 26 August 1893.
4. *Blackburn Times*, 29 June 1889.
5. J. H. Fox, 'The social origins, careers and characteristics of entrepreneurs in South Lancashire during the nineteenth century', unpublished MA dissertation, University of Lancaster, 1970.
6. *Textile Mercury*, 3 September 1892.
7. G. Trodd, 'Political change and the working class in Blackburn and Burnley 1880–1914', unpublished PhD thesis, University of Lancaster, 1978.
8. G. Trodd, 'The local elite of Blackburn and the response of the working class to its social control 1880–1890', unpublished MA dissertation, University of Lancaster, 1974.
9. *Blackburn Times*, 26 June 1893.
10. Trodd, 'The local elite of Blackburn'.
11. Trodd, 'Political Change', table 10.
12. *Daily News*, December 1883, quoted in *Blackburn Standard*, 29 December 1883.
13. *Blackburn Times*, 16 September 1875.
14. Trodd, 'The local elite of Blackburn', p. 14.
15. P. Joyce, *Work, Society and Politics* (Harvester Press, London, 1980), p. 123.
16. *Blackburn Standard*, 3 April 1880, and *Blackburn Times*, 24 October 1885.
17. *Blackburn Labour Journal*, December 1900.
18. *Blackburn Times*, 18 September 1875.
19. *Blackburn Standard*, 24 March 1869.
20. W. Abrams, 'Social conditions and political prospects of the Lancashire workman', *Fortnightly Review*, October 1868, p. 437.
21. P. Joyce, 'Popular Toryism in Lancashire 1860–1890', unpublished DPhil thesis, University of Oxford, 1975.
22. Quoted in J. C. Lowe, 'Parliamentary Elections in Blackburn and the Blackburn Hundred 1865–1880', unpublished MLitt thesis, University of Lancaster, 1970.
23. For full discussion of the paternalism of Blackburn's mill-owners see Joyce, *Work, Society and Politics*.
24. Quoted in Trodd, 'The local elite of Blackburn'.
25. For the full story of this petition see J. Liddington and J. Norris, *One Hand Tied Behind Us* (London, 1978), chapter 10.
26. Liddington and Norris, *One Hand Tied*, p. 226.
27. Liddington and Norris, *One Hand Tied*, p. 251.
28. Quoted in Stephen G. Jones, *Sport, Politics and the Working Class* (Manchester University Press, Manchester and New York, 1988), p. 33.

*Notes to Chapter 4: Law and order, popular protest and crime, 1750–1914*

1. J. Aikin, *A Description of the Country from 30–40 miles around Manchester*, London, 1795.
2. *Blackburn Mail*, 20 April 1796.
3. J. D. Marshall, 'Colonization as a factor in the planting of towns in North-West England', in H. J. Dyos (ed.), *The Study of Urban History* (Edward Arnold, London, 1968), p. 228.
4. St Matthew's Church centenary booklet, Blackburn Library Community History collection.
5. D. Walsh, 'Working-class development, control and new conservatism: Blackburn, 1820–1850', unpublished MA dissertation, University of Salford, 1986.
6. P. Joyce, *Work, Society and Politics* (Harvester Press, London, 1980).
7. A. Howe, *The Cotton Masters 1830–1860* (Clarendon Press, Oxford, 1984).
8. D. R. Beattie, 'The origins, implementation and legacy of the Addison Housing Act 1919, with special reference to Lancashire', unpublished PhD thesis, University of Lancaster, 1986, chapter 2.
9. G. Trodd, 'Political change and the working class in Blackburn and Burnley 1880–1914', unpublished PhD thesis, University of Lancaster 1978.
10. P. A. Whittle, *Blackburn As It Is* (privately published, Preston, 1852).
11. Whittle, *Blackburn As It Is*.
12. John Withers, *Report on the Sanitary Condition of Blackburn* (Blackburn, 1852).
13. *Annual Report of the Medical Officer of Health 1890*.
14. A. Greenwood, *Report on the Housing of the Working Classes in Blackburn 1908*, in Blackburn Library Local History Collection.
15. School Medical Officer's Report 1907.
16. Bannister Eccles to 'Enquiry into the conditions prevailing in the northern districts', quoted in Walsh, 'Working-class development'.
17. J. C. Doherty, 'Short-distance migration in mid-Victorian Lancashire: Blackburn and Bolton 1851–1871', unpublished PhD thesis, University of Lancaster, 1985, pp. 333–53.
18. Trodd, 'Political change'.
19. Beattie, 'Addison Housing Act', chapter 2.
20. Walsh, 'Working-class development'.
21. Trodd, 'Political change'.
22. A worker in Blackburn Calico Printing Works, quoted in Trodd, 'Political change'.
23. Trodd, 'Political change'.
24. J. Clay, 'The Tramways of Blackburn 1851–1949', unpublished BA dissertation, Lancashire Polytechnic, 1984.
25. What follows is mainly based on A. Granath, 'The Irish in mid-nineteenth-century Lancashire', unpublished MA dissertation, University of Lancaster, 1975.
26. Withers, *Sanitary Condition of Blackburn* p. 22.
27. Trodd, 'Political change'.
28. W. A. Abram, *A History of Blackburn Parish* (J. G. & J. Toulmin, Blackburn, 1877).
29. Whittle, *Blackburn As It Is*, p. ix.
30. Eileen Cooper, 'Medical Provision in Blackburn 1790–1870' Unpublished dissertation Chorley College of Education 1973.
31. *Blackburn Standard*, 12 May 1841 and 10 August 1842.
32. J. Withers, 'A report upon the sanitary condition of the Borough of Blackburn 1853', Blackburn Library Local History Collection.
33. J. B. McCallum, *Report on the Municipal and Sanitary*

*Works of Blackburn* (Blackburn, 1885).

34. Memorandum in support of application for constituting the County Borough of Blackburn a City, undated (1934?), in author's possession.

35. Blackburn Centenary Souvenir, Blackburn Town Council, Blackburn, 1951.

36. School Medical Officer's Report 1907.

37. Extracted from the annual reports of the Medical Officer of Health and the Annual report of Blackburn's School Medical Officer 1911.

38. *Annual Reports of the Medical Officer of Health.*

39. Cooper, *Medical Provision.*

40. *A History of Blackburn and East Lancs. Royal Infirmary 1865–1965* (Blackburn, 1965).

41. *Description of the Fever Hospital with Plans* (Blackburn, 1894).

## Notes to Chapter 5; *Law and order, popular protest and crime, 1750–1914*

1. Colin Hey, 'A History of the Police in the County Borough of Blackburn', unpublished work in Blackburn Library Local History Collection.

2. Personnel records of Blackburn Borough Police Force 1889–1907, Blackburn Library Local History Collection.

3. *Blackburn Mail*, 7 August 1808.

4. See, for example, *Blackburn Mail*, 14 September 1808 and 6 February 1828.

5. Letter to Vicar of Blackburn 13 May 1829 quoted in G. C. Miller, *Blackburn: Evolution of a Cotton Town* (Blackburn Town Council, Blackburn, 1951).

6. G. Trodd, 'The local elite of Blackburn and the response of the working class to its social control 1880–1900', unpublished MA dissertation, University of Lancaster, 1974, Appendix 1.

7. W. A. Abram, *A History of Blackburn Parish* (J.G. & J. Toulmin, Blackburn, 1877).

8. 'Brief History of working-class movements in Blackburn', unpublished and unattributed manuscript in Blackburn Library Local History Collection.

9. Major Eckersley, military commander in Manchester, 16 April 1826, PRO. H.O. 40 19/1, quoted in R. A. Light, 'The Lancashire power-loom breaking riots of 1826', unpublished MA dissertation, University of Lancaster, 1982.

10. See Light, 'Powerloom breaking riots', and Abram, *History of Blackburn Parish* and *Annual Register 1826* for the story of these riots. Also William Turner, *Riot: The Story of the East Lancashire Loom Breaking in 1826* (Lancashire County Books, Preston, 1992).

11. Michael Jones, 'Deference and the Blackburn Working Class: Operatives Struggles 1852–1878' unpublished MA thesis, University of Warwick, 1984. For the story of the 1878 riot see also J. E. King, '"We could eat the police": Popular Violence in the North Lancashire Cotton Strike of 1878', *Victorian Studies*, vol. 28 (Spring, 1985).

12. *Blackburn Gazette*, 26 June 1839.

13. Quoted in W. Durham, *History of Blackburn A.D. 31 7–1868* (T.H.C.L. Books, Blackburn, 1988 reprint).

14. See D. Walsh, 'Working-class development, control and new Conservatism: Blackburn 1820–1850', unpublished MSc dissertation, University of Salford, 1986; D. Gadian, 'A comparative study of popular movements in north west industrial towns 1830–1850', unpublished PhD thesis, University of Lancaster, 1976.

15. *Blackburn Mail*, 12 September 1827 and 26 September 1827.

16. Alan Booth, 'Reform, repression and revolution: radicalism and loyalism in the north west of England 1789–1807', unpublished PhD thesis, University of Lancaster, 1979.

17. *Blackburn Standard*, 4 May 1842.

18. *Northern Star*, 30 March 1839, quoted in Duncan Bythell, *The Handloom Weavers* (Cambridge University Press, Cambridge, 1969).

19. Bythell, *Handloom Weavers*.

20. Walsh, 'Working-class development'.

21. Walsh, 'Working-class development'.

22. Gadian, 'Popular movements in North West'.

23. *Blackburn Standard*, 10 July 1839.

24. *Blackburn Times*, 7 November 1868.

25. Chief Constable's reports to the Watch committee, 1861–1879, and Criminal and statistical returns of the Blackburn Borough Police 1881–1885.

26. Rev. John Whittaker's report of Blackburn to the Bishop of Chester 1835, quoted in Miller, *Evolution of a Cotton Town*, pp. 28–9.

27. Annual report of the chaplain of Preston Goal, 1833, quoted in Miller, *Evolution of a Cotton Town*.

## Notes to Chapter 6: *'Behind every other town in England': education, 1750–1914*

1. Quoted in G. C. Miller, *Blackburn: Evolution of a Cotton Town* (Blackburn Town Council, Blackburn, 1951).

2. Report of Chester Diocesan Board of Education, 1839, (Blackburn Deanery) cited in B. J. Biggs, 'Education in Blackburn 1870–1914', unpublished MEd dissertation, University of Durham, 1961.

3. Biggs, 'Education in Blackburn'.

4. A newspaper cutting of 1805 cited in Miller, *Evolution of a Cotton Town*.

5. Report of the Committee of Blackburn's National Society Schools, 1828, quoted in B. Lewis, *Life in a Cotton Town: Blackburn 1818–48* (Carnegie Press, Preston, 1985), p. 60.

6. The National Schools were formed by the National Society for the Promoting of the Education of the Poor in the Principles of the Established Church set up in 1811. This was in answer to the schools, opened by the Royal Lancastrian Society formed in 1808 and renamed the British Foreign Schools Society in 1814, which took in all children regardless of religion and taught a Christian education not tied to any particular church. They were, however, predominantly allied to the Nonconformists.

7. Extracted from Census of Children made for Blackburn Board of Education, 1871, Blackburn Library Local History Collection.

8. Mill Hill Congregational Church Souvenir Handbook, 1921, in Blackburn Library Local History Collection.

9. D. Walsh, 'Working-class development, control and new conservatism: Blackburn 1820 1850', unpublished MSc dissertation, University of Salford, 1986.

10. C. Birtwistle, 'A history of the education of children in the Blackburn Hundred to 1870', unpublished MA dissertation, University of London, 1952, pp. 121, 141; collection of Church and Chapel Centenary booklets in Blackburn Library Local History Collection.

11. Biggs 'Education in Blackburn', and P. Joyce, *Work,*

*Society and Politics* (Harvester Press, London, 1980).

12. Birtwistle, 'History of Education'.
13. Minute Book of Blackburn Mechanics Institute 1844 46, Blackburn Library Local History Collection.
14. Biggs, 'Education in Blackburn'.
15. G. Trodd, 'Political change and the working class in Blackburn and Burnley 1880–1914', unpublished PhD thesis, University of Lancaster, 1978.
16. Biggs, 'Education in Blackburn'.
17. Biggs, 'Education in Blackburn'.
18. *Inter Departmental Committee on Partial Exemption from School Attendance* PP 1909 xvii pp. 1018–22.
19. Census of Children.
20. Biggs, 'Education in Blackburn'.
21. A. Howe, *The Cotton Masters 1830–1860* (Clarendon Press, Oxford, 1984).
22. Board of Education Inspector quoted in Penny Summerfield, 'Cultural Reproduction in the Education of Girls: a Study of Girls' Secondary Schooling in Two Lancashire Towns, 1900–1950,' in Felicity Hunt (ed.), *Lessons For Life: The Schooling of Girls and Women 1850–1950* (Basil Blackwell, Oxford, 1987), p. 153.
23. J. W. Hudson, *History of Adult Education* (London, 1851), quoted in M. B. Smith, 'The growth and development of popular entertainment and pastimes in Lancashire cotton towns 1830–1870,' unpublished MLitt thesis, University of Lancaster, 1970.
24. *Blackburn Standard*, 13 November 1867 and 16 December 1868.

## Notes to Chapter 7: 'A passionate love of sport': leisure, 1750–1914

1. R. W. Malcolmson, *Popular Recreations in English Society 1700–1850* (Cambridge University Press, Cambridge, 1977); Peter Bailey, *Leisure and Class in Victorian England: Rational Recreation and the Contest for Control* (Routledge & Kegan Paul, London, 1978); Hugh Cunningham, *Leisure in the Industrial Revolution 1780–1880* (Croom Helm, London, 1980); J. M. Golby and A. W. Purdue, *The Civilisation of the Crowd* (Batsford, London, 1984).
2. Bailey, *Leisure and Class in Victorian England*.
3. John Walton and Robert Poole, 'The Lancashire Wakes in the Nineteenth Century' in Robert Storch (ed.), *Popular Culture and Custom in Nineteenth-century England* (London and Canberra, 1982).
4. *Blackburn Times*, 23 January 1904.
5. *Blackburn Standard*, 22 February 1837 and January 1839.
6. *Blackburn Standard*, 15 February 1837.
7. *Blackburn Standard*, 1 April 1840.
8. *Blackburn Standard*, June 1844.
9. *Cotton Factory Times*, 1 June 1888.
10. *Blackburn Standard*, 10 May 1887.
11. R. J. Poole, 'Wakes, Holidays and Pleasure Fairs in the Lancashire Cotton District c.1790–1890', unpublished PhD thesis, University of Lancaster, 1985.
12. G. J. Mellor, *The Northern Music Hall* (Newcastle, 1970), p. 186. Most of the section on theatres comes from a bound collection of newspaper cuttings of theatre and cinema in Blackburn Library Community History Collection.
13. Chief Constable's Annual Reports in Blackburn Library Community History Collection.
14. W. E. Moss, *Life of Mrs Lewis* (London, 1926).
15. *Free lance (Manchester)*, 12 October 1867, quoted in Patrick Joyce, *Work, Society and Politics* (London, 1980).
16. *Blackburn Times*, 22 August 1891.
17. *Blackburn Times*, 22 August 1891.
18. Extracted from the *Annual Reports of the Medical Officer of Health*.
19. Joyce, *Work, Society and Politics*.
20. Joyce, *Work, Society and Politics*.
21. Collection of newspaper cuttings titled Blackburn Library in Community History section.
22. *Blackburn Standard* quoted in R. D. S. Wilson, *The Feildens of Witton Park* in Blackburn Library Community History Section.
23. *Pall Mall Gazette*, March 1883.
24. Janet M. Geddes, 'Music in Blackburn', Dissertation for unknown HE institution, 1958, in Blackburn Library Community History Collection.
25. H. Whittaker, *The Union Club, Blackburn 1849–1959* (Blackburn, 1950).
26. Souvenir booklet of East Lancashire Cricket Club Bazaar, 1929, Blackburn Library Local History Collection.
27. History of Blackburn Golf Club, 1954, Blackburn Library Community History Collection.
28. Fifty Years of Hockey in Blackburn 1904–1954, Blackburn Library Community History Collection.
29. C. Francis, *History of Blackburn Rovers F.C., 1875–1925* (Blackburn, 1925).
30. Blackburn Rovers F.C. Bazaar Booklet, 1895, Blackburn Library Community History Collection.
31. East Lancs. Souvenir Booklet.
32. B. Morris, 'The Growth and Development of Popular Entertainment and Pastimes in Lancashire Cotton Towns 1830–1870', unpublished MLitt thesis, University of Lancaster, 1970. See also M. I. Watson, *William Billington: The Blackburn Poet* (privately published and a copy held in Blackburn Library Community History Section); John T. Baron, *A Cotton Town Chronicle* (Accrington, 1978), and *The Poets and Poetry of Blackburn* (*Blackburn Times*, 1902).

## Notes to Chapter 8: 'Reforming manners and morals': religion, 1750–1914

1. Quoted in W. A. Abram, *A History of Blackburn* (J. G. & J. Toulmin, Blackburn, 1877).
2. *Wesleyanism in Blackburn; Bazaar Booklet* (Blackburn, 1913).
3. Quoted in B. Lewis, *Life in a Cotton Town: Blackburn 1818–1848* (Carnegie Press, Preston), 1985, pp. 56–7.
4. P. Joyce, *Work, Society and Politics* (Harvester Press, London, 1980).
5. *Blackburn Standard*, 2 July 1823.
6. *Blackburn Standard*, 16 December 1868.
7. *All Saints Church Bazaar Booklet*, Blackburn, 1900.
8. *Christ Church Jubilee Handbook*, Blackburn, 1907.
9. *James Street Congregational Church Bazaar Booklet*.
10. Barrett's Town Directory, 1939.
11. Annual Report of the Parochial Church Council, St Silas Church, 1982. My thanks to Robin Whalley for bringing this to my attention.
12. Rev. Hignett in *Blackburn Standard*, 6 December 1880.
13. *Christ Church Handbook*.
14. *St Luke's Centenary Pamphlet*, Blackburn, 1976.
15. *Blackburn Times*, 17 October 1868.
16. Quoted in *Blackburn Times*, 17 October 1868.

*Notes to Chapter 9: The Great War and after, 1914–1939*

1. G.C.Miller, Unpublished war memories, Blackburn Community History Section, Blackburn Library.
2. *Blackburn Times*, 6 February 1915.
3. *Blackburn Times*, 10 October 1914.
4. *Weekly Telegraph*, 29 October 1921.
5. *Blackburn Times*, 16 November 1918.
6. 1st Annual Report of the Local Food Control Committee, September 1918.
7. *Blackburn Times*, 26 October 1918.
8. *Blackburn Times*, 16 November 1918.
9. *Blackburn Times*, 2 November 1918.
10. Annual Reports of the Medical Officer of Health.
11. J.B.Priestley, *English Journey* (London, 1934) p. 260.
12. *Blackburn Times*, 3 October 1931.
13. R.Pope, 'The Unemployment Problem in N.E. Lancashire 1920–1938', unpublished MLitt thesis, University of Lancaster, 1974, pp. 60–84.
14. Pope, 'Unemployment in N.E. Lancs', p. 29.
15. *Blackburn Times*, 5 December 1936; Pope, 'Unemployment in N.E. Lancs', pp. 378–9.
16. Pope, 'Unemployment in N.E. Lancs', pp. 96–8.
17. Pope, 'Unemployment in N.E. Lancs', p. 93.
18. *Blackburn Times*, 16 January 1937, 15 October 1937.
19. M.Rothwell, *Industrial Heritage: A Guide to the Industrial Archaeology of Blackburn Part II Other Industries* (Hyndburn Local History Society, 1986).
20. Rothwell, *Industrial Heritage*.
21. Lancashire County Census, 1921.
22. Pope, 'Unemployment in N.E. Lancs', p. 33.
23. Denise Martin, 'Women Without Work: Textile Weavers in North East Lancashire 1919–1939', unpublished MA dissertation, University of Lancaster, 1985; Pope 'Unemployment in N.E. Lancs', pp. 54–9.
24. Pope, 'Unemployment in N.E. Lancs', pp. 179–80.
25. E.M.Gray, *The Weavers Wage* (London, 1937), p. 31.
26. S.Constantine, *Unemployment in Britain Between the Wars* (Longman, London, 1980), p. 28.
27. *Blackburn Times*, 31 January 1931.
28. Pope, 'Unemployment in N.E. Lancs', pp. 199–203.
29. J.McIvor, *Organised Capital* (Cambridge, 1996), pp. 194–9.
30. Pope, 'Unemployment in N.E. Lancs', pp. 253–4.
31. *Blackburn Times*, 16 September 1933.
32. Pope, 'Unemployment in N.E. Lancs', pp. 272–83.
33. *Blackburn Times*, 9 June 1932.
34. For the full story of this episode see Brenda Crosby, 'The Lancashire Campaign of the British Union of Fascists, 1934–35', unpublished MA dissertation, University of Lancaster, 1977.
35. *Blackburn Times*, 12 January 1935.
36. Based on occupational details listed in the *Blackburn Borough Council Handbooks*, 1913–1940, in Blackburn Library Local History Collection.
37. *Blackburn Times*, 14 December 1918.
38. Lancashire County Census 1921 and Martin, 'Women Without Work'.
39. Pope, 'Unemployment in N.E. Lancs', p. 33.
40. Pope, 'Unemployment in N.E. Lancs', pp. 44–8.
41. Martin, 'Women Without Work'.
42. Martin, 'Women Without Work'.
43. J.Clay, 'The Tramways of Blackburn 1851–1949', unpublished BA dissertation, Lancashire Polytechnic, 1984.
44. *Blackburn Times*, 28 November 1931.
45. Pilgrim Trust, *Men Without Work* (Cambridge, 1938), pp. 223, 282–5.
46. Blackburn County Borough Health Department Annual Reports, 1921–1938.
47. M.A.Hamilton, *Remembering My Good Friends* (London, 1944), p. 175.
48. Health Dept Annual Reports.
49. Blackburn Health Week Handbooks for 1927 and 1931.
50. Blackburn Health Week Handbook 1927.
51. Hamilton, *Remembering*, p. 174.
52. Pilgrim Trust, *Men Without Work*, p. 82.
53. Quoted in Historical Summary for City Status Bid 1934 (in author's possession).
54. Lancashire County Census, 1921.
55. Historical Summary for City Status Bid, 1934; Pope, 'Unemployment in N.E. Lancs', pp. 16–17.
56. Barret's Town Directory, 1939.
57. Historical Summary for City Status Bid, 1934.
58. D.Beattie, 'The Origins, Implementation and Legacy of the Addison Housing Act, 1919, with special reference to Lancashire', unpublished PhD thesis, University of Lancaster, 1986.
59. Hamilton, *Remembering*, p. 175.
60. *Blackburn Centenary Souvenir*, Blackburn, 1951.
61. Health Dept Annual Reports.
62. Clay, 'Tramways of Blackburn'.
63. Pope, 'Unemployment in N.E. Lancs', pp. 193–4.
64. See Jeffrey Richards, *The Age of the Dream Palace: Cinema and Society in Britain 1930–1939* (London, 1984), chapter 1.
65. Quoted in James J.Nott, *Music for the People* (Oxford, 2002), p. 175.
66. *Blackburn Times*, 4 July 1936.
67. *Blackburn Times* 23 June 1939
68. Mass Observation, *The Pub and the People* (London, 1987), p. 259
69. *History of Blackburn Golf Club*, 1954, Blackburn Library Local History Collection.
70. Hamilton, *Remembering*, p. 175.

*Notes to Chapter 10: Decline and stagnation in the post-war period*

1. *Blackburn Times*, 8 September 1939 and 15 September 1939.
2. 'Chronology of Air Raids near Blackburn, 1939–45', in Blackburn Library Local History Collection.
3. *Blackburn Times*, 8 September 1939.
4. *Blackburn Times*, 1 September 1939, 8 September 1939 and 21 July 1944.
5. *Blackburn Times*, 31 May 1940, 27 September 1940.
6. *Blackburn Times*, 12 July 1940 and 1 August 1952; *Lancashire Evening Telegraph*, 5 February 1979; Mullards' Jubilee Pamphlet, 1920–1970.
7. *Lancashire Evening Telegraph*, 16 July 1974, 5 February 1979 and 21 August 1980.
8. Mullards' Profile Pamphlet (1970); Mullards' Jubilee Pamphlet 1920–1970.
9. *Blackburn Times*, 1 August 1952; *Lancashire Evening Telegraph*, 24 April 1953, 3 December 1958 and 20 February 1959.
10. *Scapa News*, 40th Anniversary Issue 1927–1967.
11. Collection of Advertising Literature in Blackburn Library Local History Collection.
12. Brian Conduit, *Blackburn 1934–1987: Historical Summary*

for *City Status Bid* (in author's possession); census statistics; *The Changing Face of Blackburn and Darwen* (second edition, Blackburn and Darwen Borough Council, 1990).

13. Blackburn Borough Planning Department, *Blackburn Statistics 1983*.
14. *Blackburn Statistics* and *City Status Bid*.
15. *The Changing Face of Blackburn and Darwen* (3rd edition, May 1994) p. 35.
16. Annual Reports of the Medical Officer of Health.
17. *Blackburn Times*, 24 June 1955.
18. *Blackburn Times*, 31 July 1953.
19. N. Andrews, 'Housing obsolescence: a case study of housing renewal in Blackburn', unpublished BA Dissertation, Liverpool Polytechnic, 1981, pp. 34–7.
20. Figures from The Chartered Institute of Public Finance and Accountancy, 1982 quoted in Vaughan Robinson, *Transients, Settlers and Refugees: Asians in Britain* (Clarendon Press, Oxford, 1986), p. 222.
21. W. D. Hamilton, 'Survey of Blackburn housing and factors affecting improvement or clearance', BA Social Science project for unknown HE institution, 1971; *Blackburn Statistics*; 'Housing Strategy Statement', p. 7.
22. Andrews, 'Housing obsolescence', pp. 34–7; W. D. Hamilton, 'Survey of Blackburn's housing and factors affecting improvements or clearance', unpublished BA dissertation in Blackburn Library Local History Collection; Census statistics 1971.
23. Andrews, 'Housing obsolescence', pp. 36–7.
24. Blackburn Housing Department, 'Housing strategy statement and housing investment programme submission, 1991–92'.
25. Ronalyn Hargreaves, 'The Changing Population of Blackburn 1861–1971', unpublished dissertation 1974, p. 21, in Blackburn Library Local History Collection, and *City Status Bid*, p. 9.
26. City Status Bid, p. 6; Mary Smallbone, 'Blackburn Centre Redevelopment – Phase II Completed' in *Environment North West*, 23, January 1972.

27. *Blackburn Times*, 17 August 1973
28. City Status Bid, pp. 2, 4, 7.
29. *Blackburn Times*, 6 May 1955, *Lancashire Evening Telegraph*, 10 Jan. 1972 and *Lancashire Evening Telegraph*, 6 May 1976.
30. *Lancashire Evening Telegraph*, 27 March 1975.
31. For most of the following facts see *City Status Bid*, pp. 3–9.
32. Asian Household Survey Team, *Asians in Blackburn: The Socio-Economic Conditions of Blackburn's largest Ethnic Minority Grouping*, p. 11, Blackburn Library Local History Collection; Robinson, *Transients, Settlers and Refugees*, pp. 116–21.
33. Survey Team, *Asians in Blackburn*, p. 11; Asian Household Survey Team, *Some Basic Characteristics of Blackburn's Asian Population*, p. 24, Blackburn Library Local History Collection.
34. Robinson, *Transients, Settlers and Refugees*, p. 239.
35. Survey Team, *Basic Characteristics*, p. 41.
36. Rolf Erikson, *Survey of Ethnic Groups in Districts with Large Ethnic Populations in the County of Lancashire*, LCC Social Services Department, 1987, pp. 82–102.
37. *Changing Face*, Section 5; Hargreaves, 'Changing Population'; Robinson, *Transients, Settlers and Refugees*, pp. 116, 222.
38. Survey Team, *Basic Characteristics*, p. 28.
39. *Changing Face*, Section 11; Conduit, *Historical Summary*, p. 5.
40. Housing Department, *Housing Strategy Statement* p. 2.
41. *Changing Face of Blackburn*, p. 68.
42. *Changing Face of Blackburn*, p. 80.
43. *Britain First*, Issue No. 11, 2–15 October 1971; *Spearhead*, December 1971.
44. *Lancashire Evening Telegraph*, 30 December 1975.
45. *Lancashire Evening Telegraph*, 24 May 1976, 10 June 1976 and 11 September 1976.
46. *Lancashire Evening Telegraph*, 13 September 1976.
47. *Lancashire Evening Telegraph*, 13 September 1976.

*Notes to Chapter 11: Renaissance*

1. For most of the statistics in this section I have to thank Adam Scott, the Director of Regeneration, and two of his team, Claire Turner and Garth Hodgkinson.
2. *Review of 96–97 and Development Plan for 98–99* published by Blackburn Partnership pp. 10–12.
3. *East Lancashire Guardian Angel Entrepreneurs Network*.

Leaflet published by Blackburn Partnership.
4. *The Wolstenholme International School Friends Project*. Leaflet published by Blackburn Partnership.
5. My thanks to Alison Milner for this information.
6. First results from the 2001 Census and Key Statistics for Local Authorities supplied by Council Statistics Section.

# Index